Volume 2

Apocalypse Soon

Originally published as *Wolf* #5–9

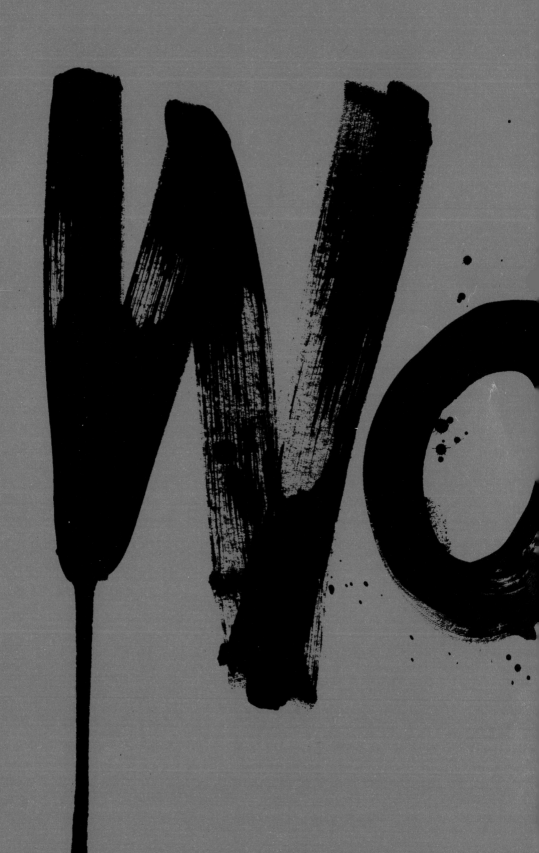

Volume 2

Apocalypse Soon

Writer	**Ales Kot**
Artist	**Ricardo López Ortiz**
Colorist	**Lee Loughridge**
Letterer	**Clayton Cowles**
Designer	**Tom Muller**

Chapter 5

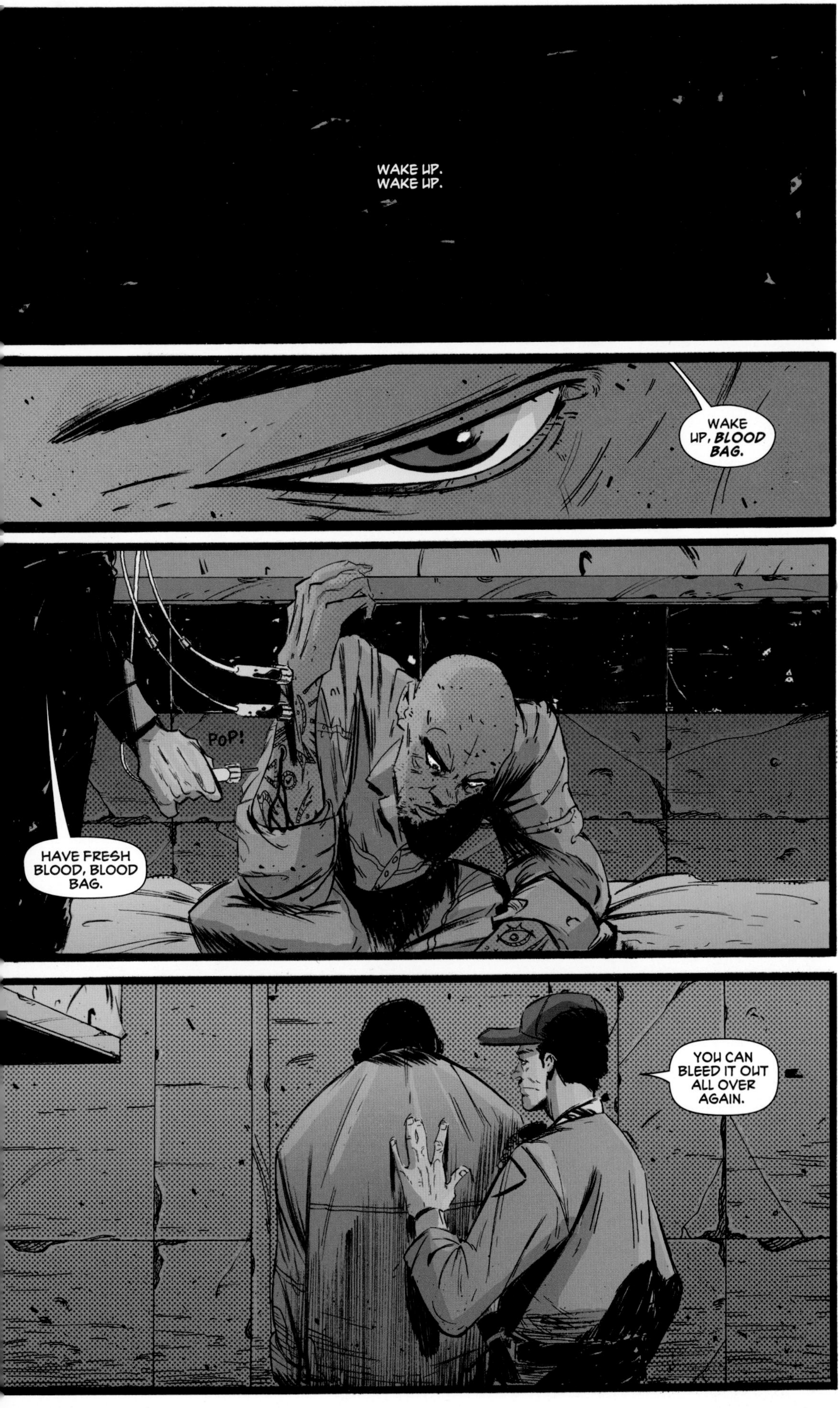

WAKE UP.
WAKE UP.
WAKE UP, BLOOD BAG.
POP!
HAVE FRESH BLOOD, BLOOD BAG.
YOU CAN BLEED IT OUT ALL OVER AGAIN.

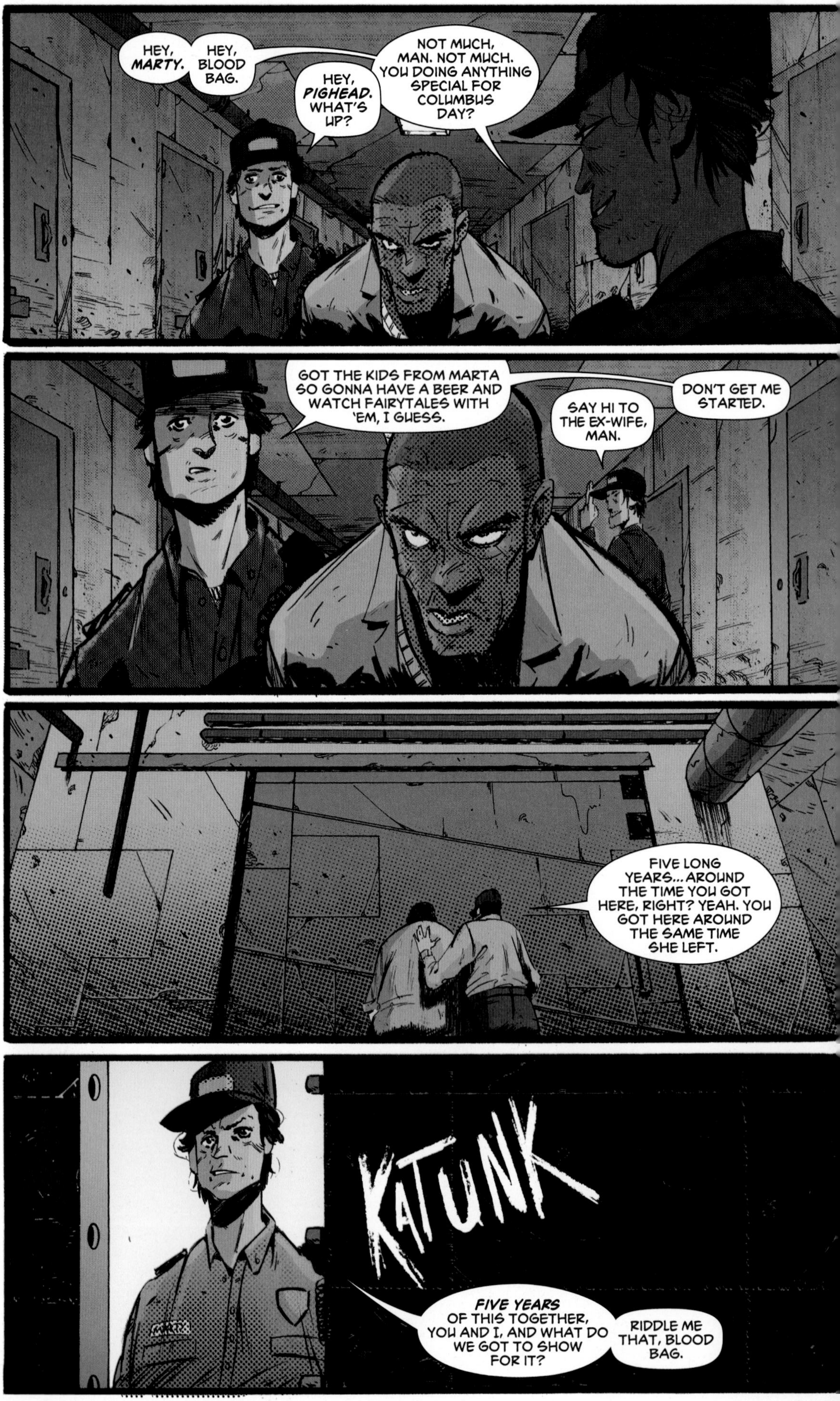

HEY, MARTY.
HEY, BLOOD BAG.
HEY, PIGHEAD. WHAT'S UP?
NOT MUCH, MAN. NOT MUCH. YOU DOING ANYTHING SPECIAL FOR COLUMBUS DAY?
GOT THE KIDS FROM MARTA SO GONNA HAVE A BEER AND WATCH FAIRYTALES WITH 'EM, I GUESS.
SAY HI TO THE EX-WIFE, MAN.
DON'T GET ME STARTED.
FIVE LONG YEARS... AROUND THE TIME YOU GOT HERE, RIGHT? YEAH. YOU GOT HERE AROUND THE SAME TIME SHE LEFT.
KATUNK
FIVE YEARS OF THIS TOGETHER, YOU AND I, AND WHAT DO WE GOT TO SHOW FOR IT?
RIDDLE ME THAT, BLOOD BAG.

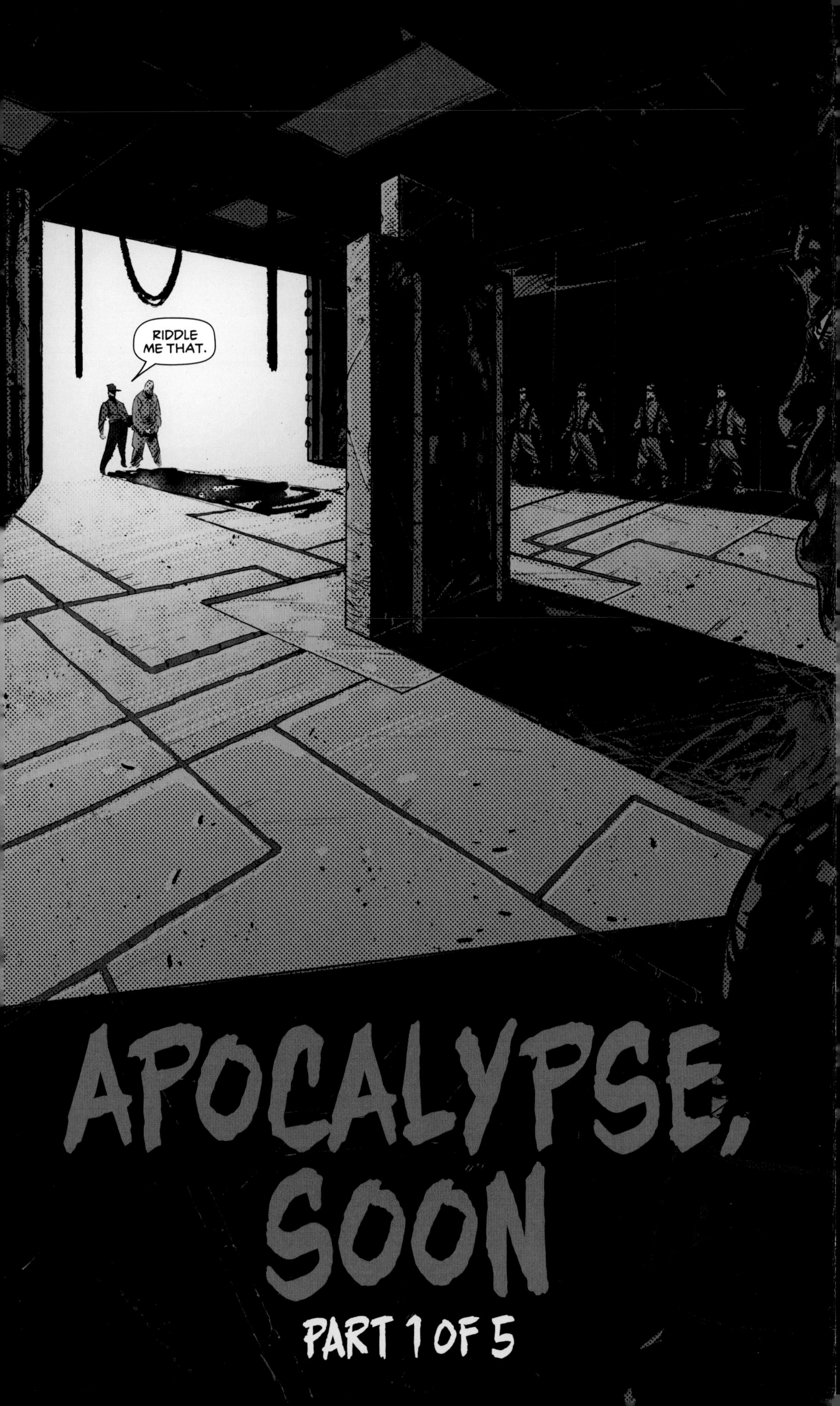
RIDDLE ME THAT.
APOCALYPSE, SOON
PART 1 OF 5

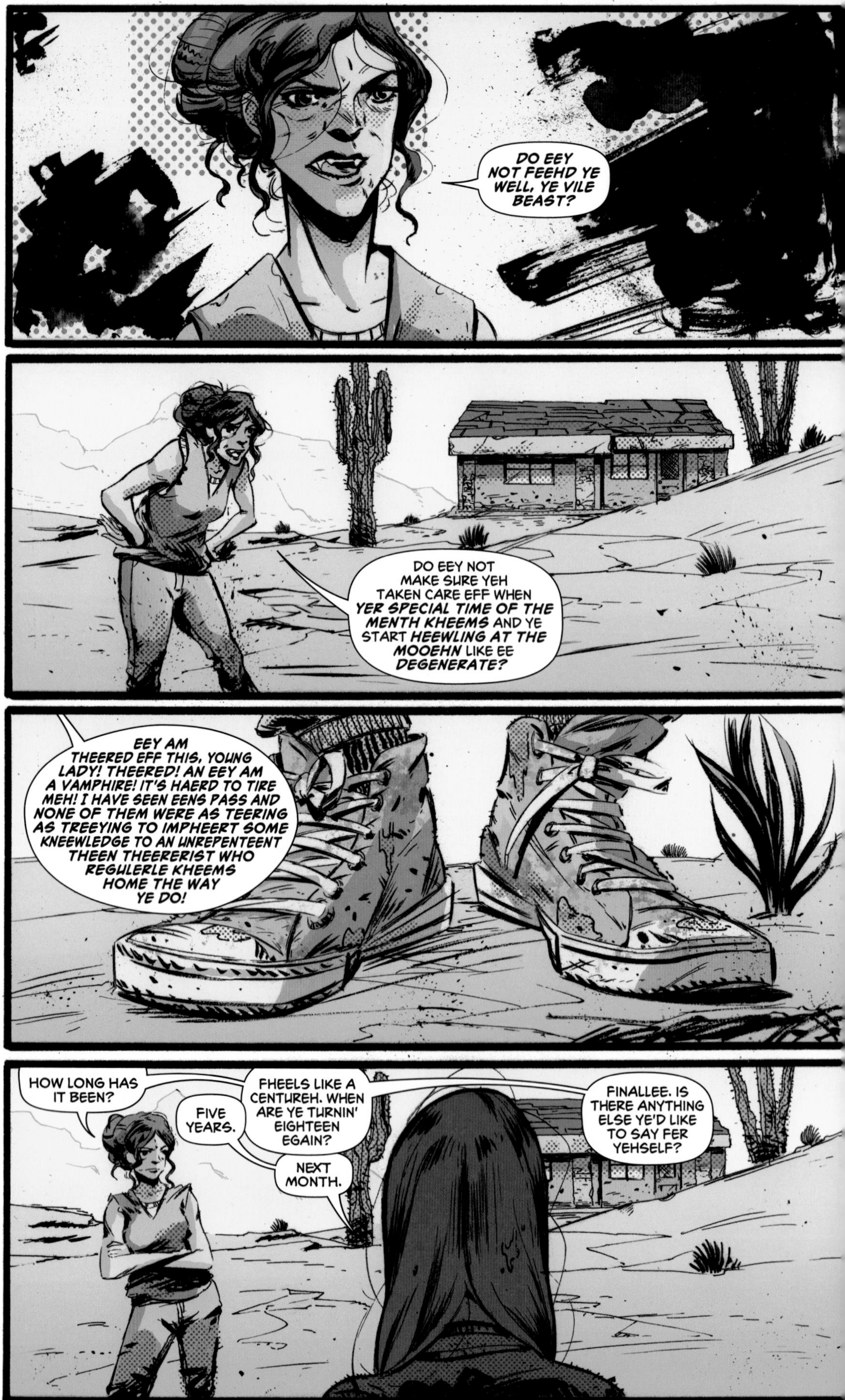
DO EEY NOT FEEHD YE WELL, YE VILE BEAST?
DO EEY NOT MAKE SURE YEH TAKEN CARE EFF WHEN YER SPECIAL TIME OF THE MENTH KHEEMS AND YE START HEEWLING AT THE MOOEHN LIKE EE DEGENERATE?
EEY AM THEERED EFF THIS, YOUNG LADY! THEERED! AN EEY AM A VAMPHIRE! IT'S HAERD TO TIRE MEH! I HAVE SEEN EENS PASS AND NONE OF THEM WERE AS TEERING AS TREEYING TO IMPHEERT SOME KNEEWLEDGE TO AN UNREPENTEENT THEEN THEERERIST WHO REGULERLE KHEEMS HOME THE WAY YE DO!
HOW LONG HAS IT BEEN?
FIVE YEARS.
FHEELS LIKE A CENTUREH. WHEN ARE YE TURNIN' EIGHTEEN EGAIN?
NEXT MONTH.
FINALLEE. IS THERE ANYTHING ELSE YE'D LIKE TO SAY FER YEHSELF?

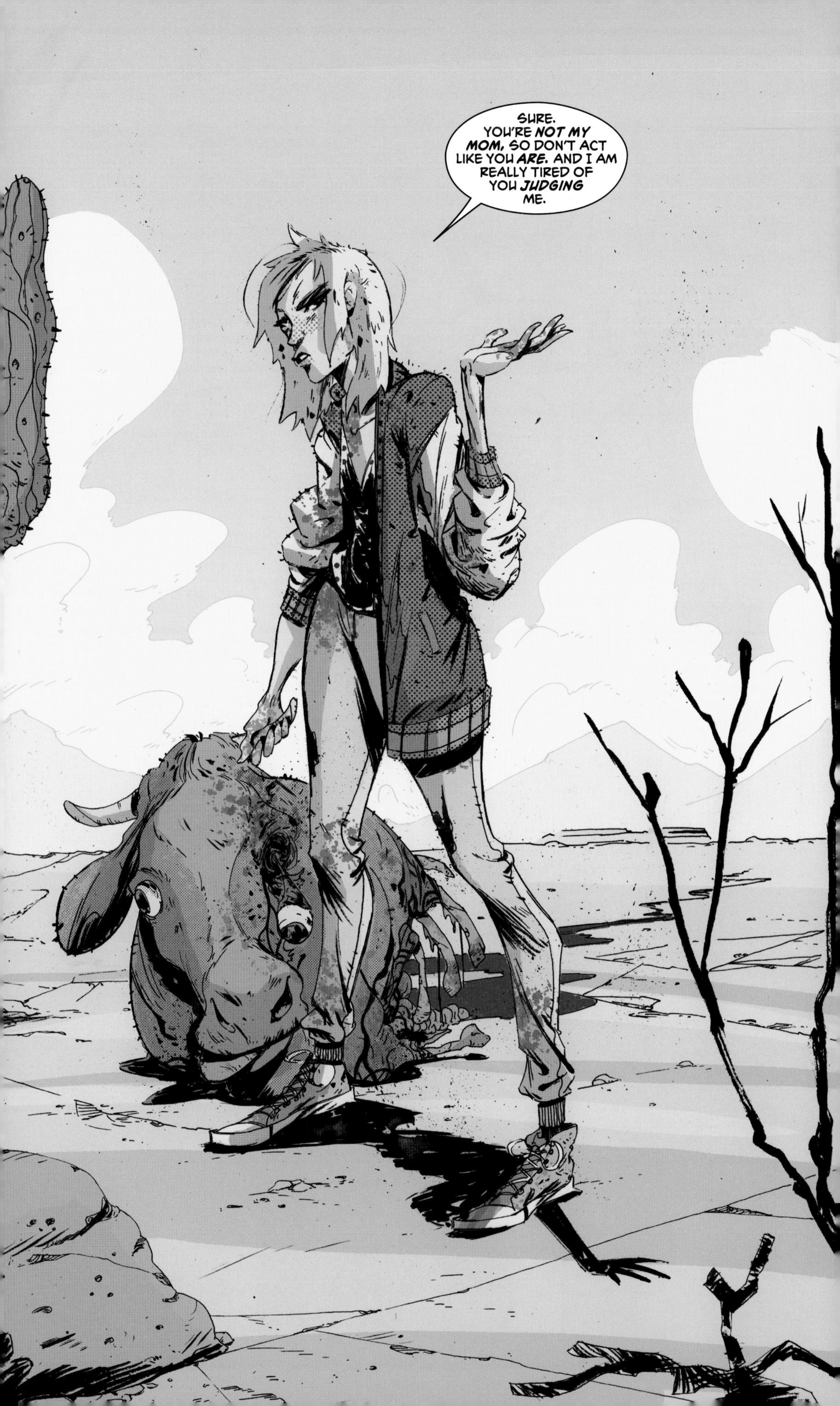
SURE. YOU'RE NOT MY MOM, SO DON'T ACT LIKE YOU ARE. AND I AM REALLY TIRED OF YOU JUDGING ME.

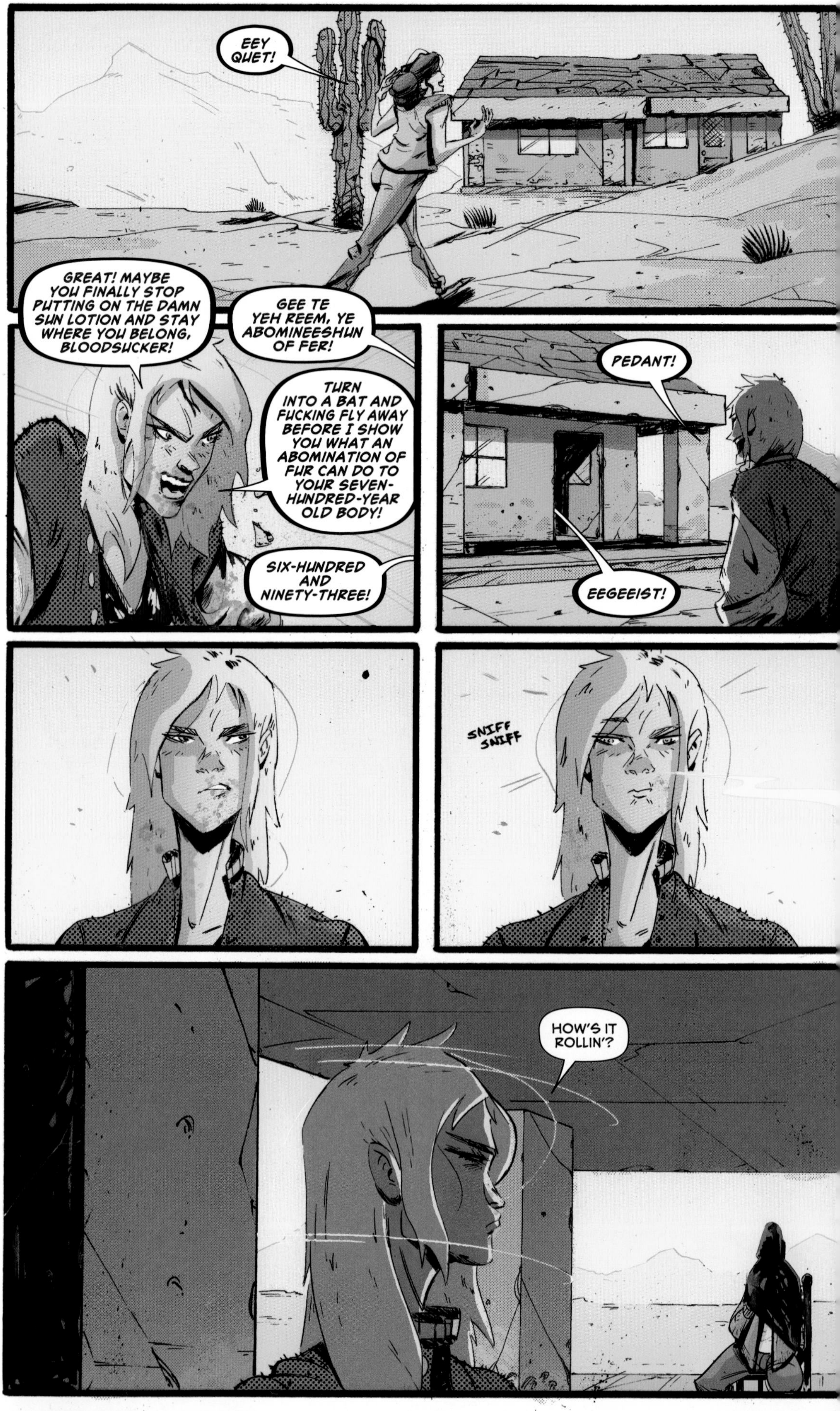
EEY QUET!
GREAT! MAYBE YOU FINALLY STOP PUTTING ON THE DAMN SUN LOTION AND STAY WHERE YOU BELONG, BLOODSUCKER!
GEE TE YEH REEM, YE ABOMINEESHUN OF FER!
TURN INTO A BAT AND FUCKING FLY AWAY BEFORE I SHOW YOU WHAT AN ABOMINATION OF FUR CAN DO TO YOUR SEVEN-HUNDRED-YEAR OLD BODY!
SIX-HUNDRED AND NINETY-THREE!
PEDANT!
EEGEEIST!
SNIFF SNIFF
HOW'S IT ROLLIN'?

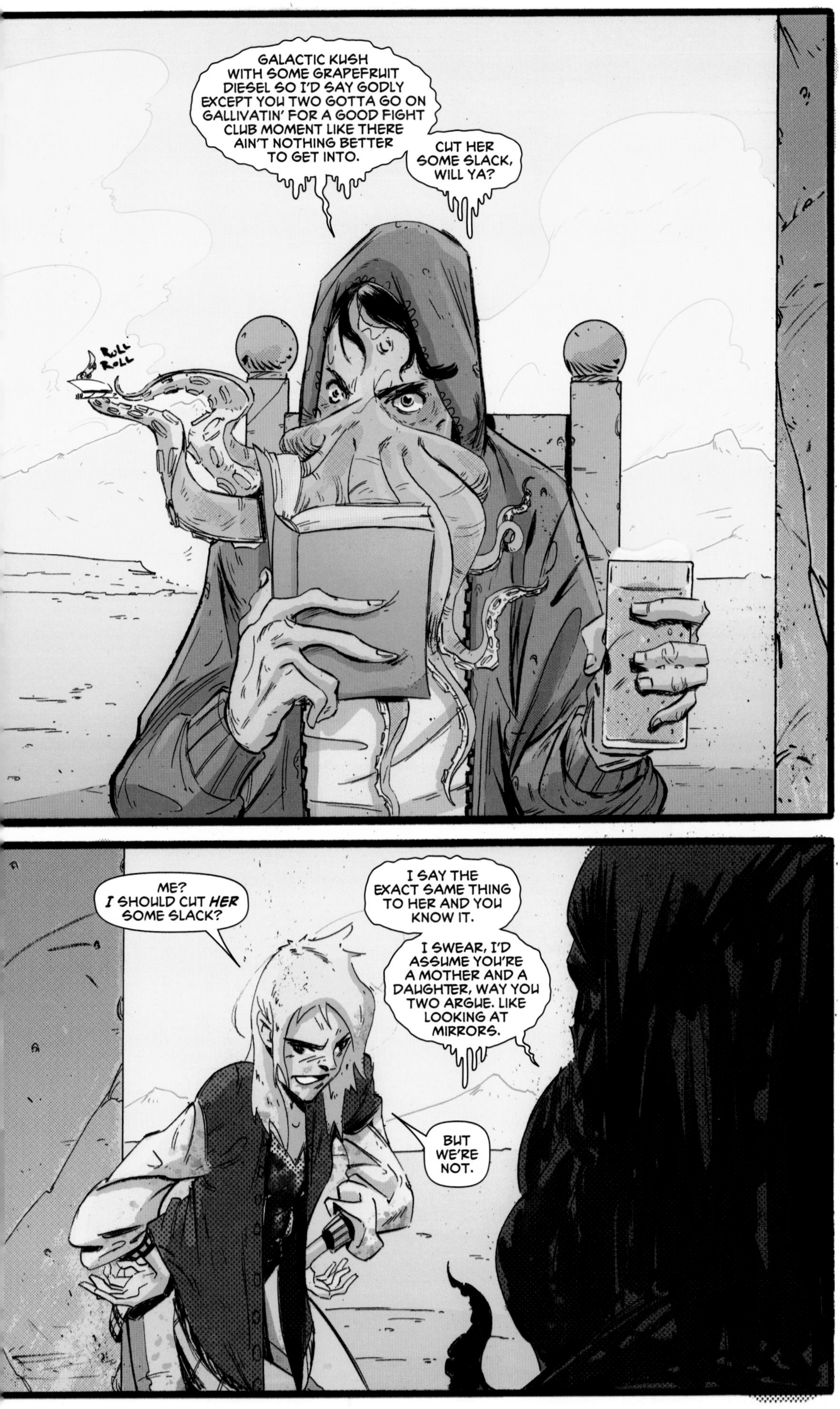
GALACTIC KUSH WITH SOME GRAPEFRUIT DIESEL SO I'D SAY GODLY EXCEPT YOU TWO GOTTA GO ON GALLIVATIN' FOR A GOOD FIGHT CLUB MOMENT LIKE THERE AIN'T NOTHING BETTER TO GET INTO.
CUT HER SOME SLACK, WILL YA?
ROLL ROLL
ME? *I* SHOULD CUT *HER* SOME SLACK?
I SAY THE EXACT SAME THING TO HER AND YOU KNOW IT.
I SWEAR, I'D ASSUME YOU'RE A MOTHER AND A DAUGHTER, WAY YOU TWO ARGUE. LIKE LOOKING AT MIRRORS.
BUT WE'RE NOT.

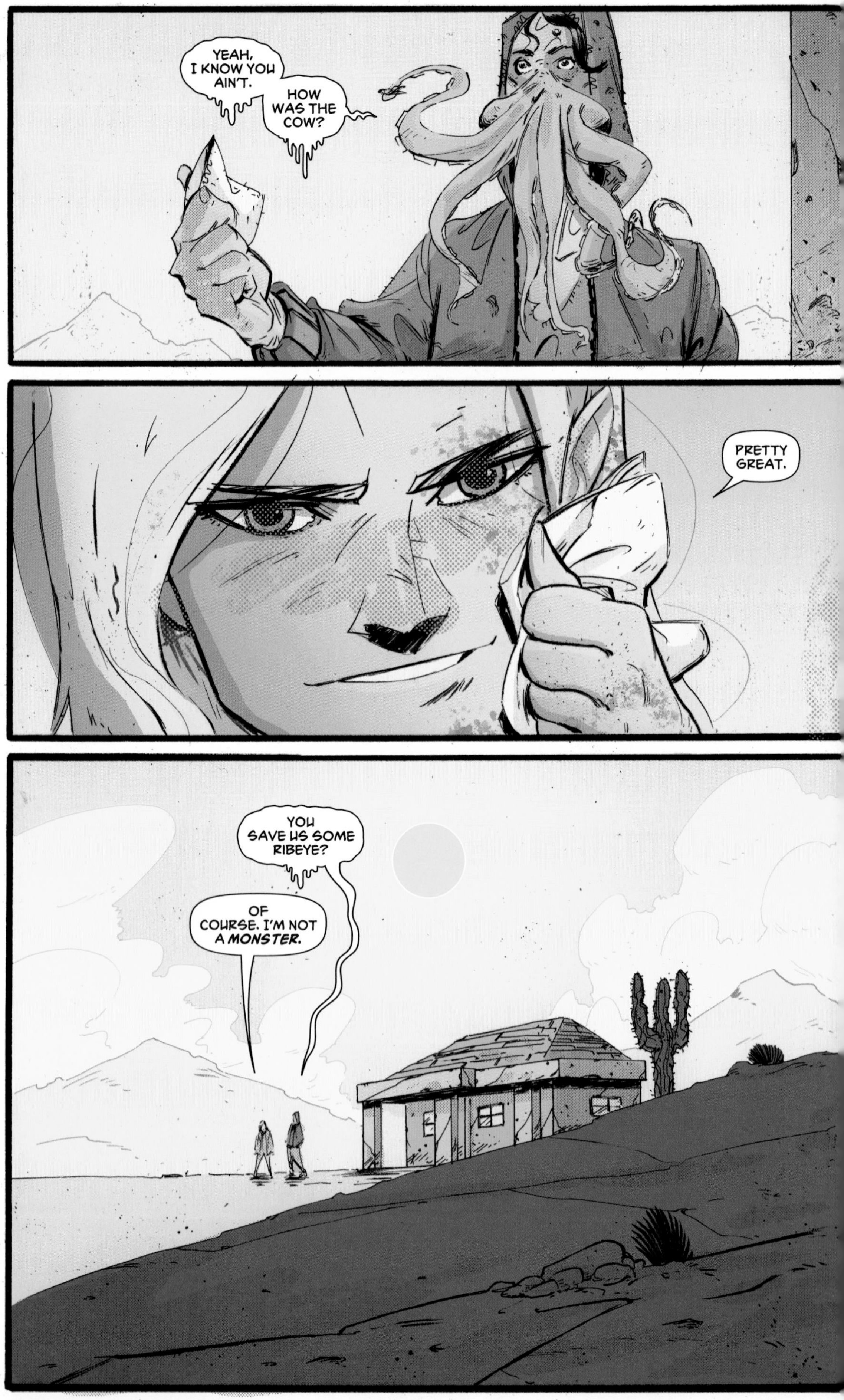
YEAH, I KNOW YOU AIN'T.
HOW WAS THE COW?
PRETTY GREAT.
YOU SAVE US SOME RIBEYE?
OF COURSE. I'M NOT A *MONSTER*.

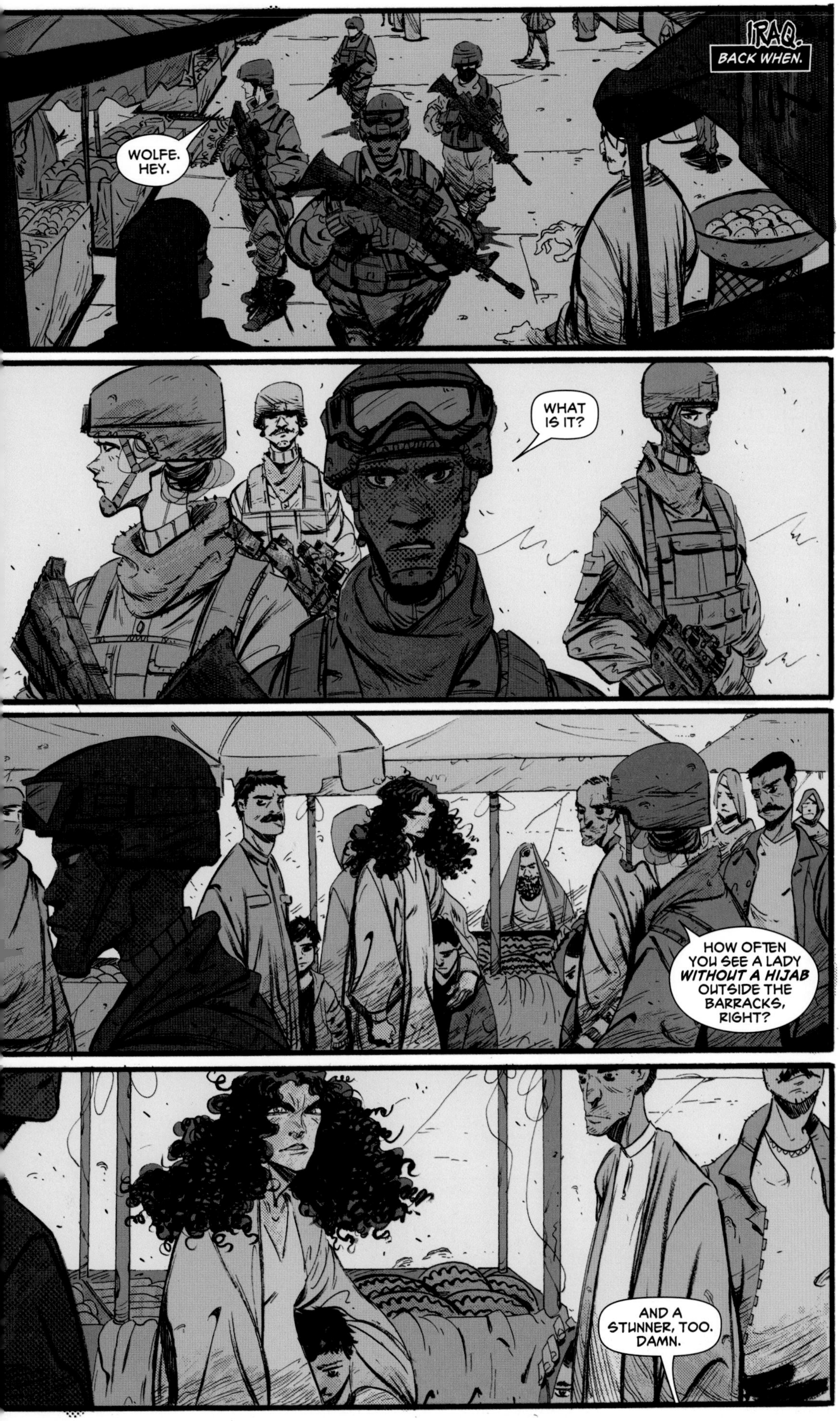
IRAQ.
BACK WHEN.
WOLFE. HEY.
WHAT IS IT?
HOW OFTEN YOU SEE A LADY *WITHOUT A HIJAB* OUTSIDE THE BARRACKS, RIGHT?
AND A STUNNER, TOO. DAMN.

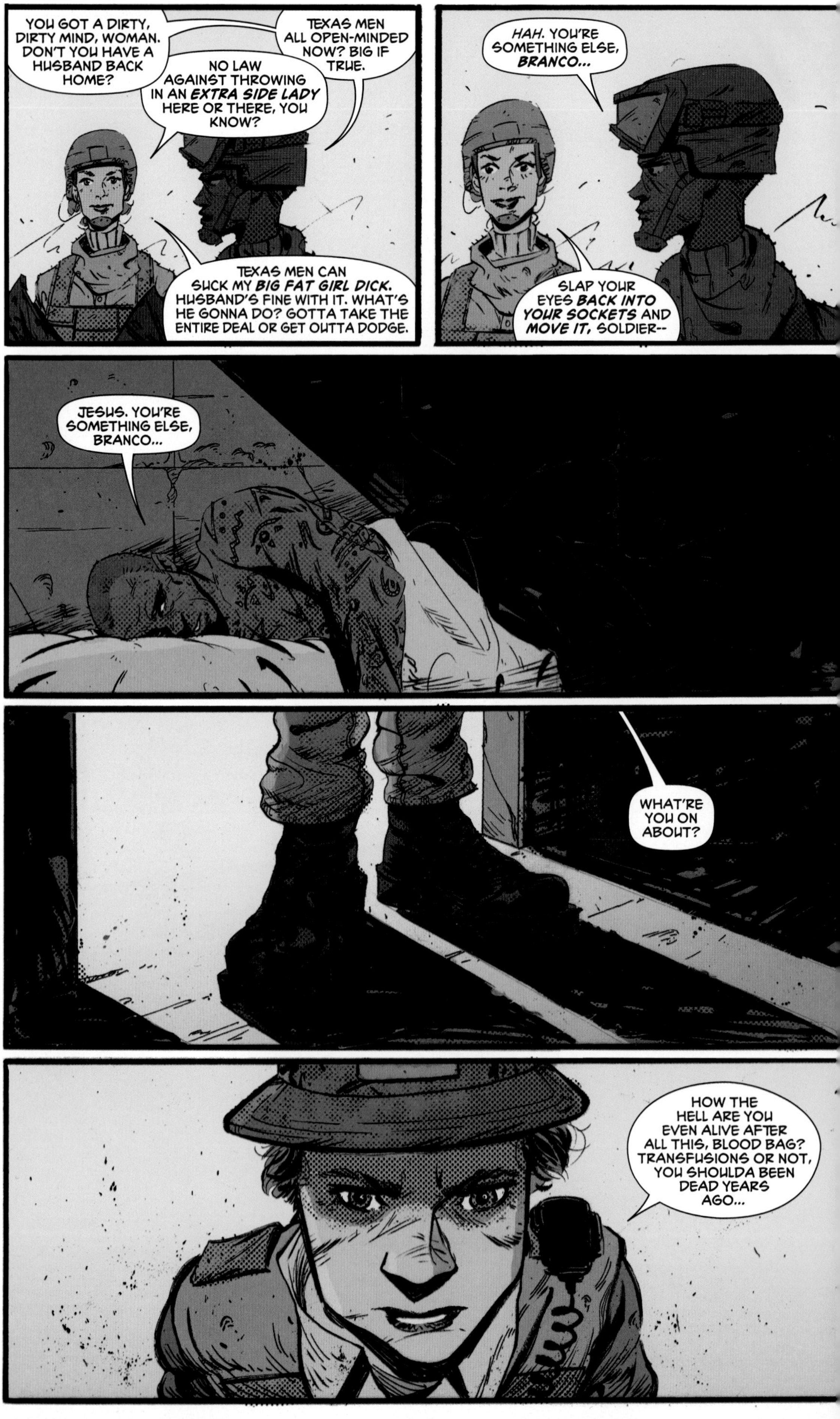
YOU GOT A DIRTY, DIRTY MIND, WOMAN. DON'T YOU HAVE A HUSBAND BACK HOME?
TEXAS MEN ALL OPEN-MINDED NOW? BIG IF TRUE.
NO LAW AGAINST THROWING IN AN *EXTRA SIDE LADY* HERE OR THERE, YOU KNOW?
TEXAS MEN CAN SUCK MY *BIG FAT GIRL DICK.* HUSBAND'S FINE WITH IT. WHAT'S HE GONNA DO? GOTTA TAKE THE ENTIRE DEAL OR GET OUTTA DODGE.
HAH. YOU'RE SOMETHING ELSE, *BRANCO...*
SLAP YOUR EYES *BACK INTO YOUR SOCKETS* AND *MOVE IT,* SOLDIER--
JESUS. YOU'RE SOMETHING ELSE, BRANCO...
WHAT'RE YOU ON ABOUT?
HOW THE HELL ARE YOU EVEN ALIVE AFTER ALL THIS, BLOOD BAG? TRANSFUSIONS OR NOT, YOU SHOULDA BEEN DEAD YEARS AGO...

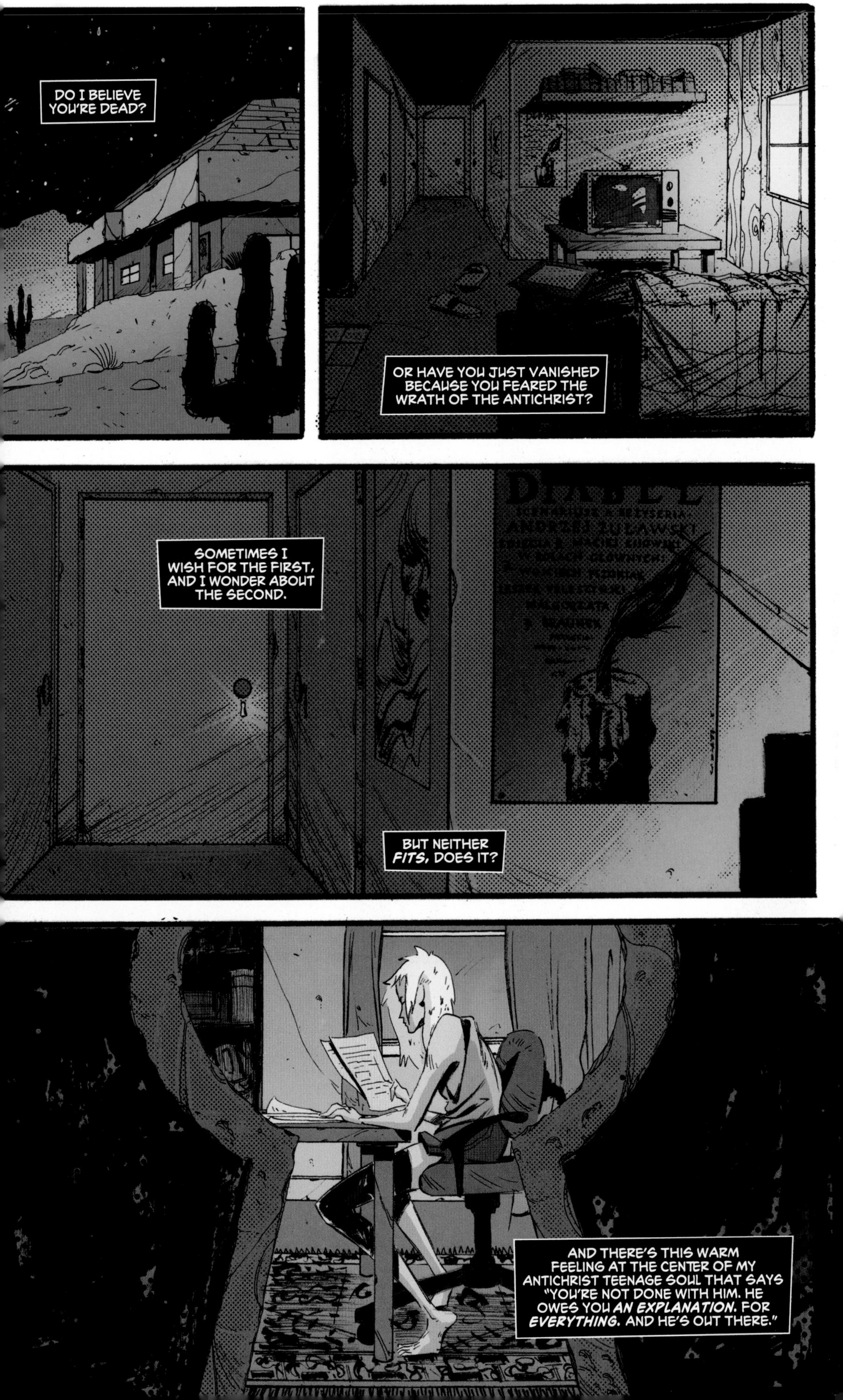
DO I BELIEVE YOU'RE DEAD?
OR HAVE YOU JUST VANISHED BECAUSE YOU FEARED THE WRATH OF THE ANTICHRIST?
SOMETIMES I WISH FOR THE FIRST, AND I WONDER ABOUT THE SECOND.
BUT NEITHER *FITS*, DOES IT?
AND THERE'S THIS WARM FEELING AT THE CENTER OF MY ANTICHRIST TEENAGE SOUL THAT SAYS "YOU'RE NOT DONE WITH HIM. HE OWES YOU *AN EXPLANATION*. FOR *EVERYTHING*. AND HE'S OUT THERE."

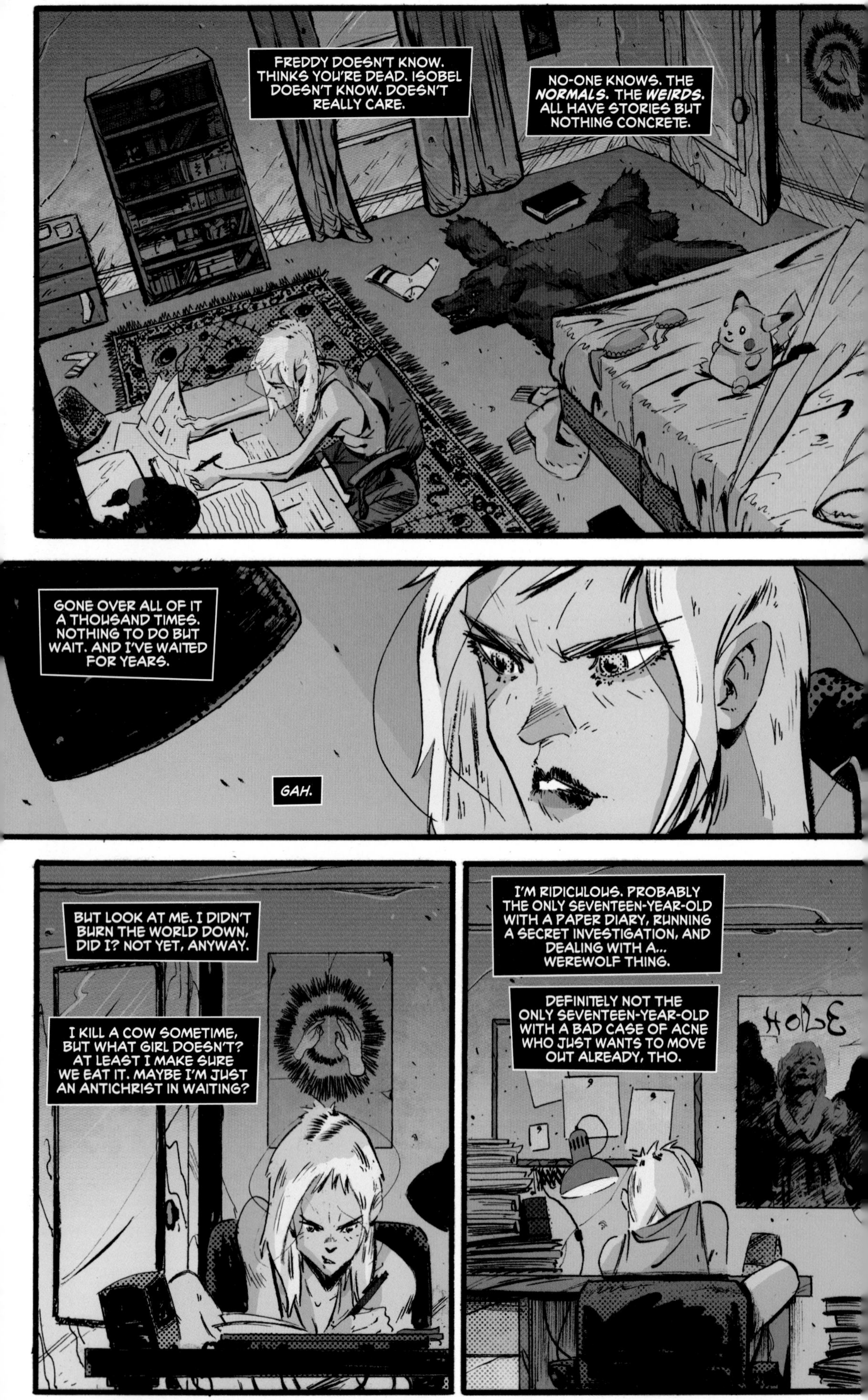

FREDDY DOESN'T KNOW. THINKS YOU'RE DEAD. ISOBEL DOESN'T KNOW. DOESN'T REALLY CARE.
NO-ONE KNOWS. THE *NORMALS*. THE *WEIRDS*. ALL HAVE STORIES BUT NOTHING CONCRETE.
GONE OVER ALL OF IT A THOUSAND TIMES. NOTHING TO DO BUT WAIT. AND I'VE WAITED FOR YEARS.
GAH.
BUT LOOK AT ME. I DIDN'T BURN THE WORLD DOWN, DID I? NOT YET, ANYWAY.
I KILL A COW SOMETIME, BUT WHAT GIRL DOESN'T? AT LEAST I MAKE SURE WE EAT IT. MAYBE I'M JUST AN ANTICHRIST IN WAITING?
I'M RIDICULOUS. PROBABLY THE ONLY SEVENTEEN-YEAR-OLD WITH A PAPER DIARY, RUNNING A SECRET INVESTIGATION, AND DEALING WITH A... WEREWOLF THING.
DEFINITELY NOT THE ONLY SEVENTEEN-YEAR-OLD WITH A BAD CASE OF ACNE WHO JUST WANTS TO MOVE OUT ALREADY, THO.

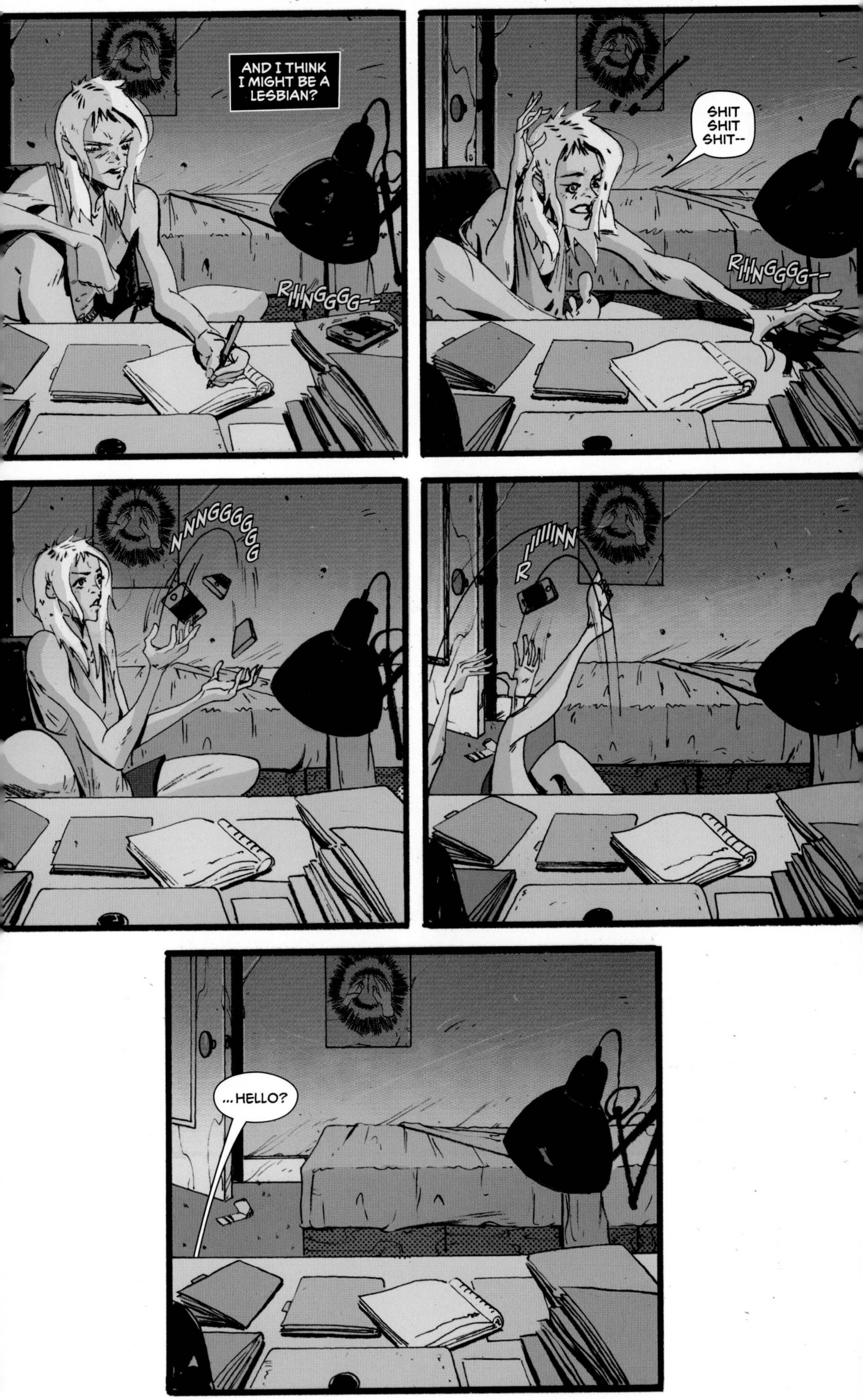
AND I THINK I MIGHT BE A LESBIAN?
RIIINGGGG--
SHIT SHIT SHIT--
RIIINGGGG--
NNNGGGGGG
RIIIIINN
...HELLO?

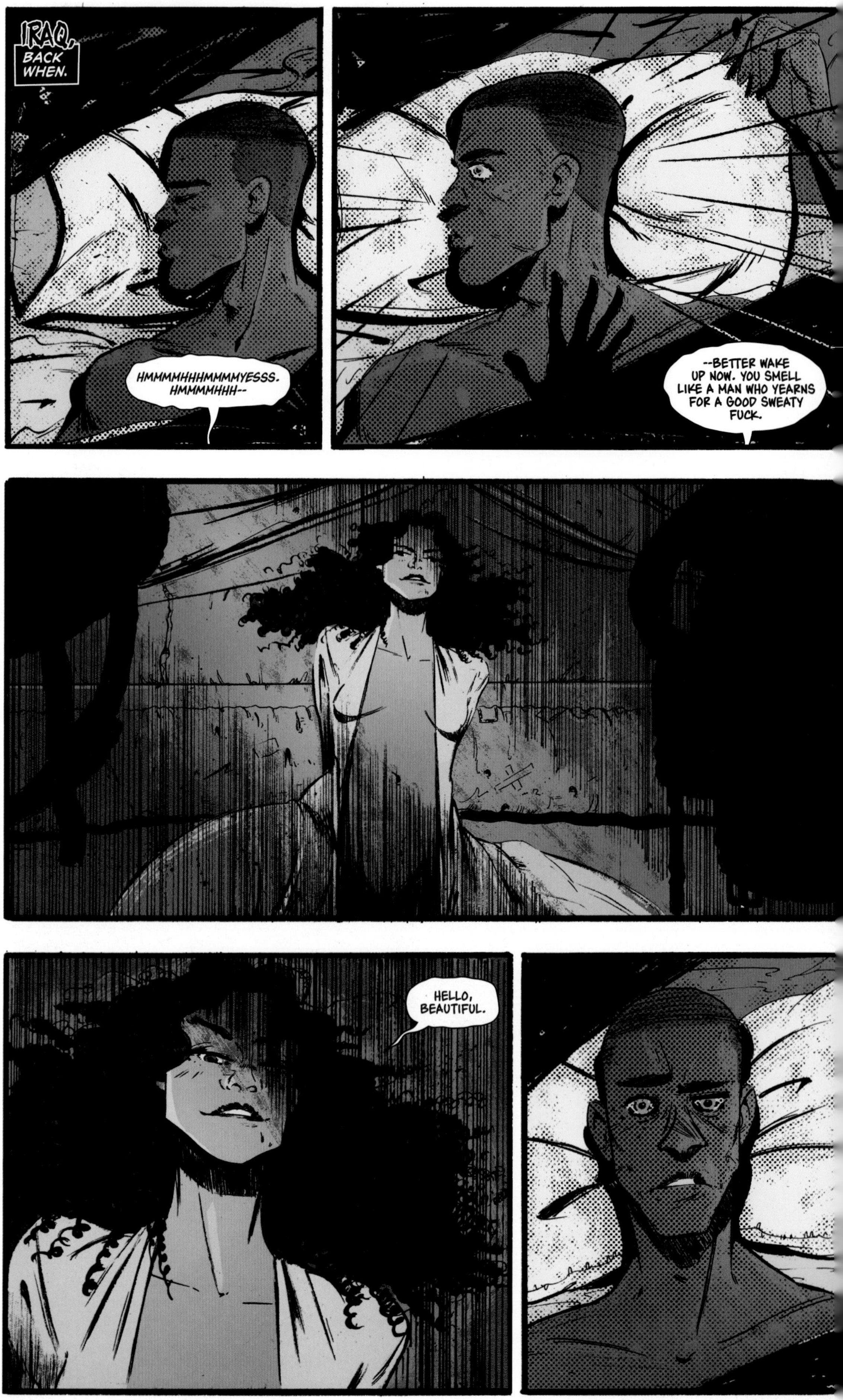
IRAQ, BACK WHEN.
HMMMMHHHMMMMYESSS. HMMMMHHH--
--BETTER WAKE UP NOW. YOU SMELL LIKE A MAN WHO YEARNS FOR A GOOD SWEATY FUCK.
HELLO, BEAUTIFUL.

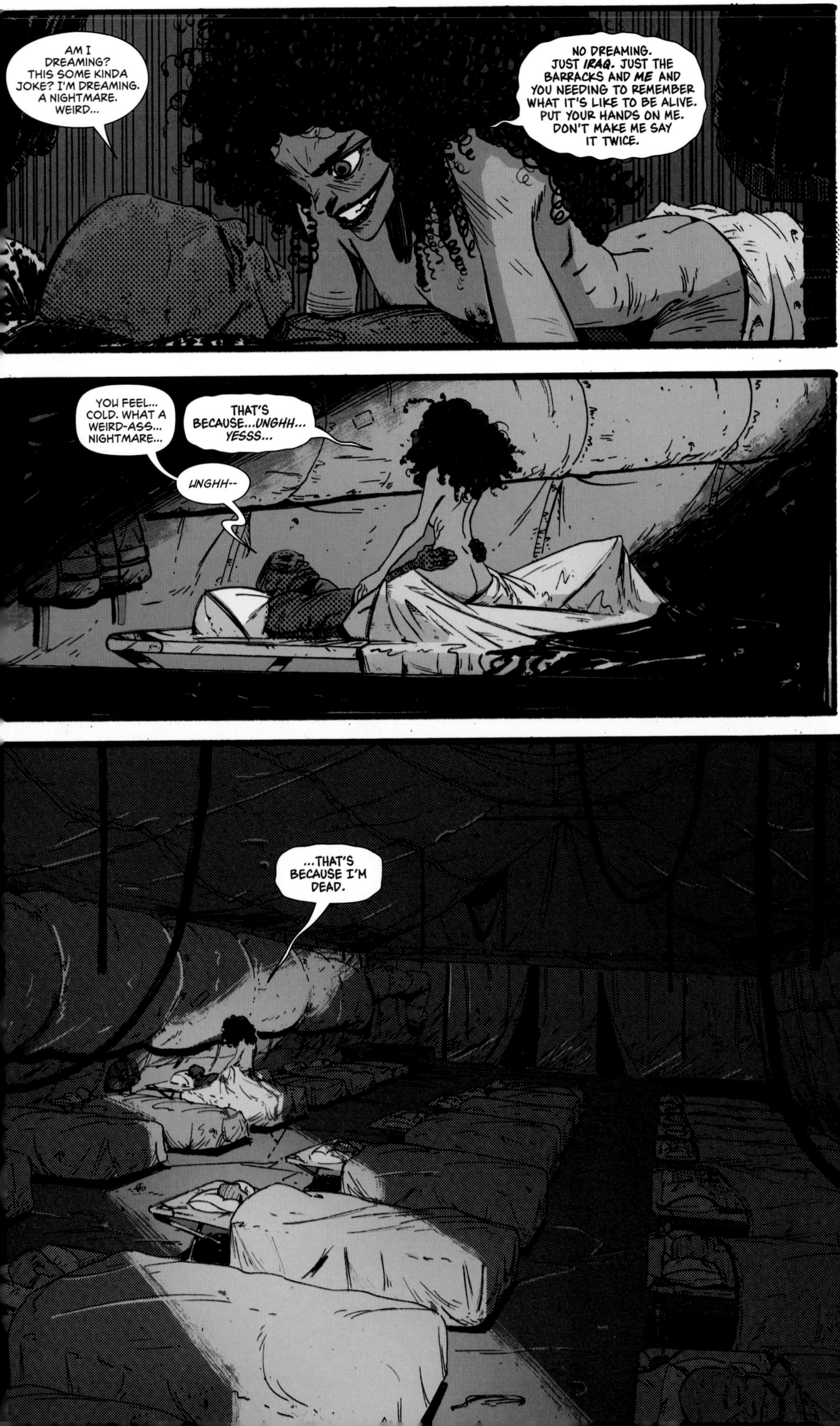
AM I DREAMING? THIS SOME KINDA JOKE? I'M DREAMING. A NIGHTMARE. WEIRD...
NO DREAMING. JUST IRAQ. JUST THE BARRACKS AND ME AND YOU NEEDING TO REMEMBER WHAT IT'S LIKE TO BE ALIVE. PUT YOUR HANDS ON ME. DON'T MAKE ME SAY IT TWICE.
YOU FEEL... COLD. WHAT A WEIRD-ASS... NIGHTMARE...
THAT'S BECAUSE...UNGHH... YESSS...
UNGHH--
...THAT'S BECAUSE I'M DEAD.

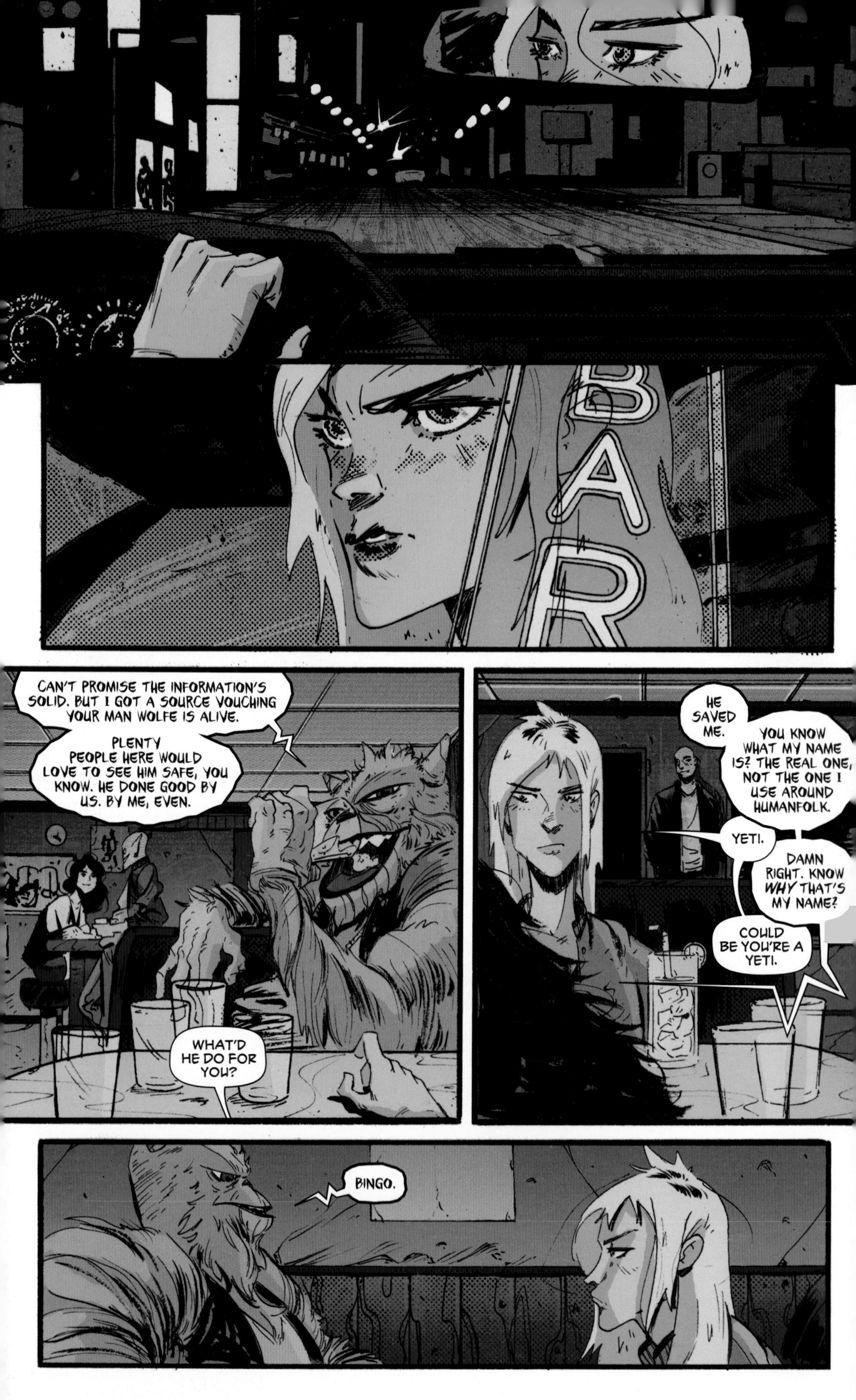
BAR
CAN'T PROMISE THE INFORMATION'S SOLID. BUT I GOT A SOURCE VOUCHING YOUR MAN WOLFE IS ALIVE.
PLENTY PEOPLE HERE WOULD LOVE TO SEE HIM SAFE, YOU KNOW. HE DONE GOOD BY US. BY ME, EVEN.
WHAT'D HE DO FOR YOU?
HE SAVED ME.
YOU KNOW WHAT MY NAME IS? THE REAL ONE, NOT THE ONE I USE AROUND HUMANFOLK.
YETI.
DAMN RIGHT. KNOW *WHY* THAT'S MY NAME?
COULD BE YOU'RE A YETI.
BINGO.

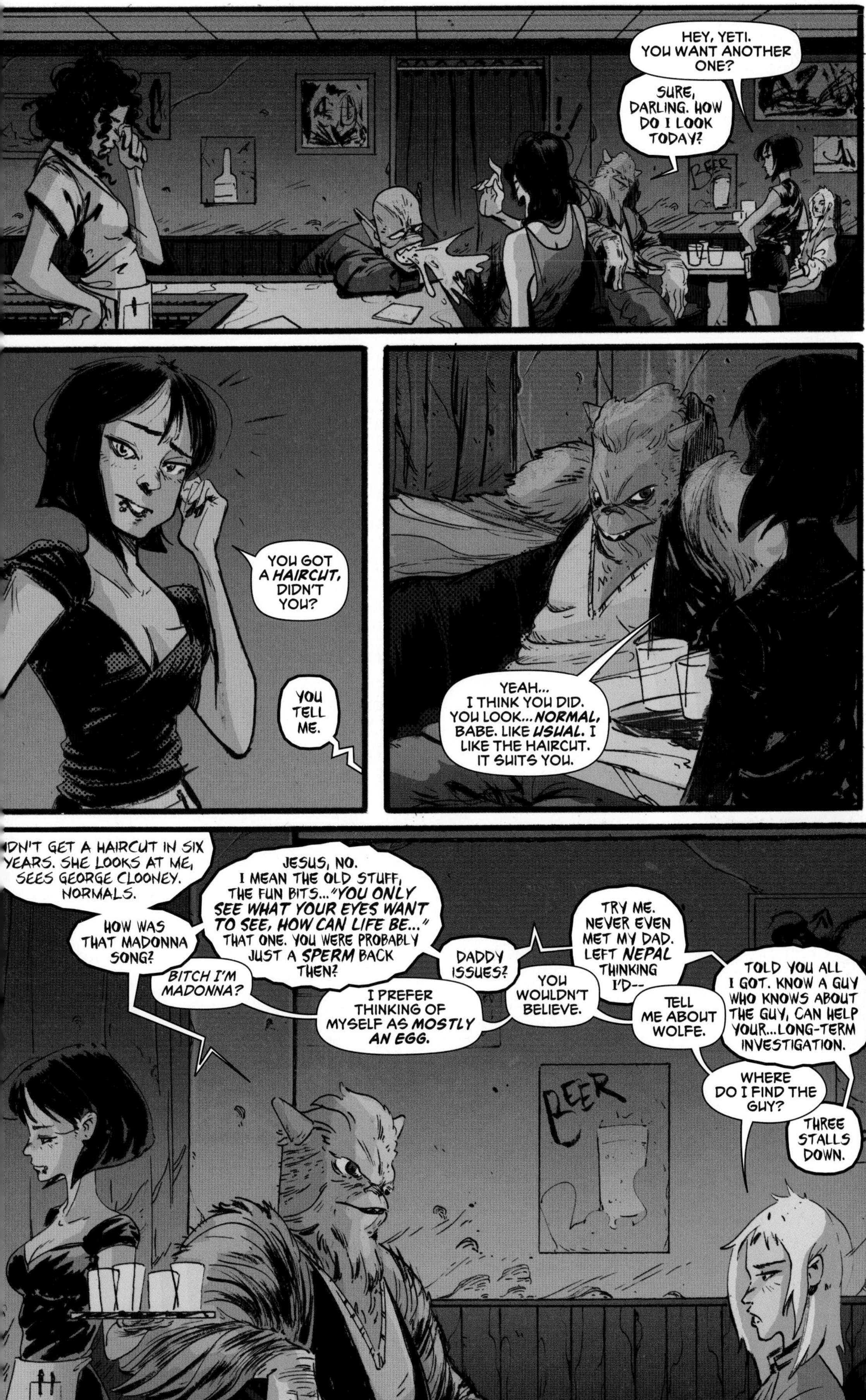
HEY, YETI. YOU WANT ANOTHER ONE?
SURE, DARLING. HOW DO I LOOK TODAY?
YOU GOT A HAIRCUT, DIDN'T YOU?
YOU TELL ME.
YEAH... I THINK YOU DID. YOU LOOK...NORMAL, BABE. LIKE USUAL. I LIKE THE HAIRCUT. IT SUITS YOU.
IDN'T GET A HAIRCUT IN SIX YEARS. SHE LOOKS AT ME, SEES GEORGE CLOONEY. NORMALS.
HOW WAS THAT MADONNA SONG?
BITCH I'M MADONNA?
JESUS, NO. I MEAN THE OLD STUFF, THE FUN BITS..."YOU ONLY SEE WHAT YOUR EYES WANT TO SEE, HOW CAN LIFE BE..." THAT ONE. YOU WERE PROBABLY JUST A SPERM BACK THEN?
I PREFER THINKING OF MYSELF AS MOSTLY AN EGG.
DADDY ISSUES?
YOU WOULDN'T BELIEVE.
TRY ME. NEVER EVEN MET MY DAD. LEFT NEPAL THINKING I'D--
TELL ME ABOUT WOLFE.
TOLD YOU ALL I GOT. KNOW A GUY WHO KNOWS ABOUT THE GUY, CAN HELP YOUR...LONG-TERM INVESTIGATION.
WHERE DO I FIND THE GUY?
THREE STALLS DOWN.

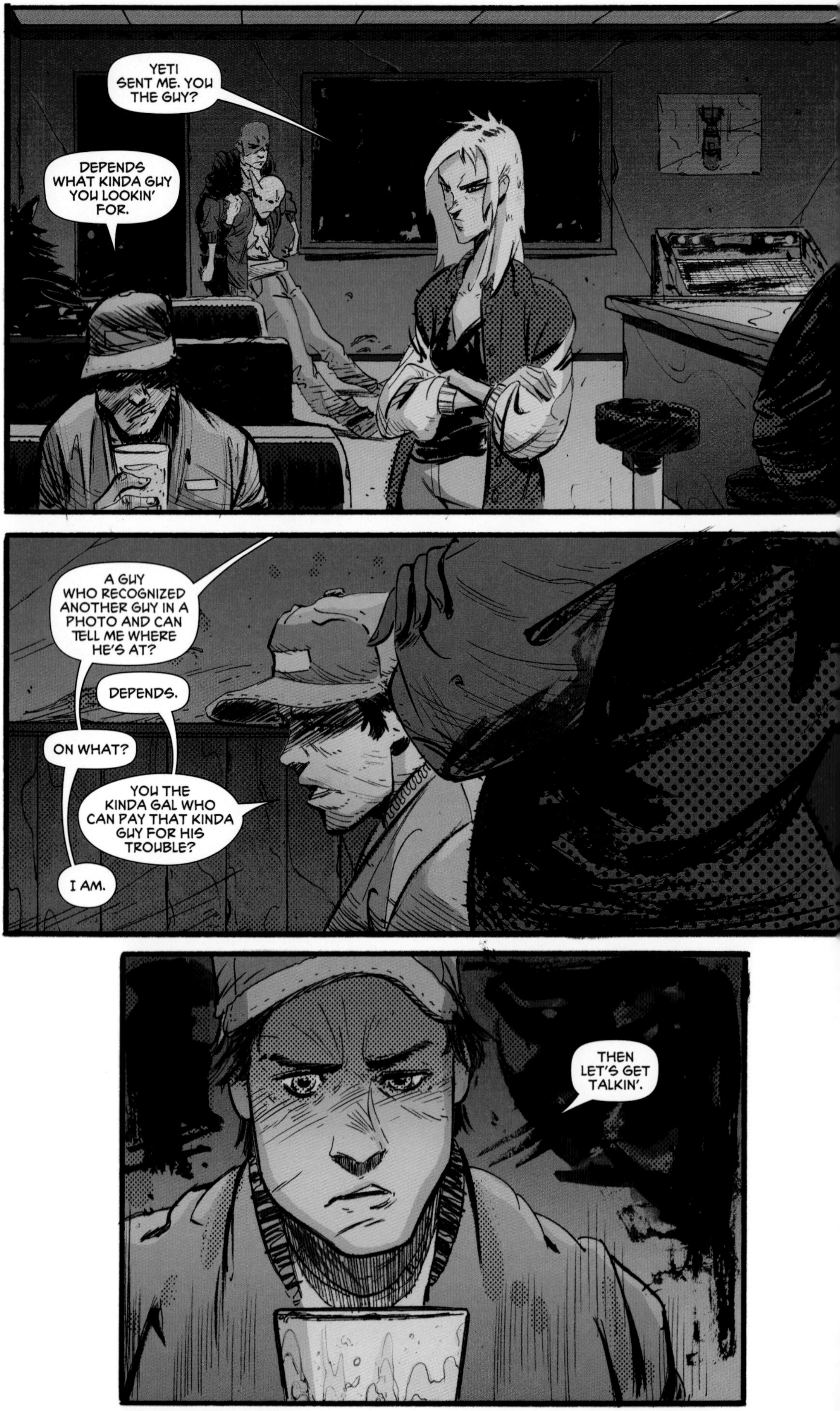
YETI SENT ME. YOU THE GUY?
DEPENDS WHAT KINDA GUY YOU LOOKIN' FOR.
A GUY WHO RECOGNIZED ANOTHER GUY IN A PHOTO AND CAN TELL ME WHERE HE'S AT?
DEPENDS.
ON WHAT?
YOU THE KINDA GAL WHO CAN PAY THAT KINDA GUY FOR HIS TROUBLE?
I AM.
THEN LET'S GET TALKIN'.

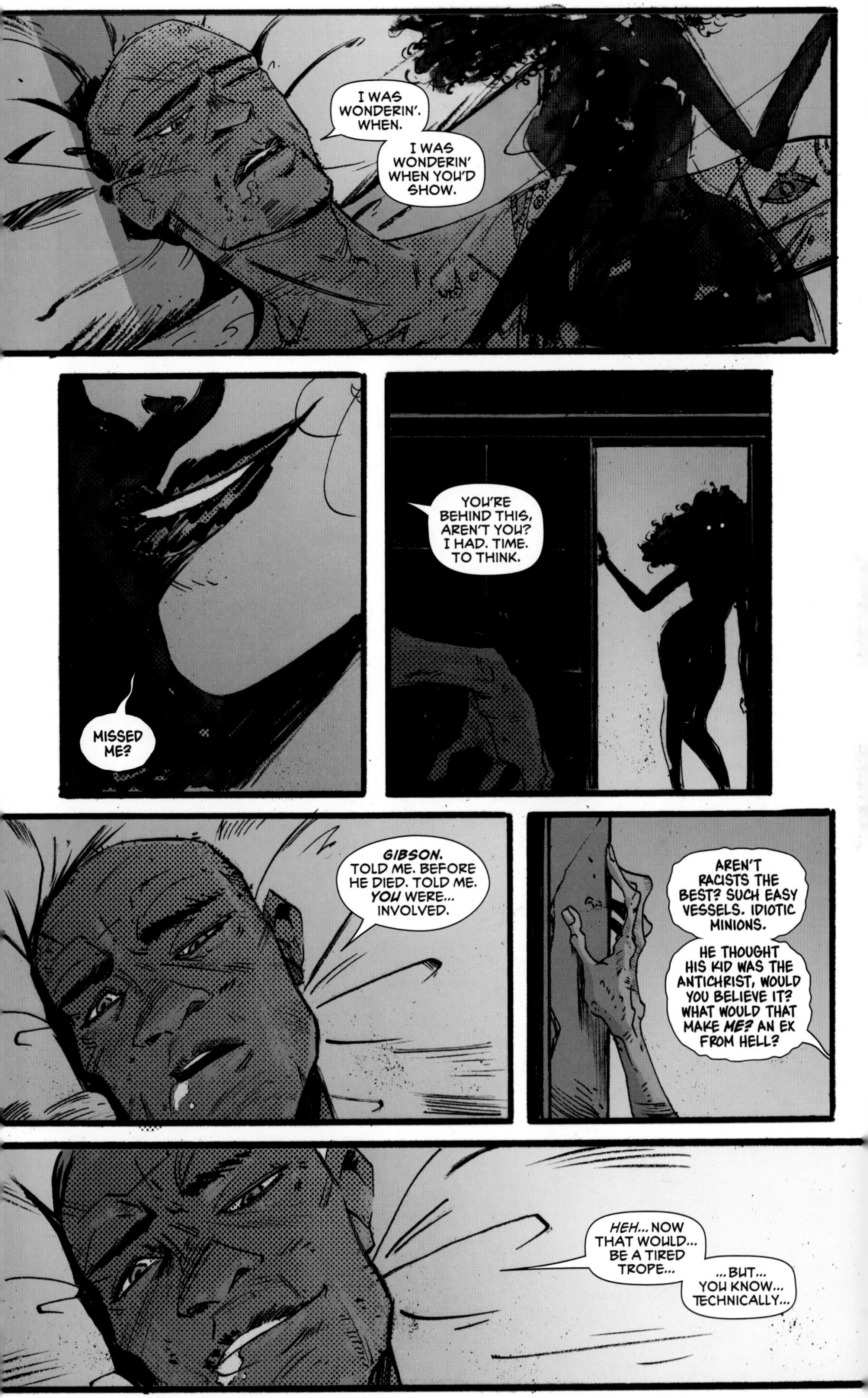
I WAS WONDERIN'. WHEN.
I WAS WONDERIN' WHEN YOU'D SHOW.
MISSED ME?
YOU'RE BEHIND THIS, AREN'T YOU? I HAD. TIME. TO THINK.
GIBSON. TOLD ME. BEFORE HE DIED. TOLD ME. YOU WERE... INVOLVED.
AREN'T RACISTS THE BEST? SUCH EASY VESSELS. IDIOTIC MINIONS.
HE THOUGHT HIS KID WAS THE ANTICHRIST, WOULD YOU BELIEVE IT? WHAT WOULD THAT MAKE ME? AN EX FROM HELL?
HEH... NOW THAT WOULD... BE A TIRED TROPE...
...BUT... YOU KNOW... TECHNICALLY...

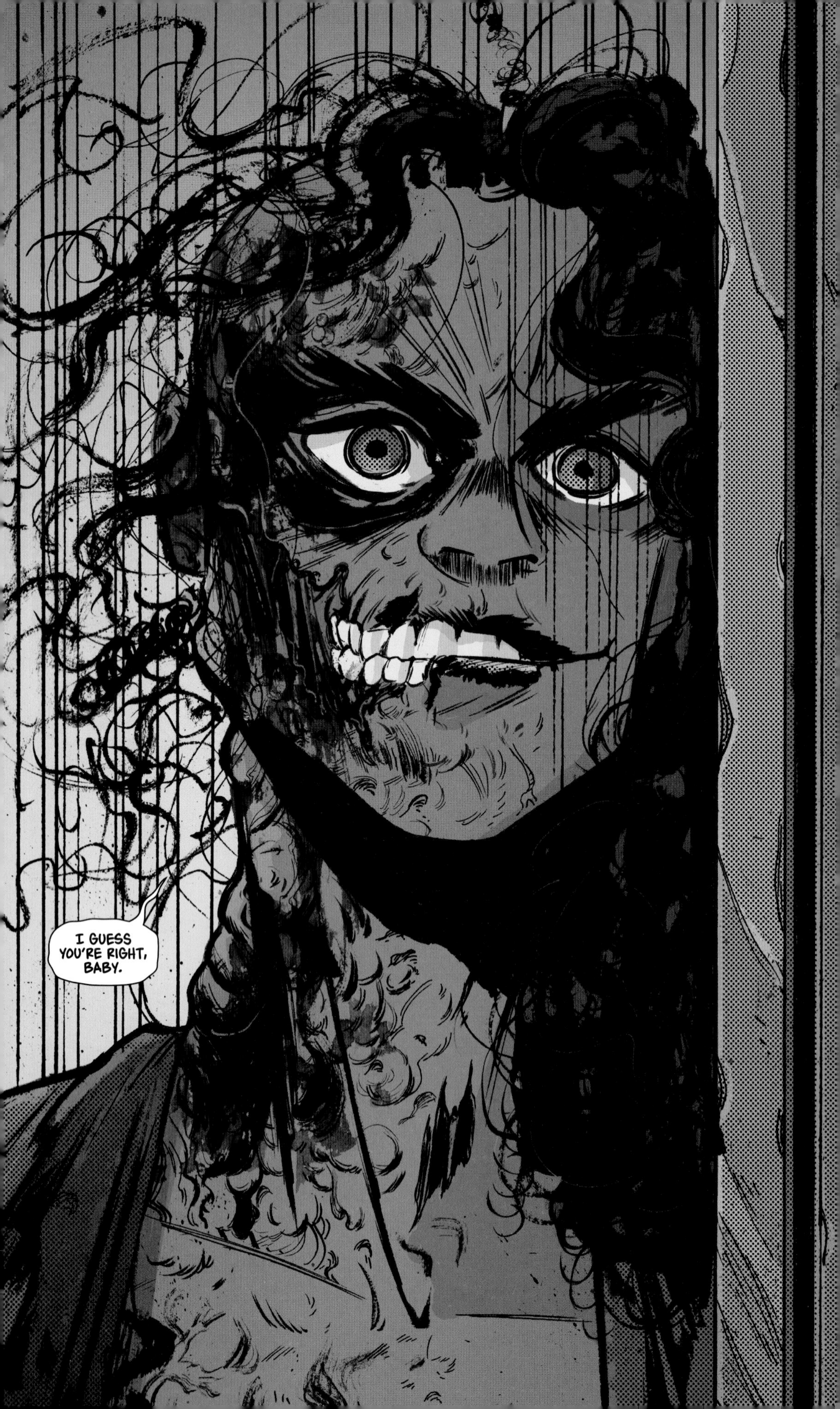
I GUESS YOU'RE RIGHT, BABY.

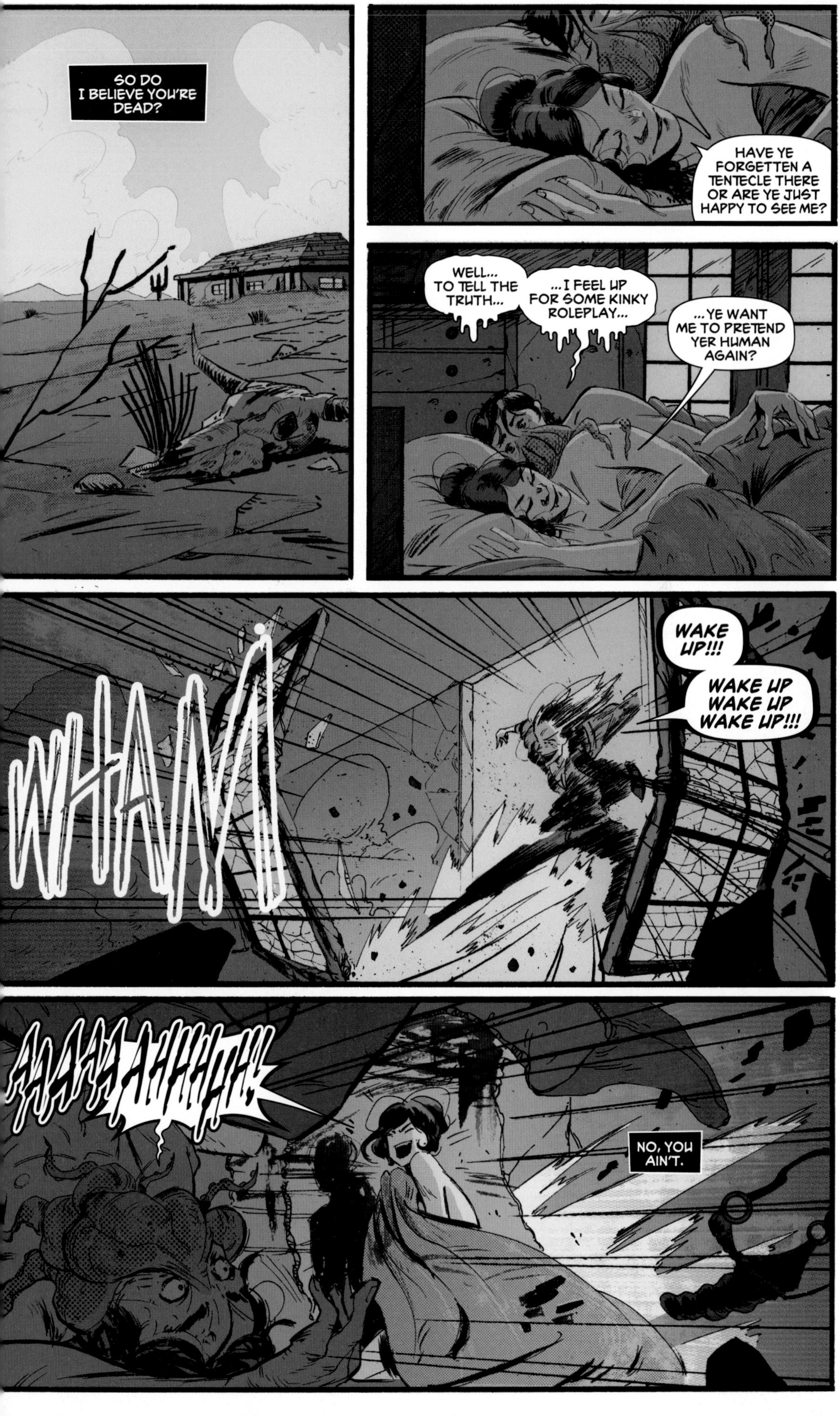

SO DO I BELIEVE YOU'RE DEAD?
HAVE YE FORGETTEN A TENTECLE THERE OR ARE YE JUST HAPPY TO SEE ME?
WELL... TO TELL THE TRUTH...
...I FEEL UP FOR SOME KINKY ROLEPLAY...
...YE WANT ME TO PRETEND YER HUMAN AGAIN?
WHAM
WAKE UP!!!
WAKE UP WAKE UP WAKE UP!!!
AAAAAAHHHH!!
NO, YOU AIN'T.

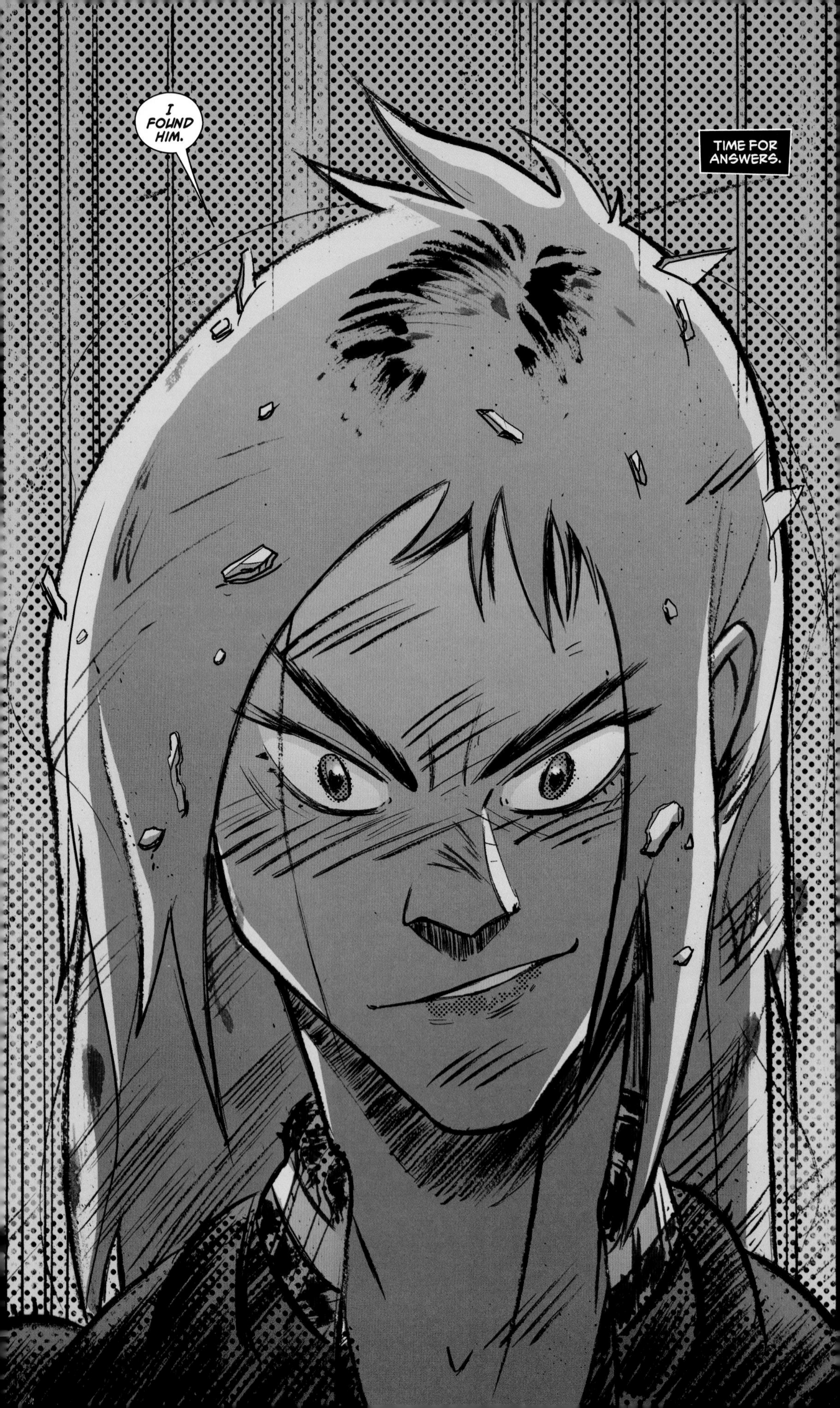
I FOUND HIM.
TIME FOR ANSWERS.

Chapter 6

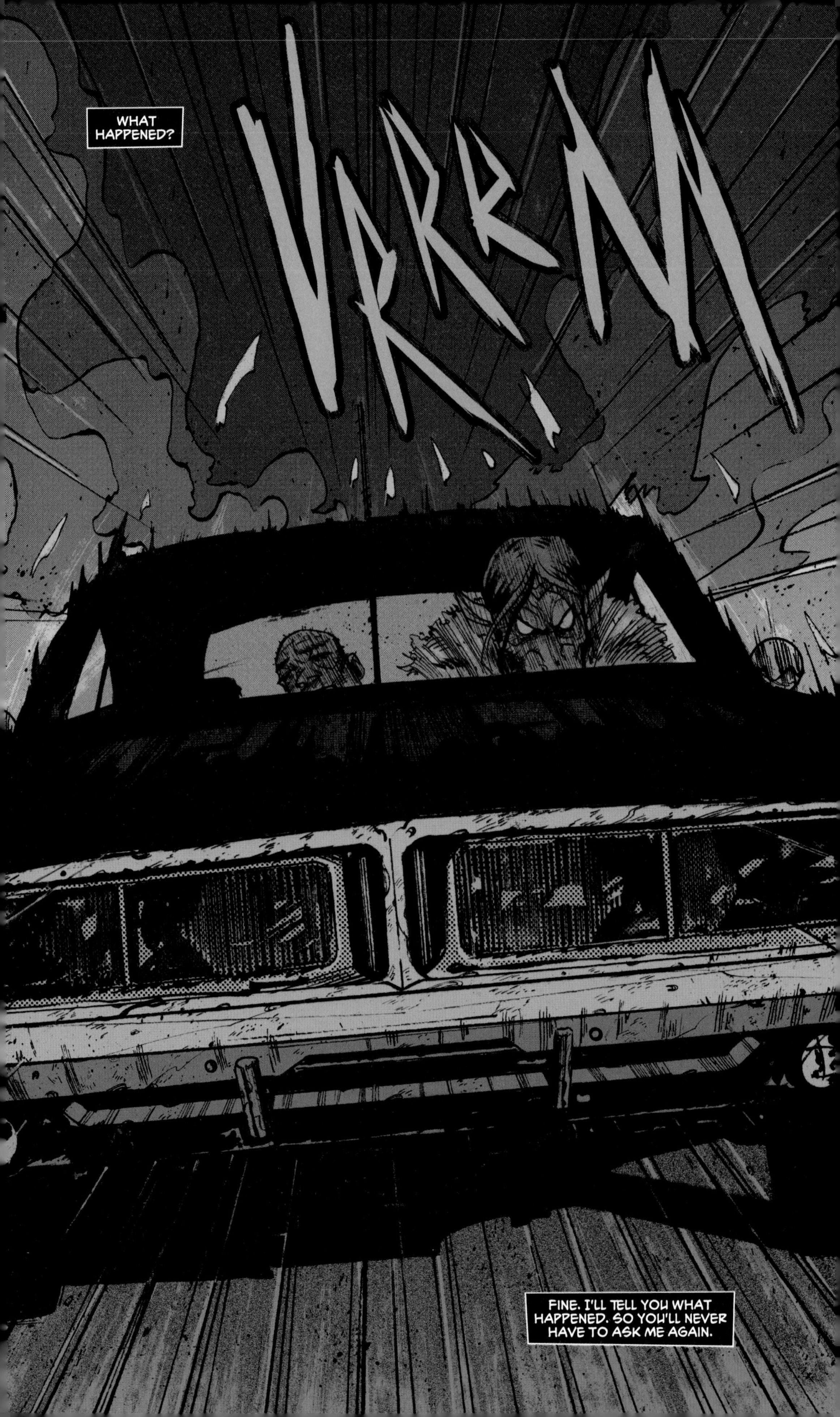
WHAT HAPPENED?
VRRRM
FINE. I'LL TELL YOU WHAT HAPPENED. SO YOU'LL NEVER HAVE TO ASK ME AGAIN.

FIVE YEARS AGO, ***WOLFE*** AND I GO INTO THE DESERT TO MEET MY NOW-DEAD BIOLOGICAL FATHER AND A TOTAL ASSHOLE ***STERLING GIBSON*** AND WHOEVER THAT OTHER GUY WAS. I GAVE THAT OTHER GUY A SCAR WHEN HE TRIED TO GRAB ME THAT TIME HE GRABBED YOU, ***FREDDY.*** SIMMONS? YEAH, ***SIMMONS. THAT*** GUY.

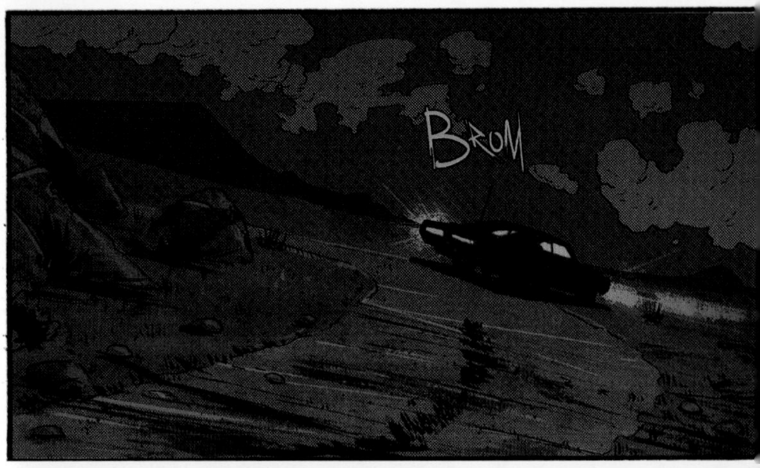
BROM

ANYWAY, WE GO INTO THE DESERT THINKING... ***I*** GO INTO THE DESERT THINKING, WOLFE HAS A ***PLAN,*** YOU KNOW? IT'S GONNA BE ***OKAY.*** I **TRUST HIM.** HE TELLS ME TO WATCH OUT AND STAND BACK AND LET THINGS HAPPEN THE WAY THEY'LL HAPPEN IF WE WANT TO SAVE YOU. WHICH WE DID.

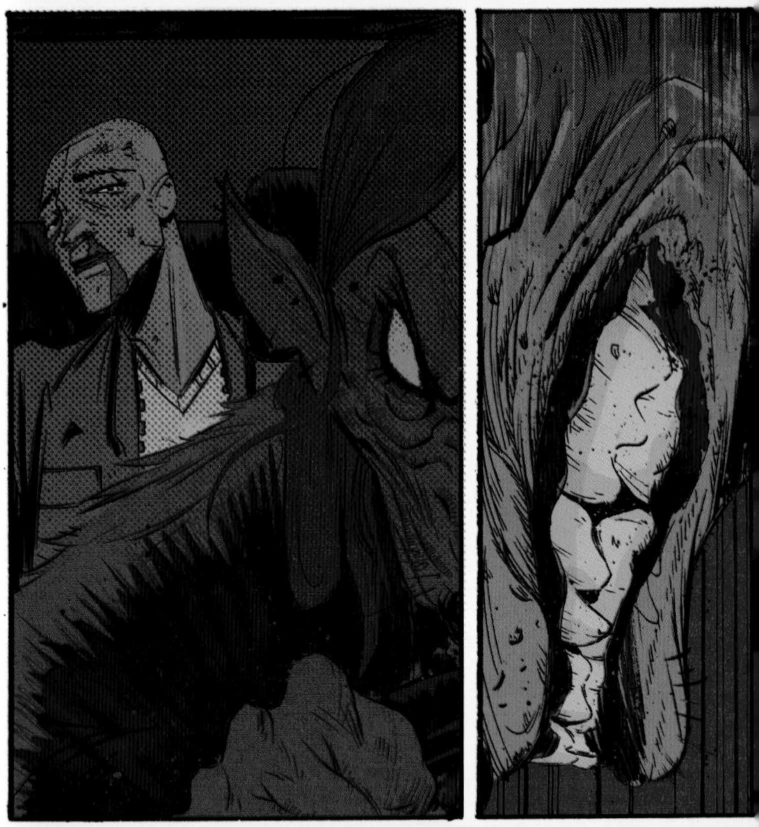

AND THEN HE ***GETS*** SHOT A FEW TIMES BUT I KNOW IT'S GONNA BE OKAY 'CAUSE HE'S IMMORTAL. AND THEN HE OPENS THIS ***BOX*** AND MY ***GRANDMA'S GHOST*** COMES OUT AND LATER ON WHILE BLEEDING IN THE CAR HE TELLS ME HE NEEDED A GHOST TO ATTRACT THOSE THINGS THAT COME WITH THE ***SANTA ANA WINDS*** BECAUSE THOSE THINGS PREY ON GHOSTS.

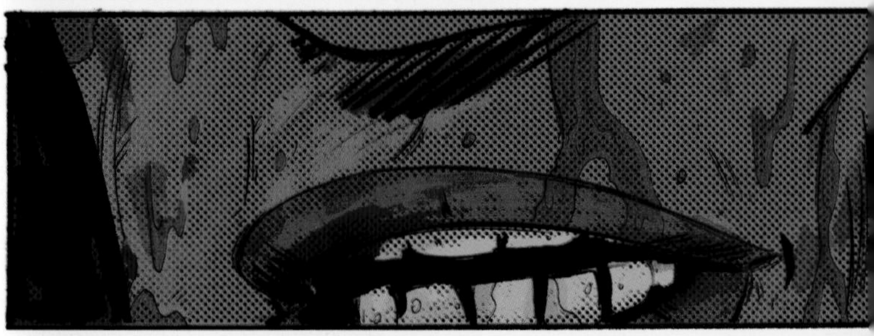

SO HE USED GRANDMA.

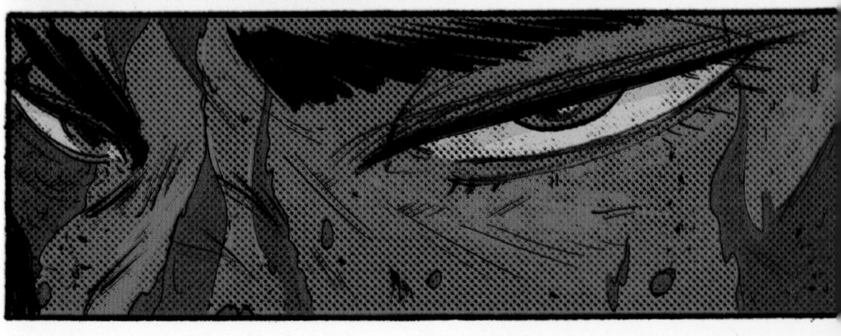

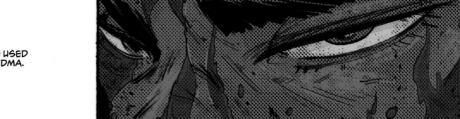

HE TELLS ME GRANDMA MUST HAVE KNOWN ABOUT WHAT MY ***DIRTBAG WEREWOLF FATHER*** HAD PLANNED FOR ME BECAUSE GRANDMA WAS AROUND HIM ALL THE TIME, TOLD WOLFE SHE WAS HAUNTING HIM, AND FATHER TOLD WOLFE HE KILLED HER AND THAT'S HOW SHE BECAME A GHOST AND STARTED HAUNTING HIM, BUT WOLFE SAID THEY WERE BOTH LYING. WOLFE SAID THEY NEEDED US BOTH FOR ***THE RITUAL.***

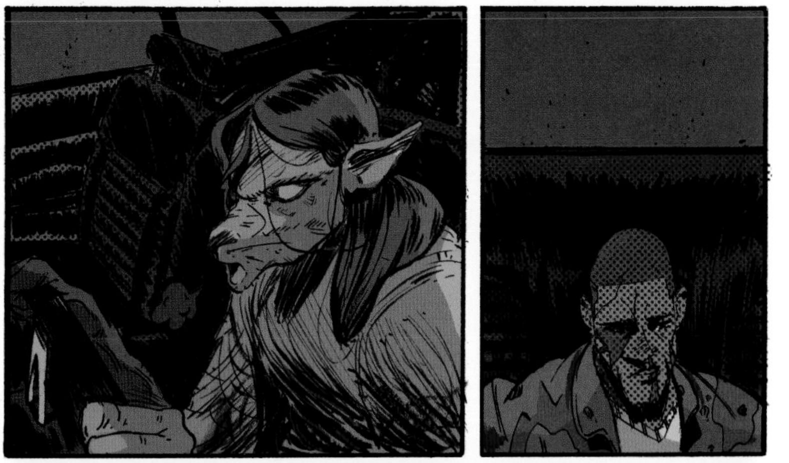

HE SAID HE KNEW I WAS A ***WEREWOLF*** AND HE KNEW I WOULD TURN AND SAVE OUR ASSES BECAUSE THAT WAS HIS ***ONLY PLAY LEFT***. HE WAS SURPRISED YOU WEREN'T THERE. THEY TOLD US YOU WERE DEAD.

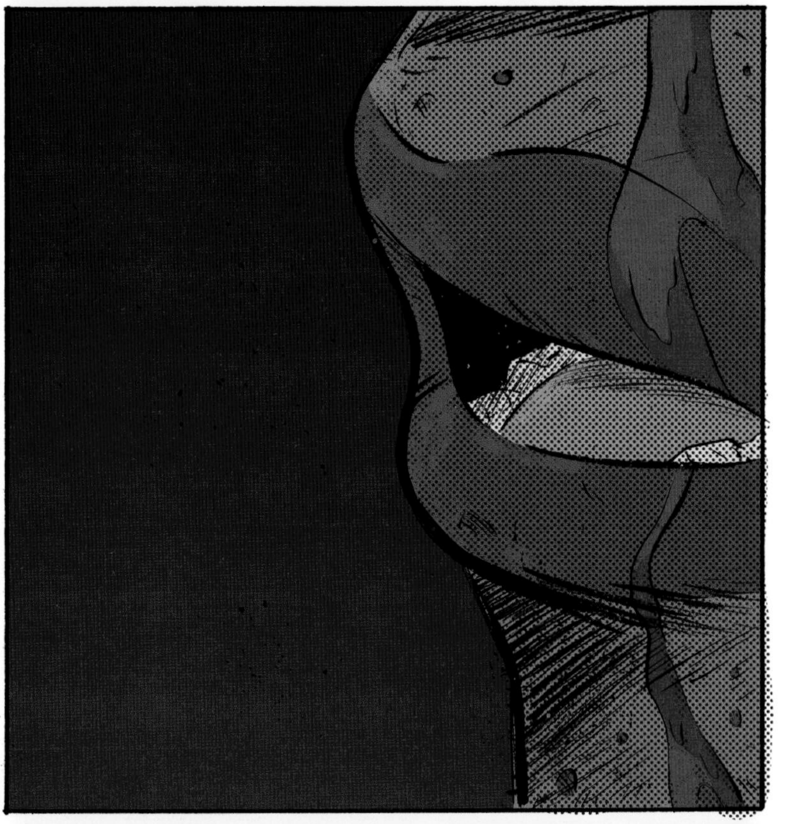

SO I TOOK CARE OF MY DEADBEAT HORROR FATHER AND HIS MINION AND I LOADED WOLFE UP INTO THE CAR AND I DROVE AWAY LIKE I HAD AN IDEA OF HOW TO DRIVE A CAR WHICH I DID NOT. GOOD THING WE WERE IN THE DESERT, YOU KNOW? AND I WAS PISSED OFF. I WAS ***REALLY*** PISSED OFF.

I THINK ***HE*** GOT THAT, TOO.

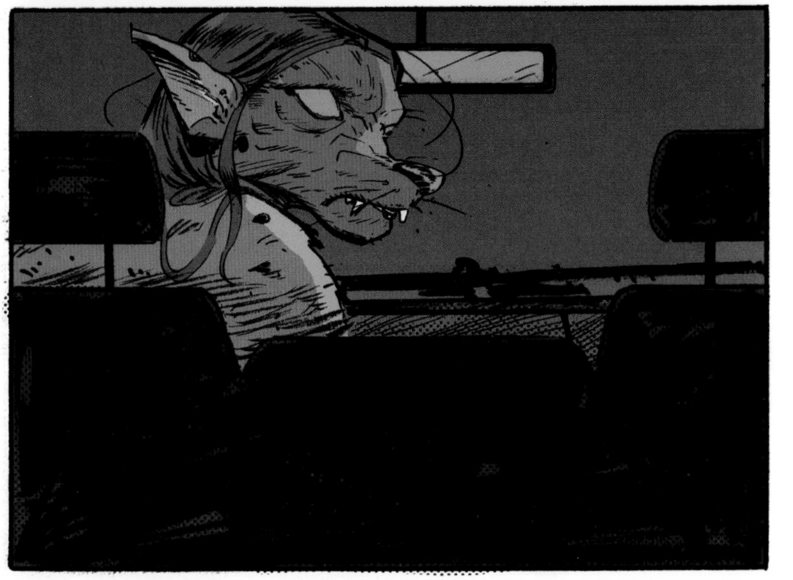

AND THEN I LEFT HIM THERE,
BLEEDING AND NOT DYING, EVER,
AND I TOLD HIM I NEVER WANTED TO
SEE HIS UGLY MUG AGAIN AND I LEFT
THE CAR BEHIND AND I RAN UNTIL I
SAW THE *CITY* LIGHTS AND I DIDN'T
STOP UNTIL I KILLED A FEW COWS
BECAUSE I WAS *ANGRY* AND
ALONE AND I'M STILL SORRY I
KILLED THOSE COWS. THEY
DIDN'T DESERVE IT AND
I DIDN'T EVEN EAT THEM.

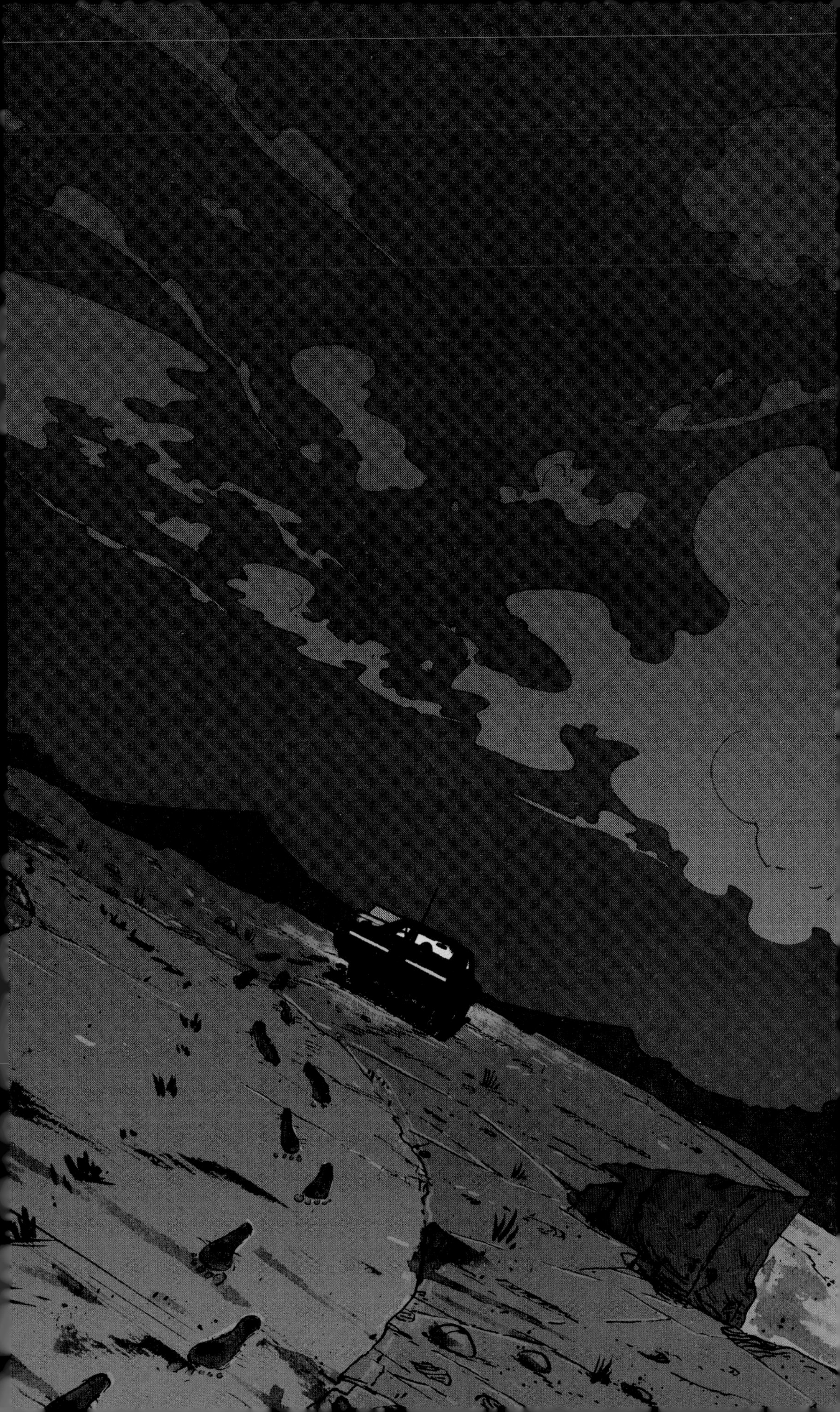

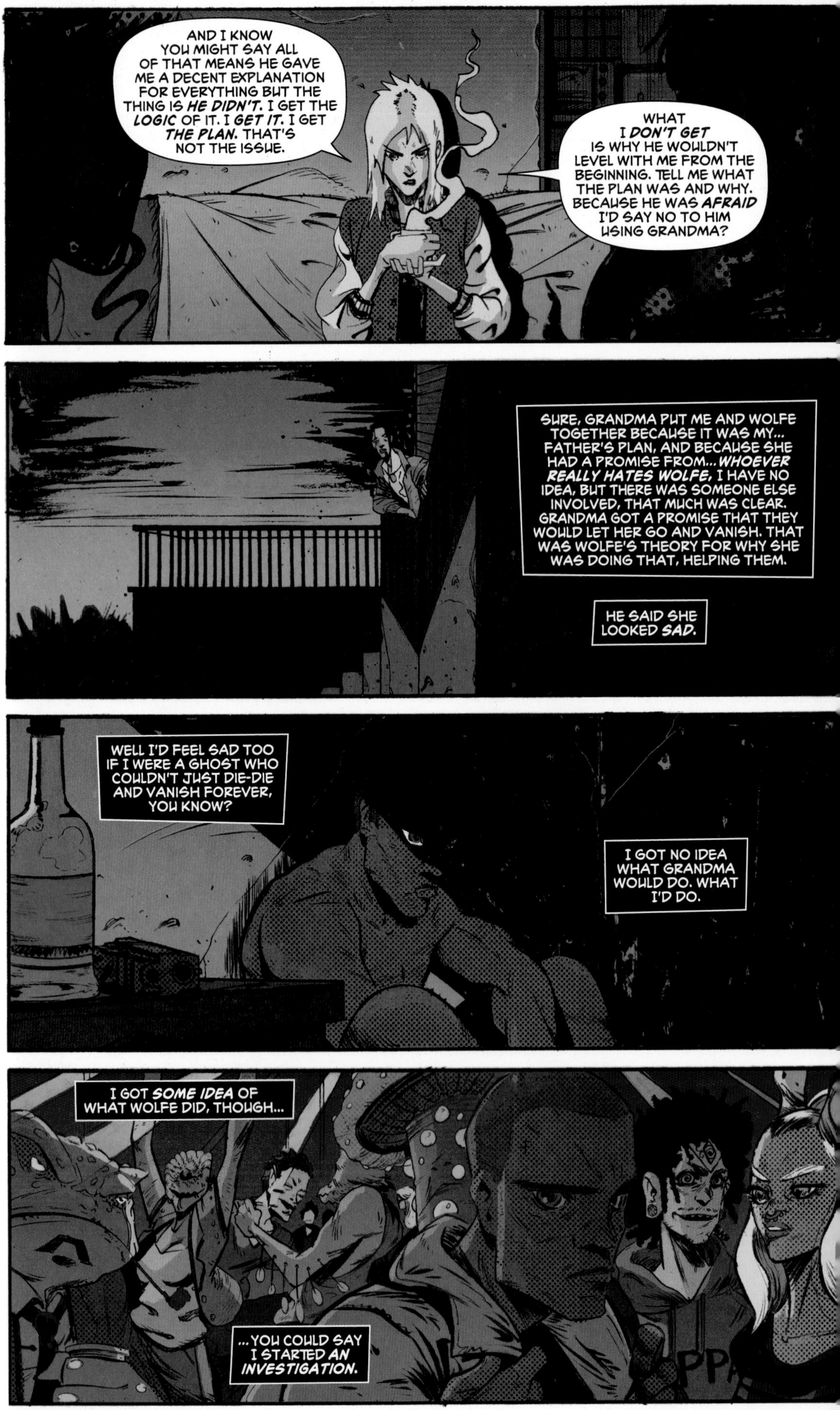
AND I KNOW YOU MIGHT SAY ALL OF THAT MEANS HE GAVE ME A DECENT EXPLANATION FOR EVERYTHING BUT THE THING IS *HE DIDN'T*. I GET THE *LOGIC* OF IT. I *GET IT*. I GET *THE PLAN*. THAT'S NOT THE ISSUE.
WHAT I *DON'T GET* IS WHY HE WOULDN'T LEVEL WITH ME FROM THE BEGINNING. TELL ME WHAT THE PLAN WAS AND WHY. BECAUSE HE WAS *AFRAID* I'D SAY NO TO HIM USING GRANDMA?
SURE, GRANDMA PUT ME AND WOLFE TOGETHER BECAUSE IT WAS MY... FATHER'S PLAN, AND BECAUSE SHE HAD A PROMISE FROM... *WHOEVER REALLY HATES WOLFE*, I HAVE NO IDEA, BUT THERE WAS SOMEONE ELSE INVOLVED, THAT MUCH WAS CLEAR. GRANDMA GOT A PROMISE THAT THEY WOULD LET HER GO AND VANISH. THAT WAS WOLFE'S THEORY FOR WHY SHE WAS DOING THAT, HELPING THEM.
HE SAID SHE LOOKED *SAD*.
WELL I'D FEEL SAD TOO IF I WERE A GHOST WHO COULDN'T JUST DIE-DIE AND VANISH FOREVER, YOU KNOW?
I GOT NO IDEA WHAT GRANDMA WOULD DO. WHAT I'D DO.
I GOT *SOME IDEA* OF WHAT WOLFE DID, THOUGH...
...YOU COULD SAY I STARTED *AN INVESTIGATION*.

YEAH, WE KNEW.

YEH'RE NOT THAT GEED ET HEIDING YER INTERESTS, YUNG DETECTIIV ANEETA CHREIST.

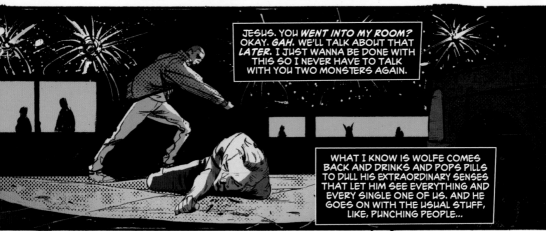

JESUS. YOU *WENT INTO MY ROOM?* OKAY. *GAH.* WE'LL TALK ABOUT THAT *LATER.* I JUST WANNA BE DONE WITH THIS SO I NEVER HAVE TO TALK WITH YOU TWO MONSTERS AGAIN.

WHAT I KNOW IS WOLFE COMES BACK AND DRINKS AND POPS PILLS TO DULL HIS EXTRAORDINARY SENSES THAT LET HIM SEE EVERYTHING AND EVERY SINGLE ONE OF US. AND HE GOES ON WITH THE USUAL STUFF, LIKE, PUNCHING PEOPLE...

...AND, LIKE, DOING MAGIC STUFF AND THINGS. FOR LIKE A WEEK OR TWO?

AND THEN HE WALKS OUT OF HIS APARTMENT WITH SOME BAGS AND HE'S MOVED MOST OF HIS STUFF SATAN-KNOWS-WHERE AND THE TRAIL VANISHES EXCEPT FOR, LIKE, *CRUMBLES.*

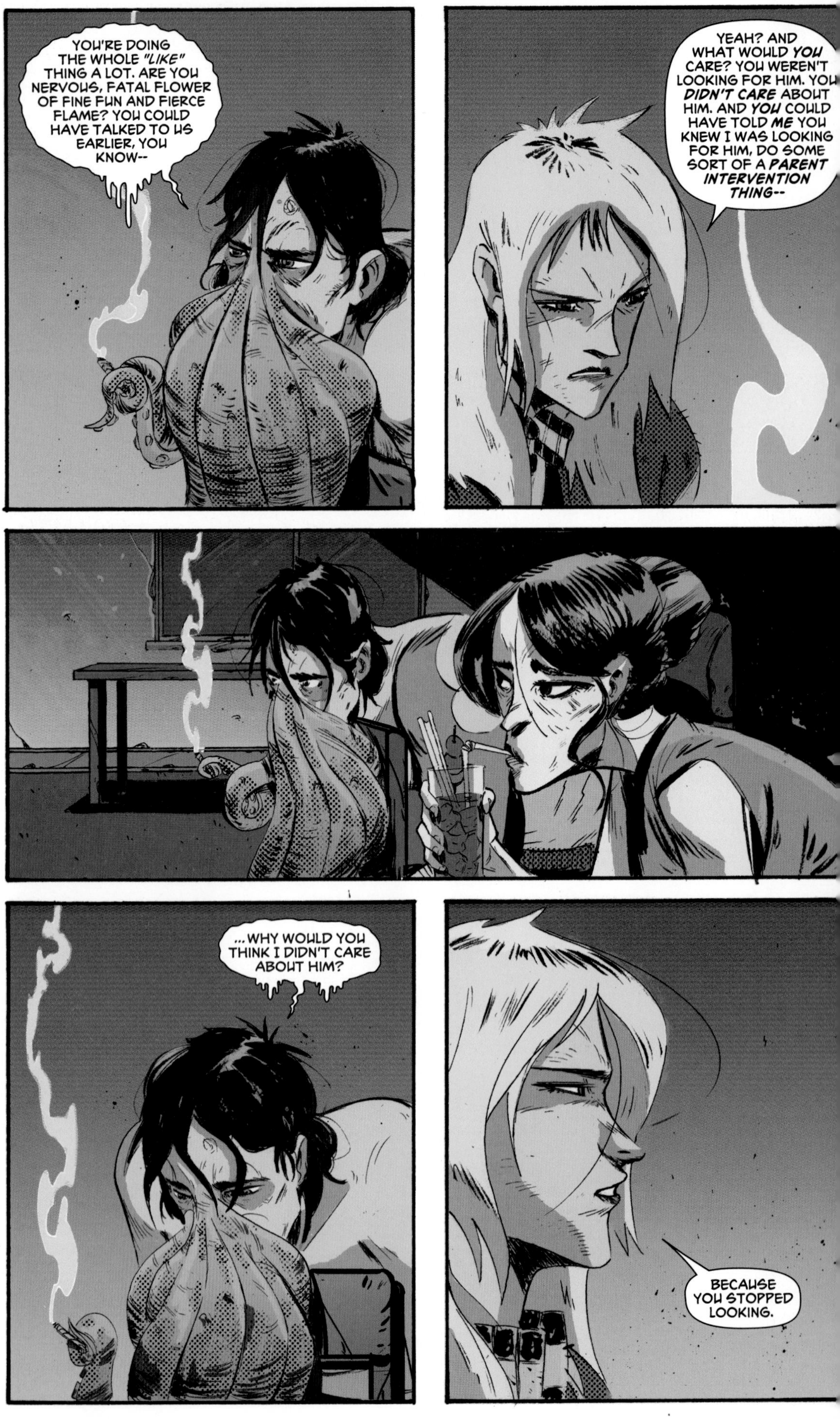
YOU'RE DOING THE WHOLE "LIKE" THING A LOT. ARE YOU NERVOUS, FATAL FLOWER OF FINE FUN AND FIERCE FLAME? YOU COULD HAVE TALKED TO US EARLIER, YOU KNOW--
YEAH? AND WHAT WOULD YOU CARE? YOU WEREN'T LOOKING FOR HIM. YOU DIDN'T CARE ABOUT HIM. AND YOU COULD HAVE TOLD ME YOU KNEW I WAS LOOKING FOR HIM, DO SOME SORT OF A PARENT INTERVENTION THING--
...WHY WOULD YOU THINK I DIDN'T CARE ABOUT HIM?
BECAUSE YOU STOPPED LOOKING.

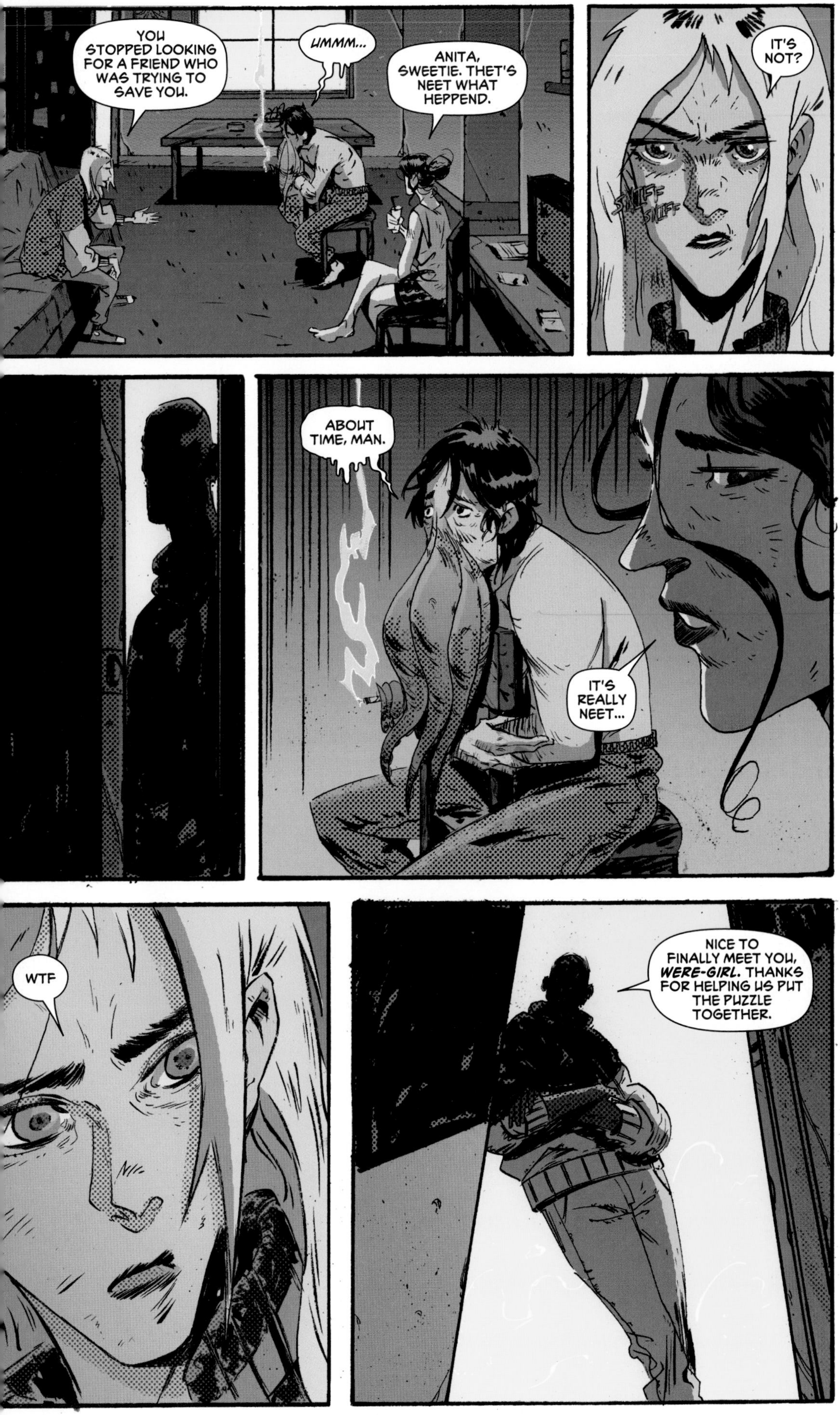

YOU STOPPED LOOKING FOR A FRIEND WHO WAS TRYING TO SAVE YOU.
UMMM...
ANITA, SWEETIE. THET'S NEET WHAT HEPPEND.
IT'S NOT?
SNIFF SNIFF
ABOUT TIME, MAN.
IT'S REALLY NEET...
WTF
NICE TO FINALLY MEET YOU, WERE-GIRL. THANKS FOR HELPING US PUT THE PUZZLE TOGETHER.

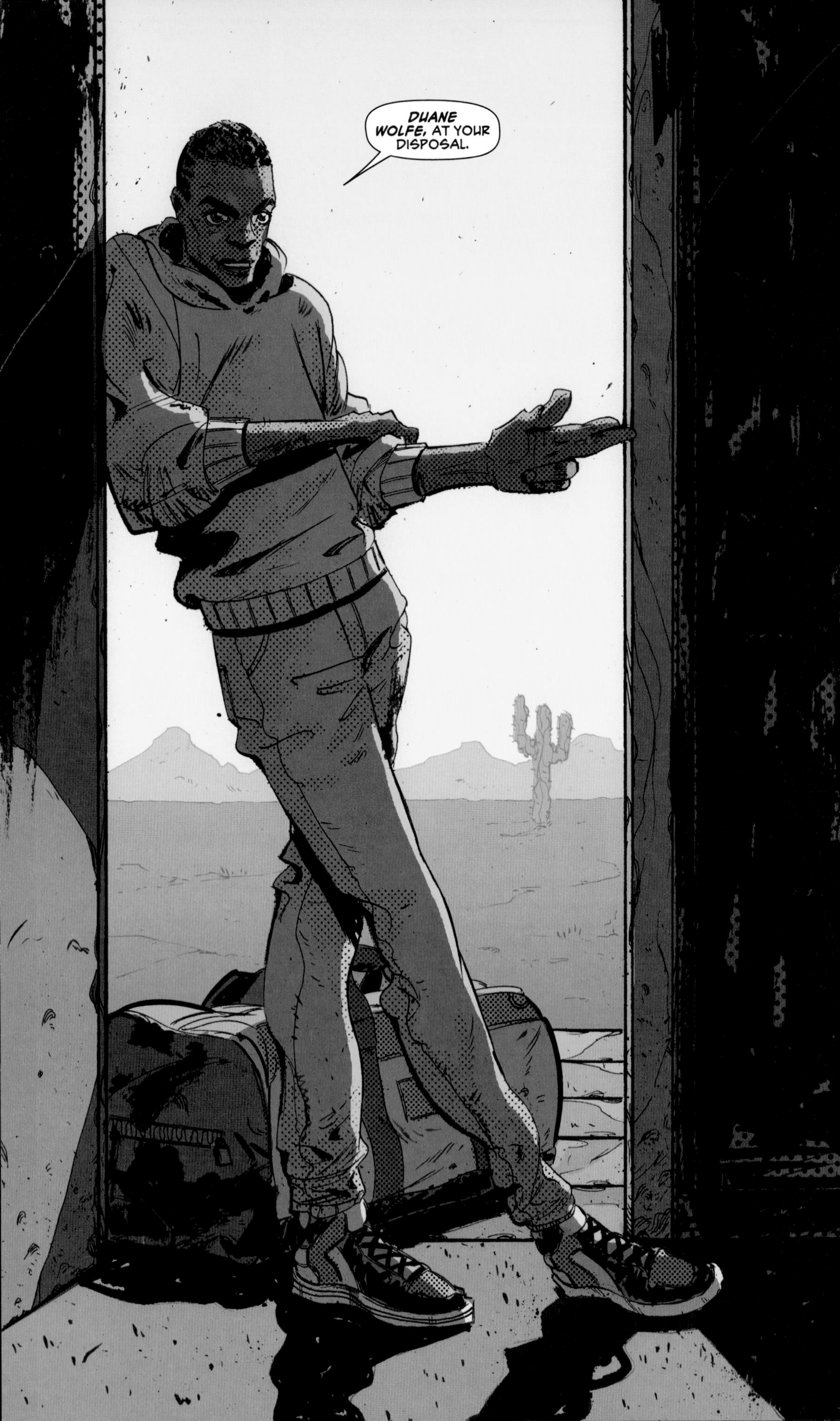
DUANE WOLFE, AT YOUR DISPOSAL.

Wolfe

5 YEARS AGO

~~DOES~~ TAKES OF WITH THE
       MONEY (iKNEW HE HAD~~$~~ iT!)
                    I SAW THE BAGS

AND? WHERE to ???
       WHAT IS THE MONEY FOR??

Mentioned a brother —
was ~~not~~ SUPPOSED TO BE iN PRISON

FIND THE BROTHER — FIND WOLFE?

Freddy ~~is~~ acting weird AGAIN —
why isn't he looking for Wolfe?
DOES HE HAVE HIM? why doesn't he
                              mention him??
WEIRD. weird weird weird!

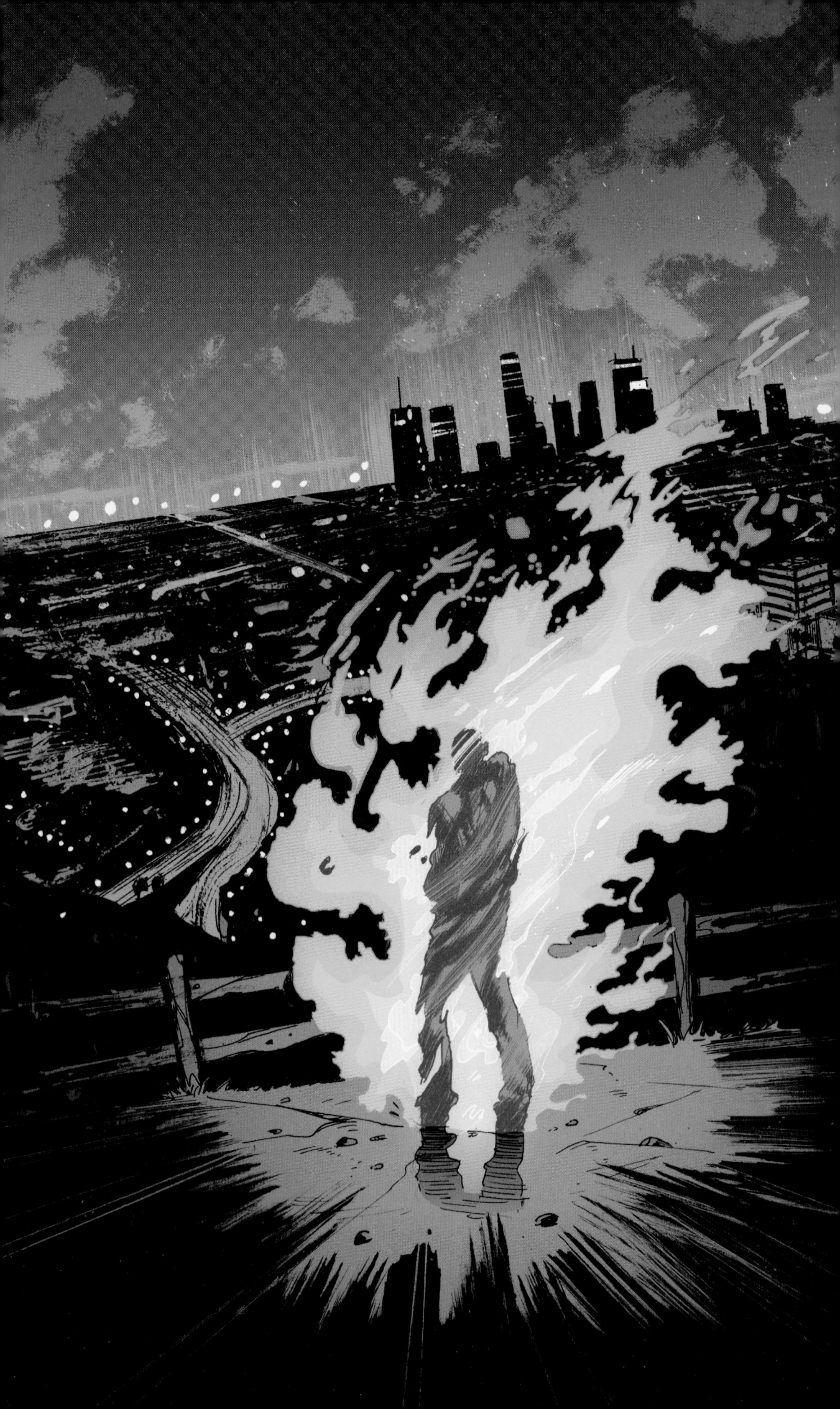

What am i not SEEING?
EVERYWHERE I look I get answers but
QUESTIONS come up twice AS ~~FAST~~
i ~~GET GET~~ GET ~~PIECES~~ PIECES —
                    BUT NOTHING CERTAIN

WHY DID YOU DO WHAT YOU DID?
    WHY DIDN'T you TRUST ME?
    WE COULD HAVE BEEN A TEAM!

I'm ~~gon~~ gonna find you. I'll ask you. I'll find out.
and maybe then i'll be able to live w/that
the feeling like I always need someone's
approval. LIKE THERE'S ~~ALWAYS~~ "ALWAYS"
    someone looking over my shoulder,
~~like~~ like someone knows better —
I know I'm lashing out at them. ~~they~~
Freddy. Isobel. I know they're trying their
best. they never wanted to be parents but
I think they're genuinely doing what they
can and I can be a handful — But they're
letting me be _me_ and I still lash out at them
I ~~HATE~~ HATE myself for that. Why do I do that?
I DON'T TRUST MYSELF. I DON'T TRUST ANYONE!
            YOU MADE ME THIS WAY —

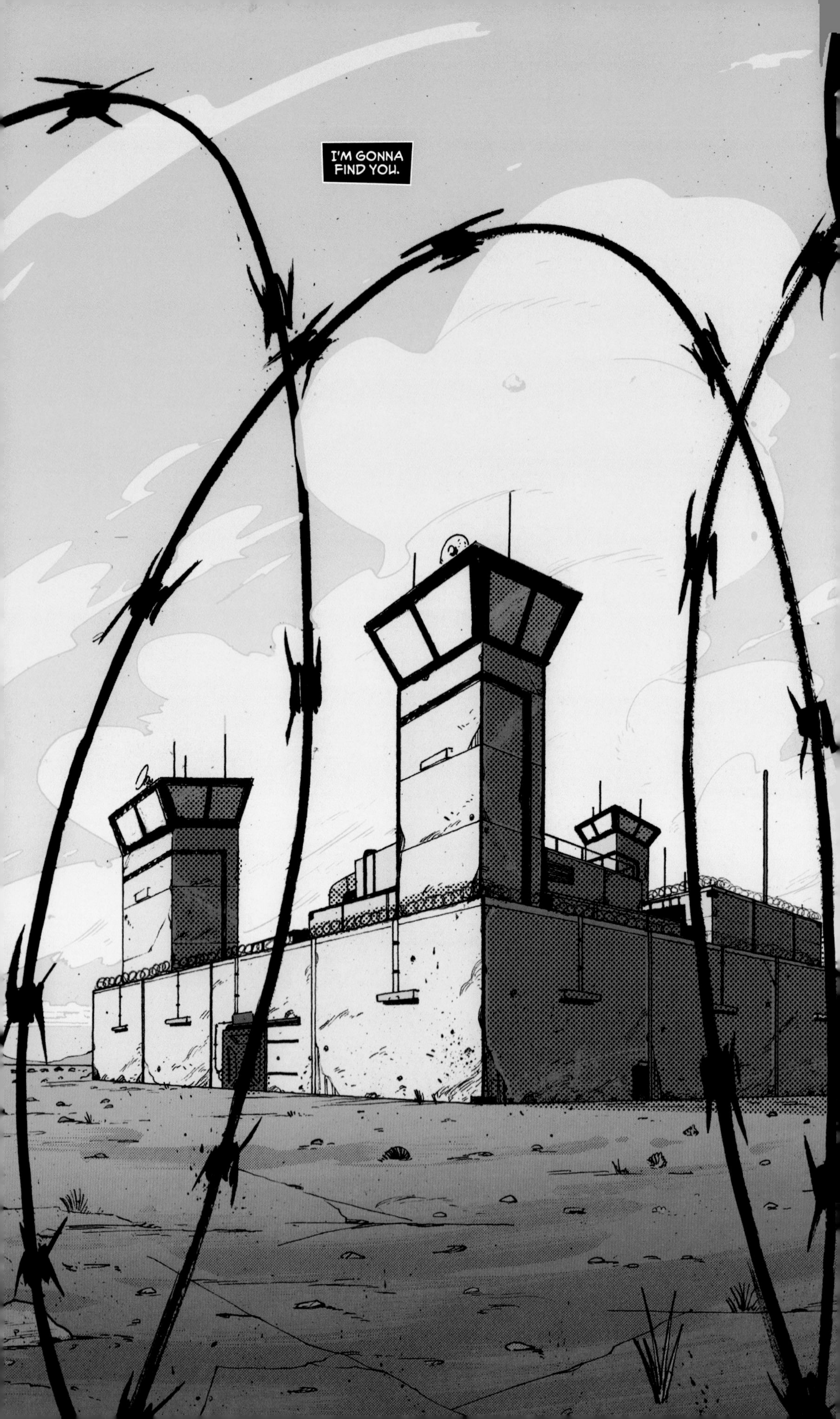
I'M GONNA FIND YOU.

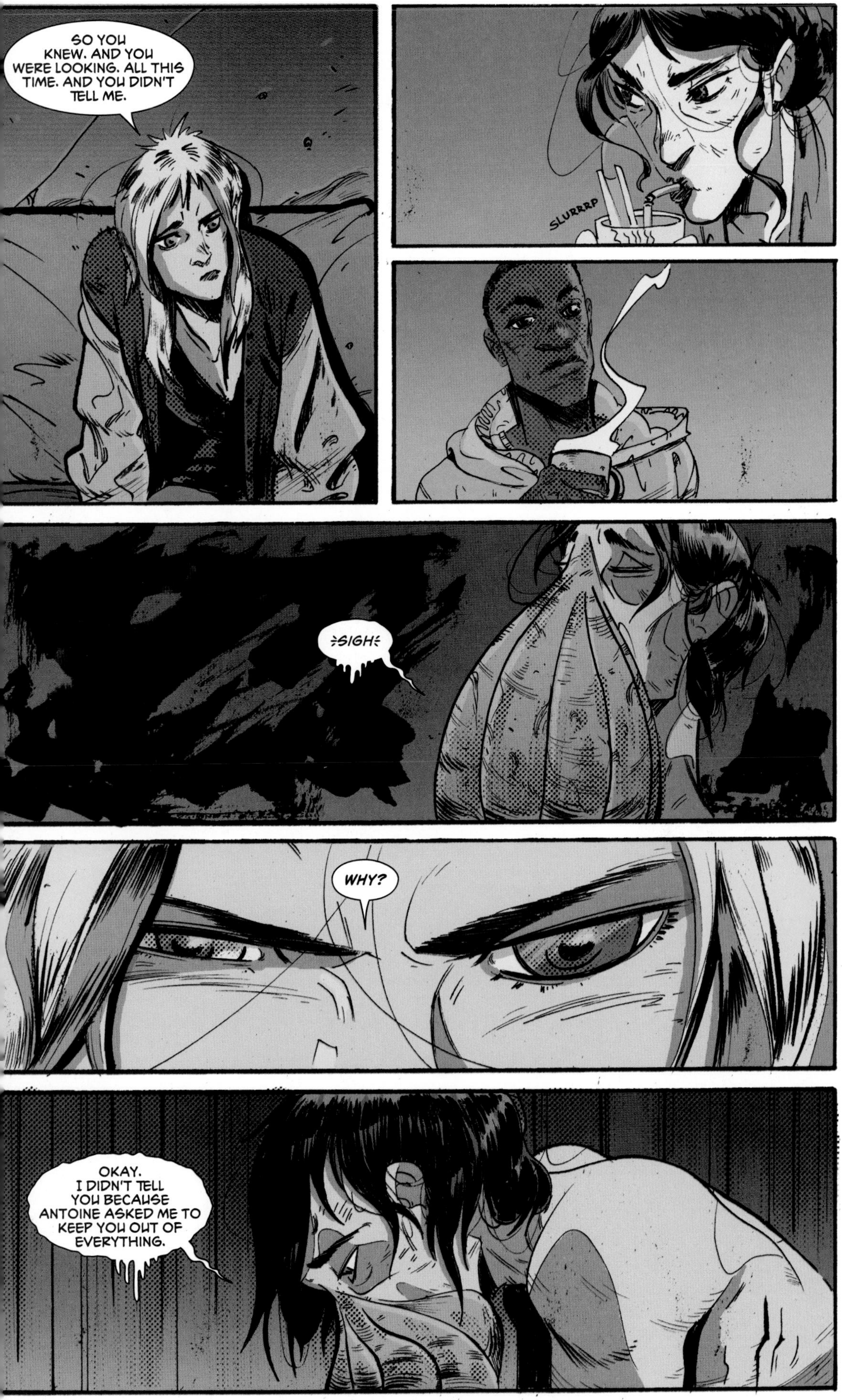
SO YOU KNEW. AND YOU WERE LOOKING. ALL THIS TIME. AND YOU DIDN'T TELL ME.
SLURRRP
SIGH
WHY?
OKAY. I DIDN'T TELL YOU BECAUSE ANTOINE ASKED ME TO KEEP YOU OUT OF EVERYTHING.

ANTOINE AND I, AS YOU KNOW, WE MEET UP SHORTLY AFTER YOU TWO PART WAYS. HE THOUGHT I WAS GONE, I THOUGHT YOU TWO MIGHT BE... WELL, NOT ALIVE. SO THE FACT THAT WE WERE ALL OKAY AND RELATIVELY WELL SORTA TOOK ME BY SURPRISE.

THEN 'TOINE REMINDS ME HE'S PAYING OFF SOME DEBT TO A MOB GUY SO HE CAN FISH DUANE HERE OUTTA PRISON WHERE HE'S AT FOR SOMETHING HE DIDN'T EVEN DO BECAUSE THE MOB GUY SET HIM UP. I MEAN, I KNEW PARTS OF THE STORY, BUT WHY DIDN'T HE TELL ME EVERYTHING? I COULD HAVE HELPED, MAYBE? HE KEEPS THINGS TO HIMSELF, HE DOES, AND I GET WHY YOU'RE ANGRY AT HIM.

HE ALSO TOLD ME YOU'D BE RUNNING AROUND L.A. LIKE THE FERAL WEREWOLF FEMALE FIEND YOU ARE, AND THAT IT WOULD BE GOOD IF I CHECKED IN ON YOU ONCE A WHILE, WERE I ABLE TO FIND YOU. AND HE GAVE ME SOME CASH TO KEEP YOU AFLOAT AND MORE CASH TO PUT INTO YOUR BANK ACCOUNT WHEN YOU'RE EIGHTEEN, WHICH IS LIKE THREE DAYS AWAY, SO I GUESS NOW YOU'RE GONNA BE EVEN MORE EXCITED ABOUT THAT.

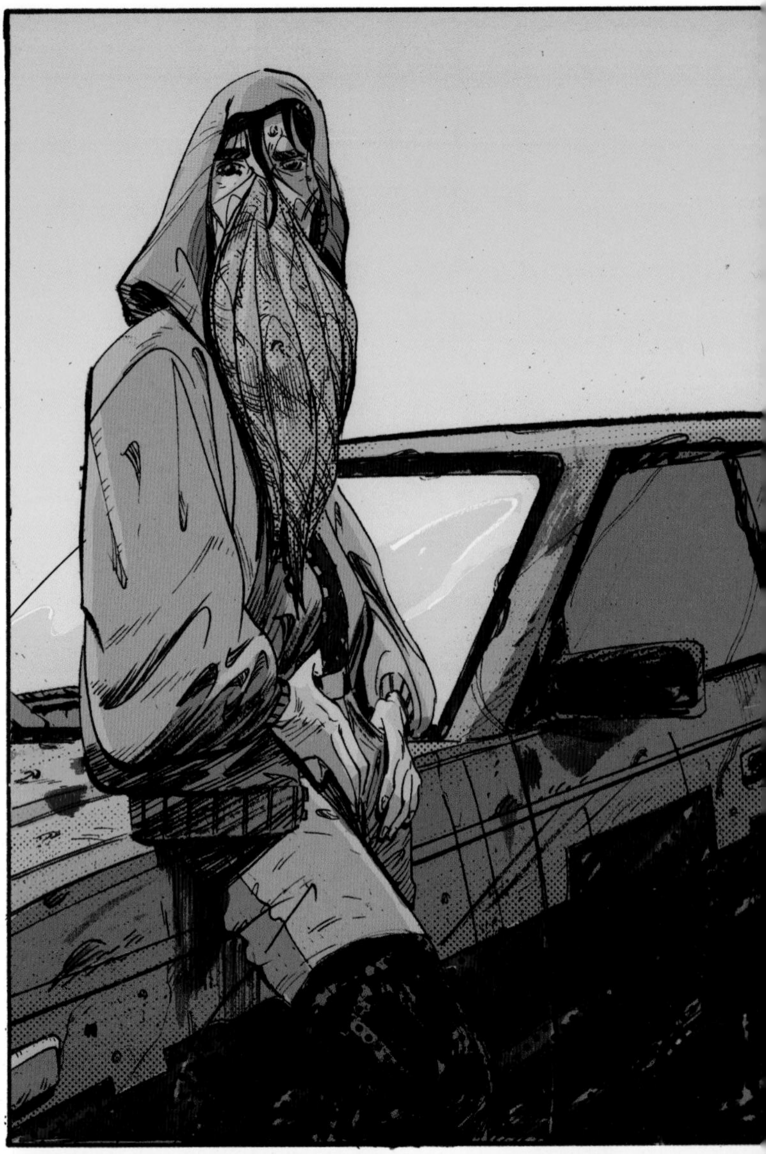

THEN, AND ALL OF THIS HAPPENS WITHIN THE FIRST TEN DAYS AFTER WE MEET AGAIN, HE SENDS ME A NOTE TELLING ME TO GO PICK UP HIS BROTHER DUANE FROM PRISON, AND I THINK, THAT'S VERY STRANGE, WHY WOULDN'T HE WANT TO DO THAT HIMSELF? BUT HE DOESN'T ANSWER.

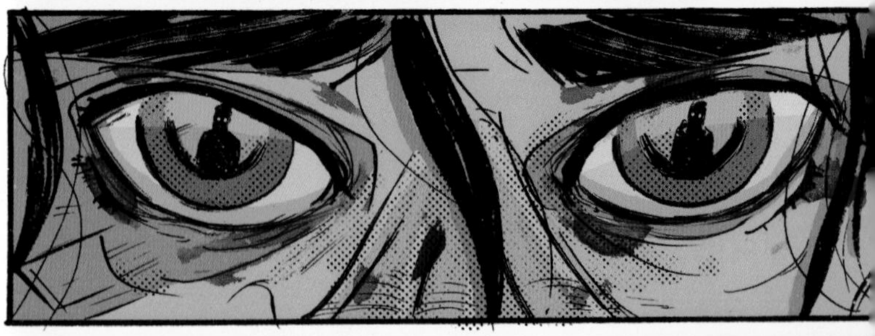

SO I GO.

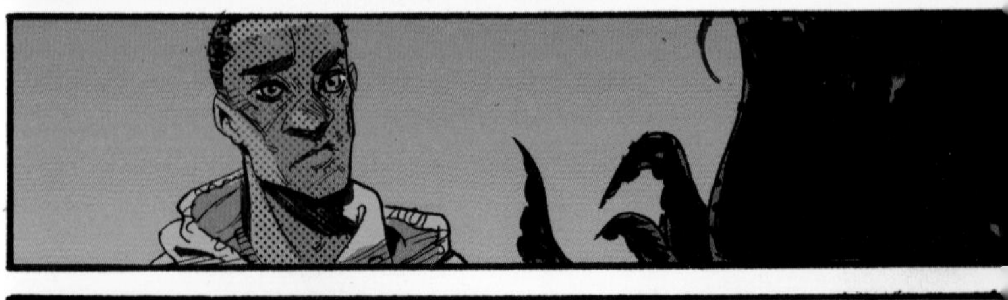

IT'S THE LAST I HEAR FROM HIM.

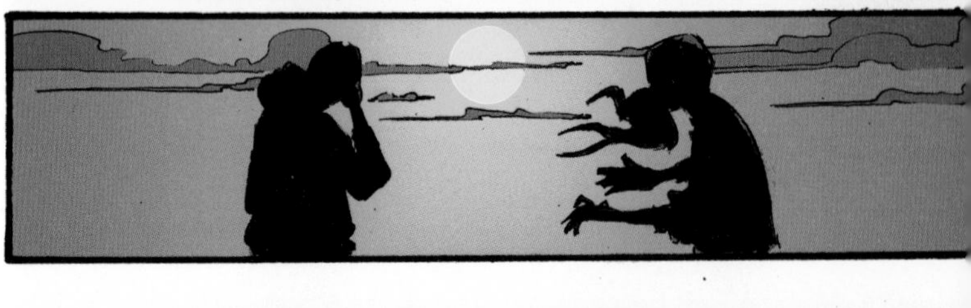

SO, Y' KNOW, DUANE AND I
GO HAVE A CUP OF TEA,
XCHANGE TALES OF TERRORS AND
RIBULATIONS, HE TELLS ME ABOUT
GROWING UP WITH 'TOINE IN
NEW ORLEANS, I TELL HIM ABOUT
GROWING UP WITH MY TENTACLED
KS, HE TELLS ME WHAT IT'S LIKE TO
EAVE HIGH SCHOOL EARLY, I TELL
HIM WHAT IT'S LIKE TO GIVE A BIG
WEET NOPE TO THE TRADITION AND
BECOME A HLIRGH INSTEAD, AND
OW MY GNAIIH AND 'FHALMA WERE
ALL BESIDE THEMSELVES...

...AND WE HAVE, YOU KNOW,
TEA, FOR A FEW DAYS, THINKING
'TOINE WILL SURELY SHOW UP
SO WE KEEP OUR EYES PEELED
AND WE STOP BY HIS PLACE AND
NOTHING HAPPENS SO WE SPEND
A FEW MORE NIGHTS JUST SORTA
WAITING FOR HIM TO MATERIALIZE
UTTA NOWHERE LIKE HE USED TO...

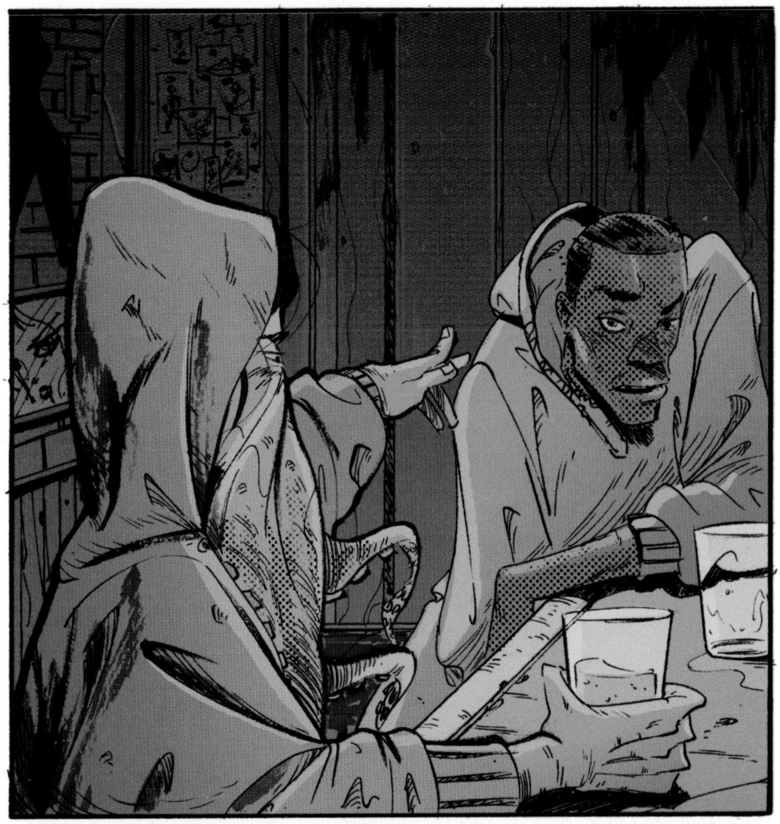

...AND NOTHING HAPPENS,
YOU KNOW? BUT BY NOW
WE'RE ALL CAUGHT UP ON
EACH OTHER'S HEFTY AND
HORRENDOUSLY HILARIOUS AND
HORRIFICALLY HARD HISTORIES,
VEN THE REALLY JUICY PARTS LIKE
WHY DUANE NEVER PURSUED A
CAREER IN MATH EVEN THOUGH
HE'S A TOTAL MATH PRODIGY,
OR WHY I HAD A RATHER
EXCELLENT CAREER IN...
OH, WELL, SOME OTHER
TIME, ACTUALLY.

ANYWAYS, OUR CHTENFF OF
TWO WONDERS WHAT'S IN
'TOINE'S LLOIG BUT WE CAN'T
TELL, YOU KNOW? SO WE GO
BACK TO HIS PLACE, ABOUT A
WEEK LATER, AND IT TURNS OUT
THIS SALVADOREAN FAMILY
MOVED IN? WHICH MEANS WOLFE
LEFT THE PLACE. WHICH MEANS
WE WASTED... HOW LONG WAS IT?

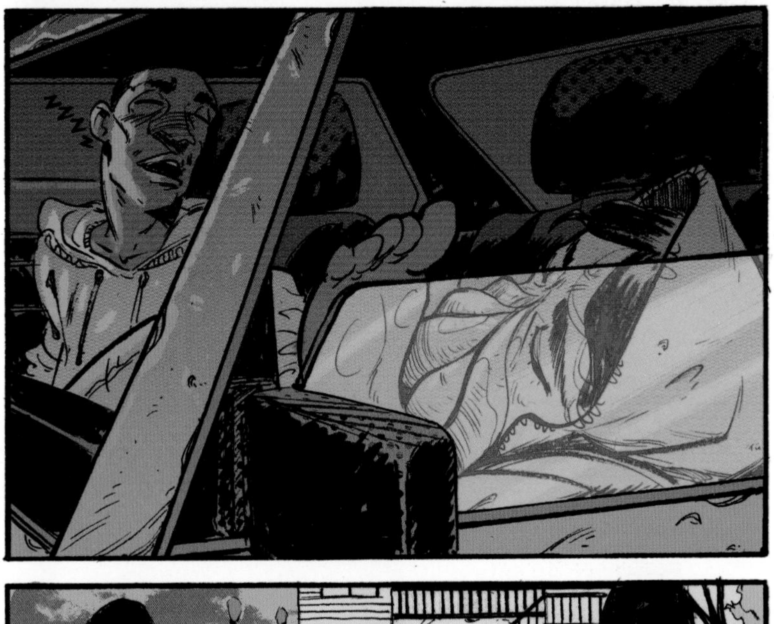
ZZZ

WE'RE NOT SURE,
WHICH HAPPENS WHEN
YOU DRINK TOO MUCH B...
CAFFEINE. TOO MUCH
CAFFEINE.

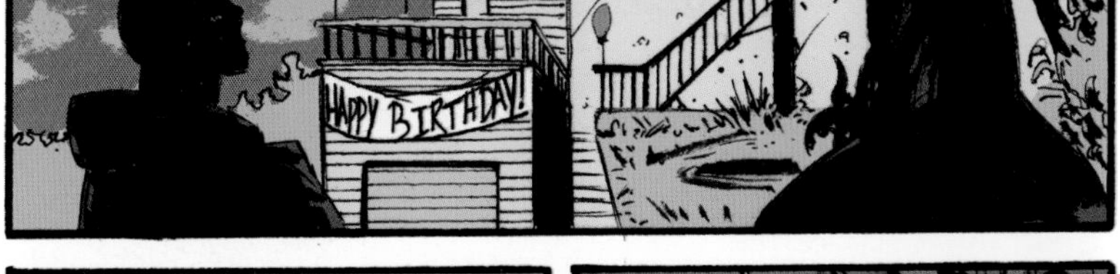
HAPPY BIRTHDAY!

AND THEN
I HAVE AN
IDEA.

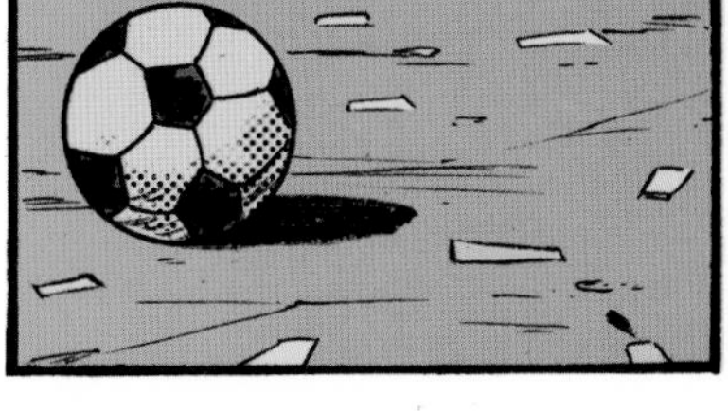

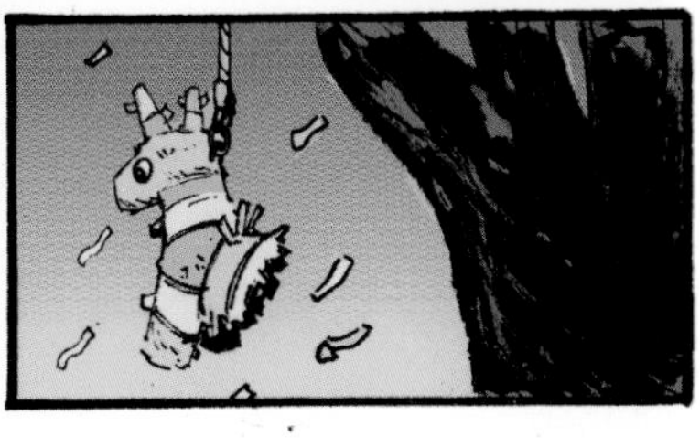

I KNOW HE USED TO HAVE AN EXTRA KEY TO HIS STORAGE UNIT HIDDEN IN THE BACK OF THE HOUSE, YOU KNOW?

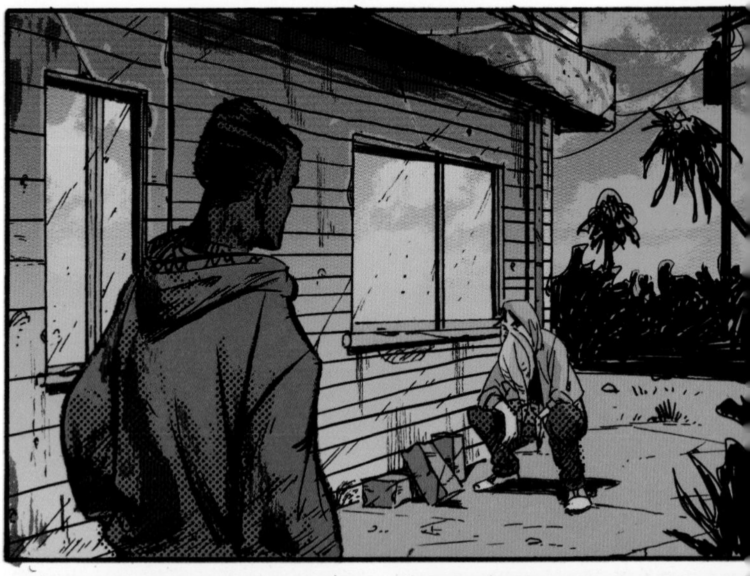

AND SURE ENOUGH!

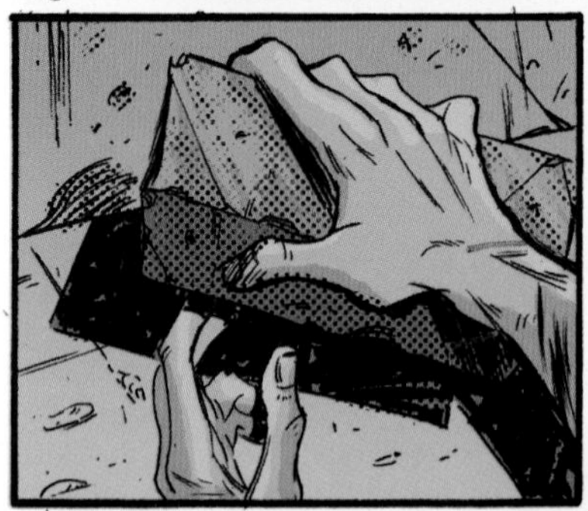

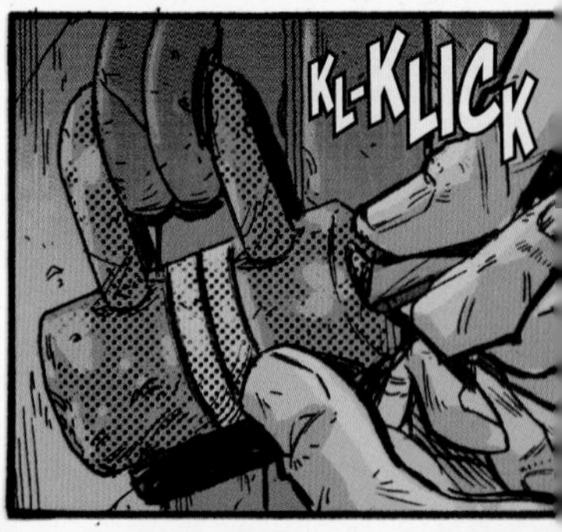
KL-KLICK

A STORAGE FULL OF OCCULT KADISHTU STUFF! AND I SWEAR, I COULD TELL HE'S GOT NEARLY EVERYTHING IN THERE. THE SECRET FILES OF SHAGG AND SHOGG, BONES OF GODS AND SUCCUBI, OLD CROSSES HE GOT FROM WHO KNOWS WHERE, AND BOOKS UPON BOOKS UPON BOOKS UPON... YOU GET THE IMAGE, RIGHT?

SO IT'S BASICALLY JUST BOXES AND BIBLES AND OCCULT STUFF AND A LOT OF DIRT. LIKE HE BARELY TOUCHED ANYTHING! AND THE FAMILY, WHEN I ASKED THEM IF THERE WERE ANY THINGS LEFT AT HIS PLACE BEFORE THEY MOVED IN, THEY SAY NOPE, THE LANDLORD WAS GIVING THE LAST BOXES WOLFE LEFT BEHIND TO SOME PEOPLE WHO SAID SOME MR. SOMETHING WOULD BE PLEASED! SO NATURALLY MY GREAT MIND GOES MR. WHO? AND TURNS OUT IT'S THE SAME GUY 'TOINE OWED THE MONEY TO BECAUSE THE GUY GOT DUANE IN PRISON FOR SOMETHING HE DIDN'T EVEN DO...

...AND THEN WE'RE IN THE STORAGE UNIT AND ONE OF THE BOOKS BREATHES AT ME AND I REALIZE IT'S ALIVE AND BASICALLY PEE MYSELF BUT THAT'S FOR ANOTHER TIME, TOO. ANYWAYS, THAT'S HOW WE PUT TWO AND TWO TOGETHER AND KNOW WOLFE JUST SORTA ***VANISHED*** AND WE KNOW THIS MR. WHATEVER HIS NAME WAS-- I'M NOT GONNA TELL YOU WHAT HIS NAME WAS BECAUSE YOU'D TRY TO TEAR OUT HIS AORTA, YOUNG LADY--WE GO PAY HIM A ***VISIT***.

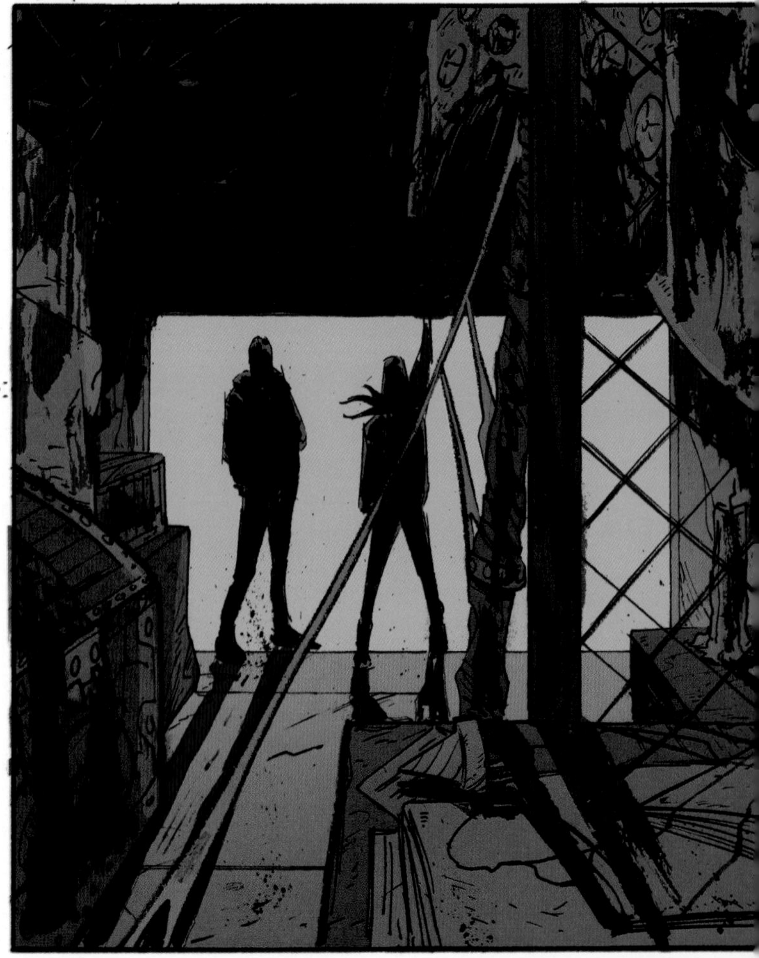

ANYWAY, HE AIN'T HAPPY TO SEE US, AND TELLS US HE KNOWS NOTHING. WE SORTA HIT A WALL WITH HIM AND HIS GUYS.

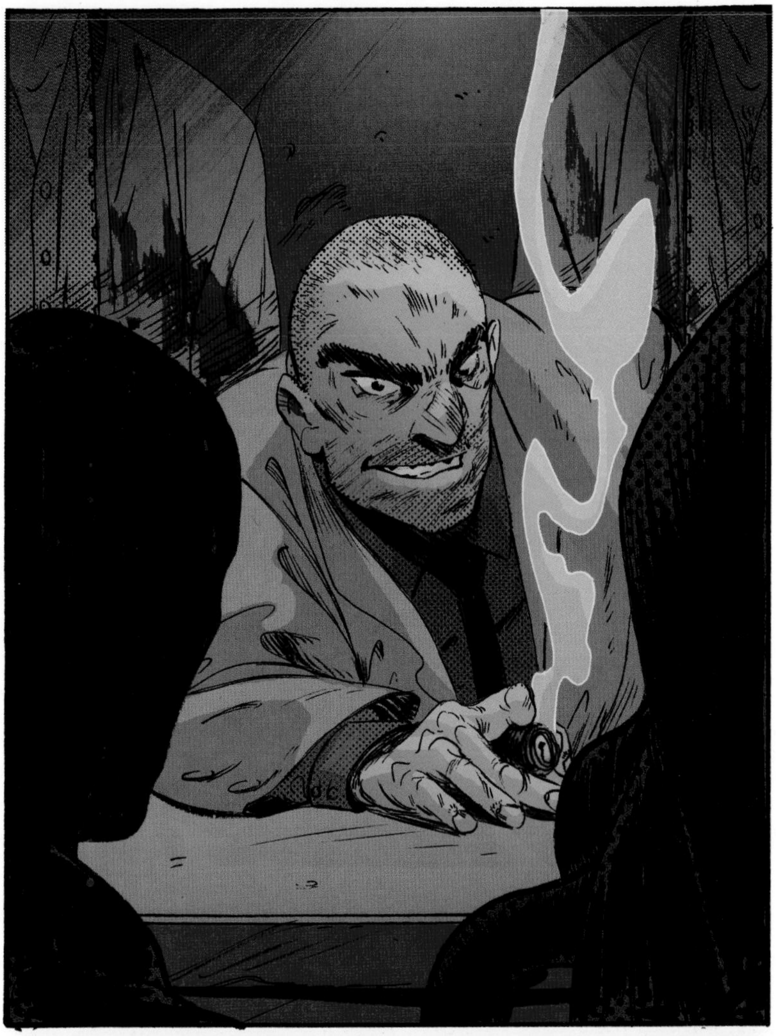

SO WE'RE THINKING, WE SHOULD ASK HARDER, YOU KNOW? MAKE SURE. AND I KNOW NORMAL FOLK AIN'T USED TO SEEING ME AS I REALLY AM, YOU KNOW? SO I LET 'EM.

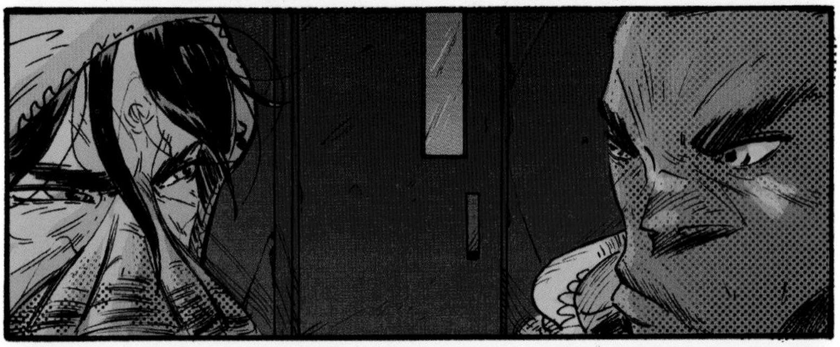

TURNS OUT HE REALLY KNOWS NOTHING.

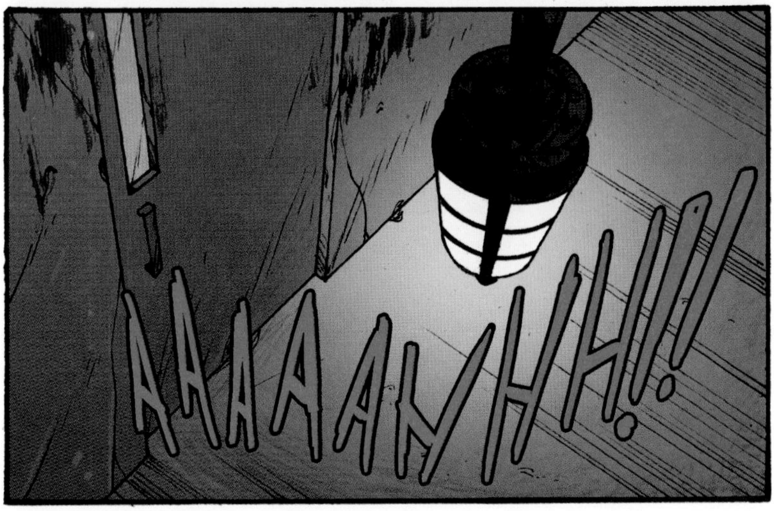
AAAAAAHH!!

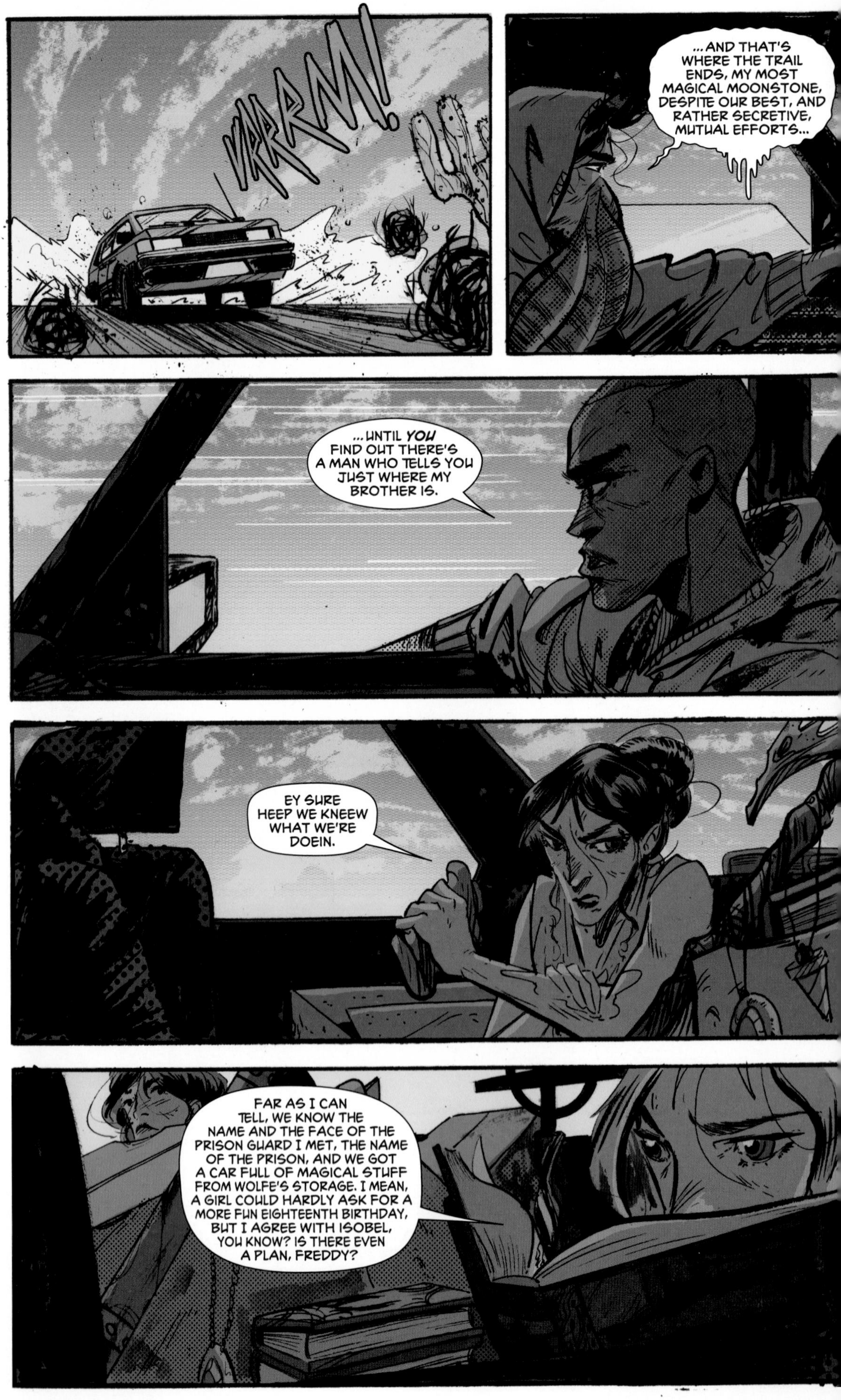
VRRRM!
...AND THAT'S WHERE THE TRAIL ENDS, MY MOST MAGICAL MOONSTONE, DESPITE OUR BEST, AND RATHER SECRETIVE, MUTUAL EFFORTS...
...UNTIL *YOU* FIND OUT THERE'S A MAN WHO TELLS YOU JUST WHERE MY BROTHER IS.
EY SURE KEEP WE KNEEW WHAT WE'RE DOEIN.
FAR AS I CAN TELL, WE KNOW THE NAME AND THE FACE OF THE PRISON GUARD I MET, THE NAME OF THE PRISON, AND WE GOT A CAR FULL OF MAGICAL STUFF FROM WOLFE'S STORAGE. I MEAN, A GIRL COULD HARDLY ASK FOR A MORE FUN EIGHTEENTH BIRTHDAY, BUT I AGREE WITH ISOBEL, YOU KNOW? IS THERE EVEN A PLAN, FREDDY?

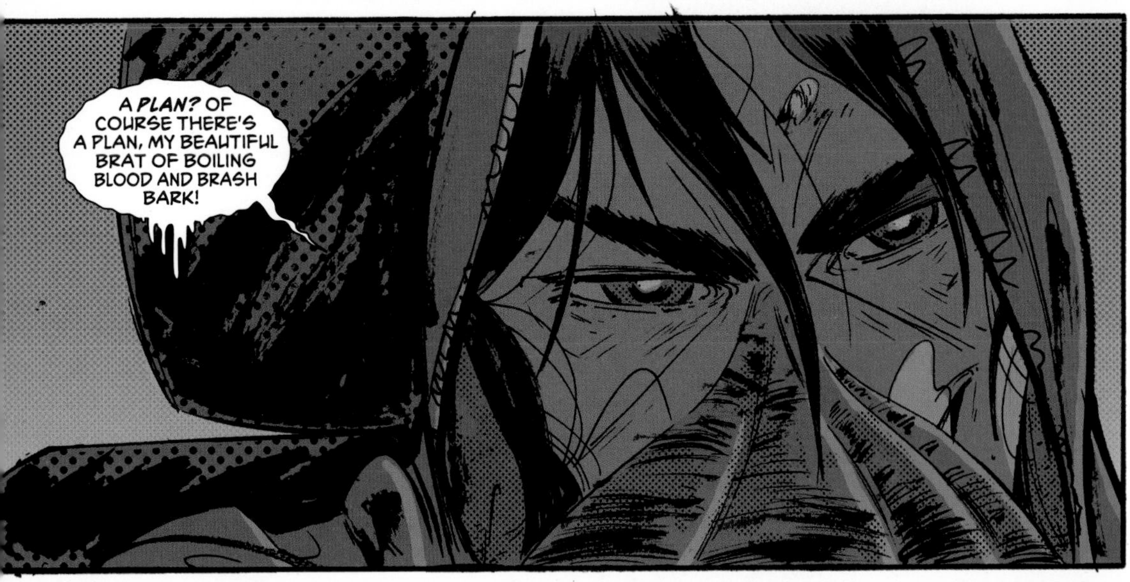
A PLAN? OF COURSE THERE'S A PLAN, MY BEAUTIFUL BRAT OF BOILING BLOOD AND BRASH BARK!

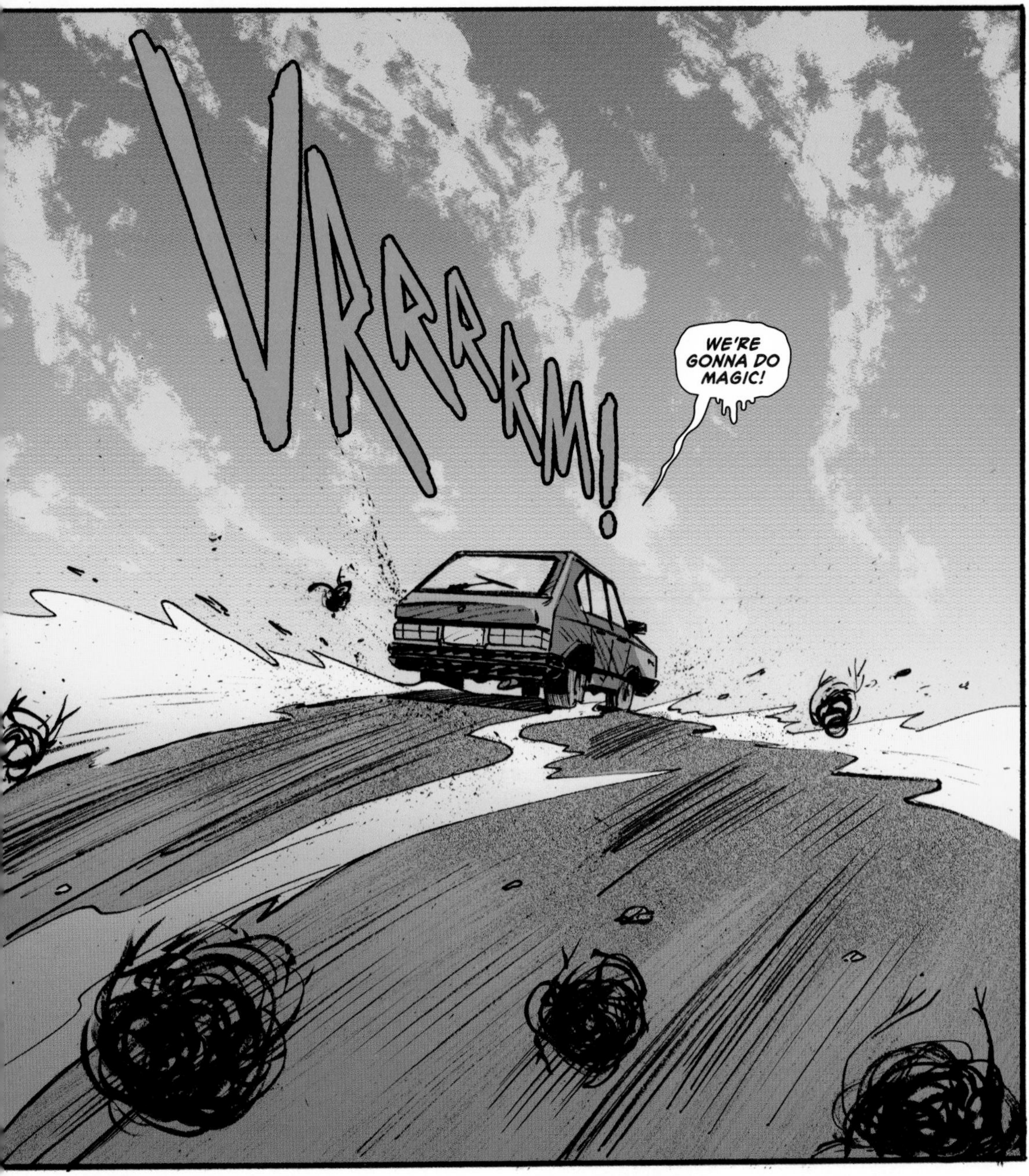
VRRRRM!
WE'RE GONNA DO MAGIC!

Chapter 7

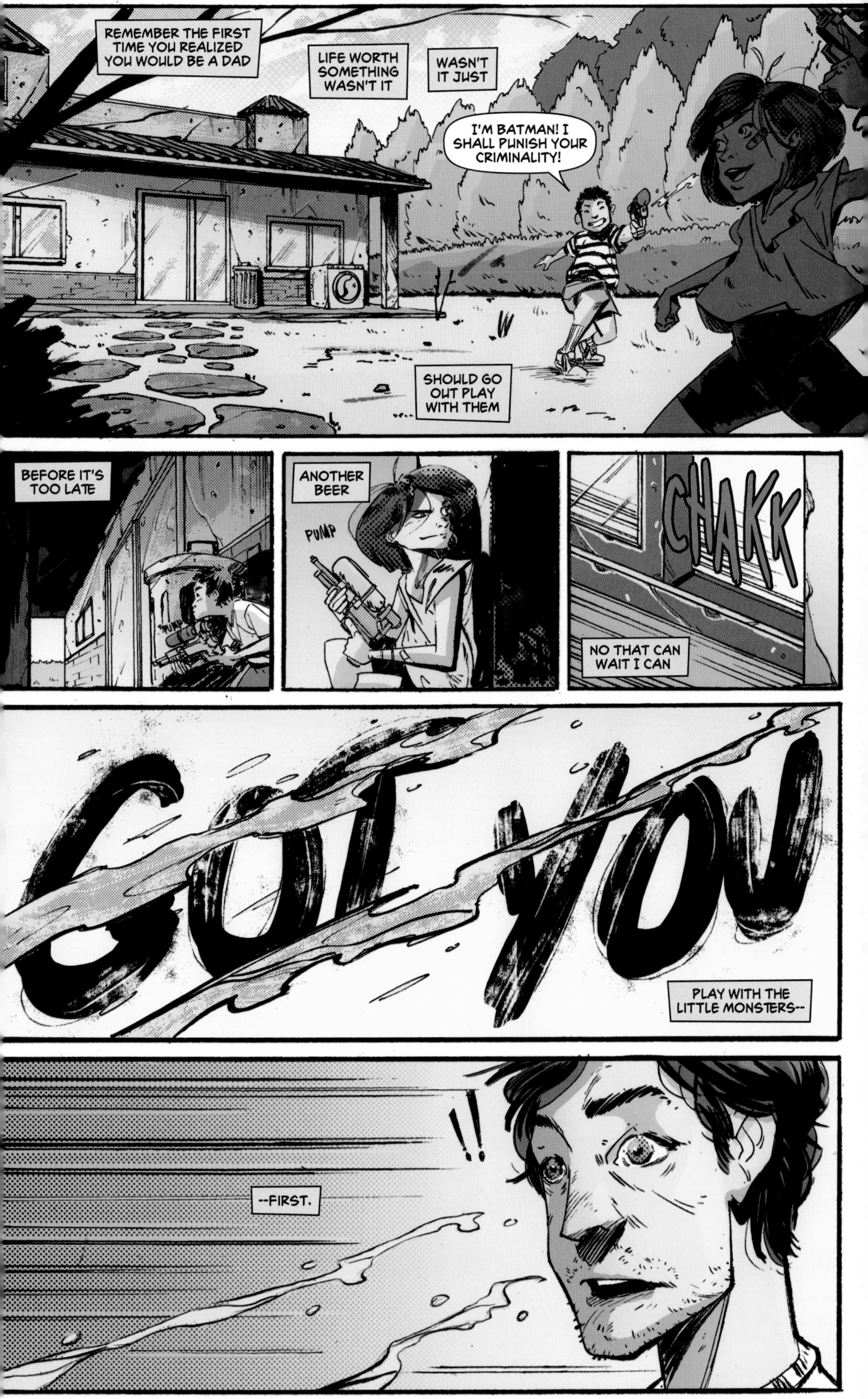
REMEMBER THE FIRST TIME YOU REALIZED YOU WOULD BE A DAD
LIFE WORTH SOMETHING WASN'T IT
WASN'T IT JUST
I'M BATMAN! I SHALL PUNISH YOUR CRIMINALITY!
SHOULD GO OUT PLAY WITH THEM
BEFORE IT'S TOO LATE
PUMP
ANOTHER BEER
PUMP
CHAKK
NO THAT CAN WAIT I CAN
GOT YOU
PLAY WITH THE LITTLE MONSTERS--
!!
--FIRST.

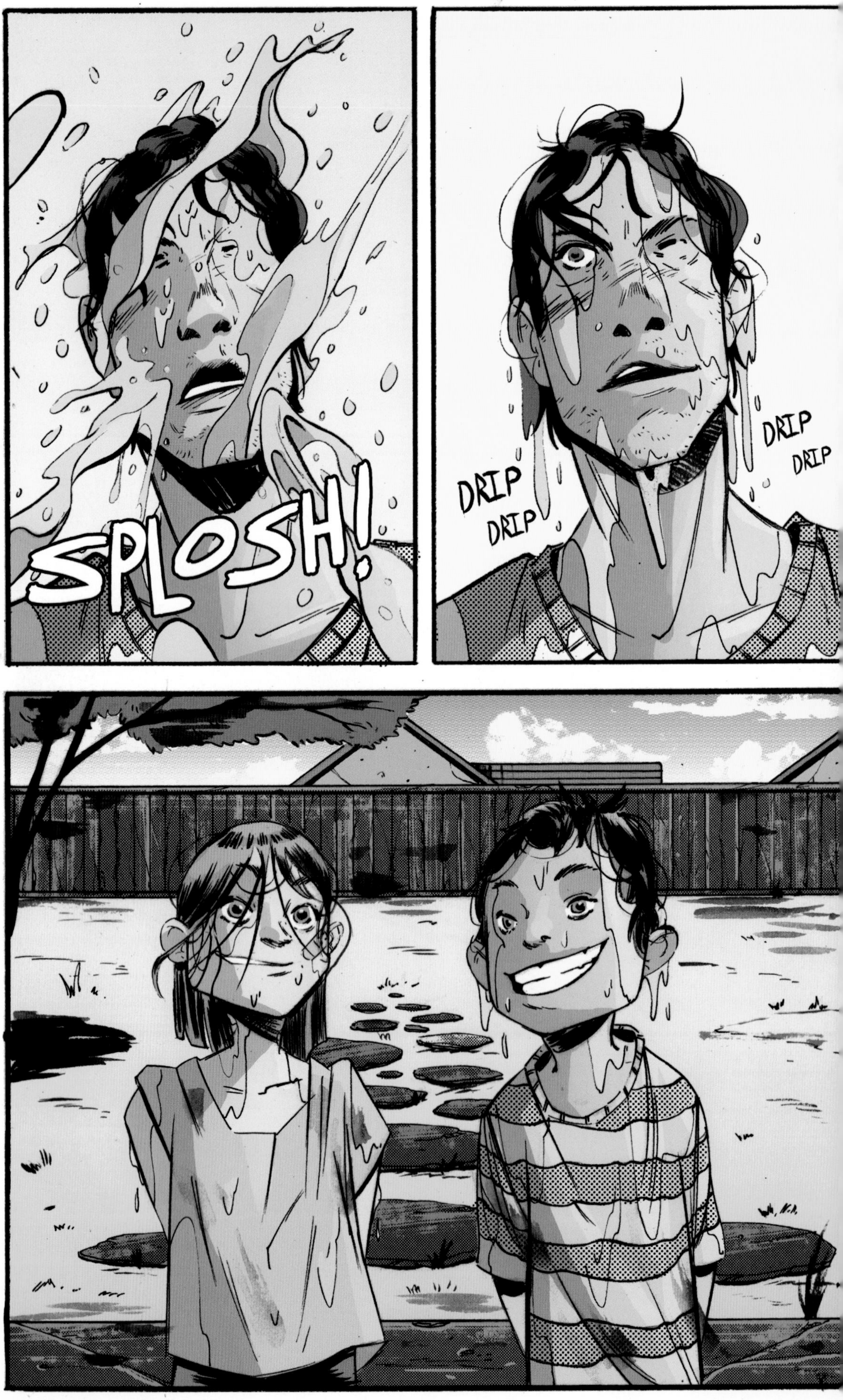
SPLOSH!
DRIP
DRIP
DRIP
DRIP

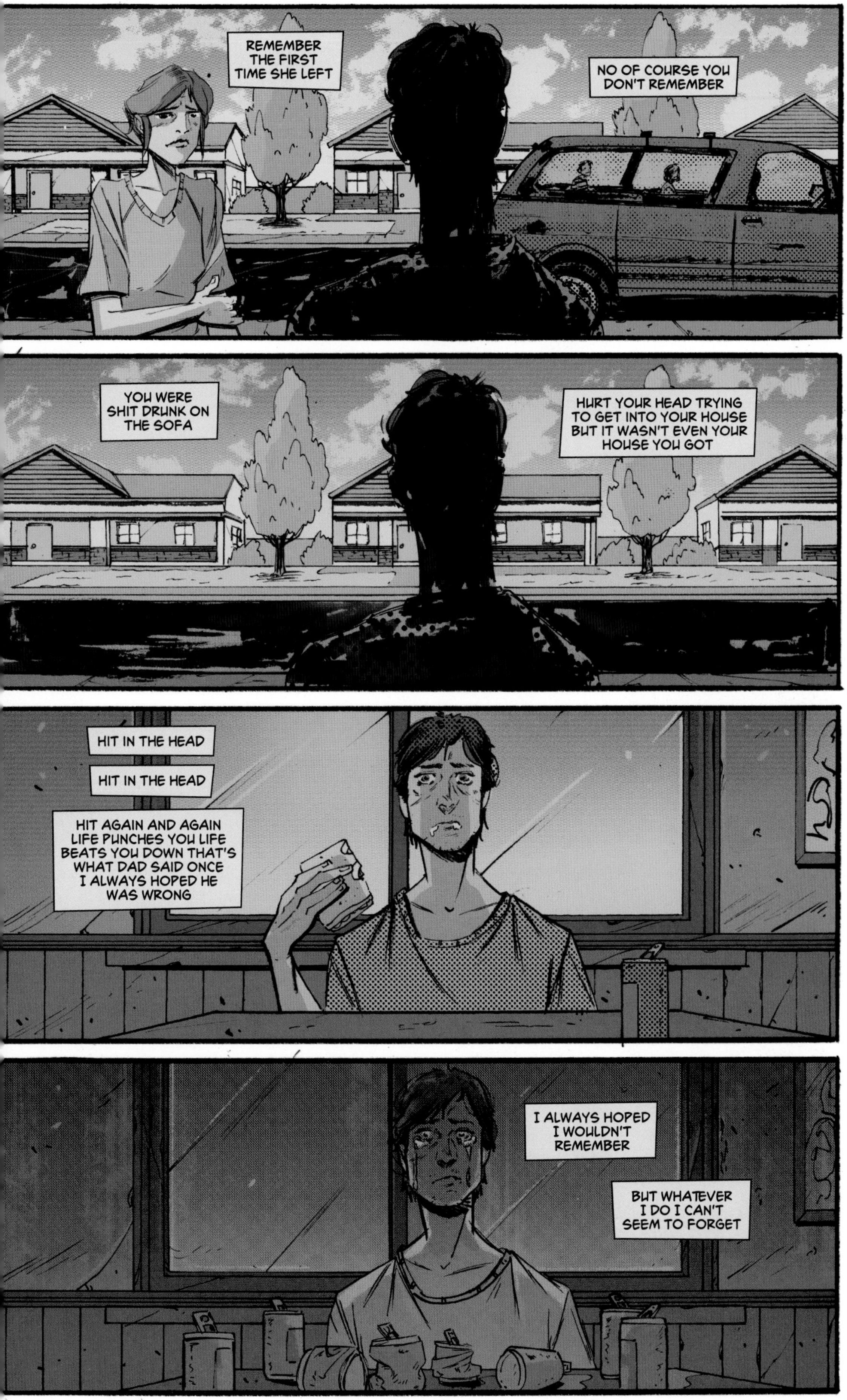
REMEMBER THE FIRST TIME SHE LEFT
NO OF COURSE YOU DON'T REMEMBER
YOU WERE SHIT DRUNK ON THE SOFA
HURT YOUR HEAD TRYING TO GET INTO YOUR HOUSE BUT IT WASN'T EVEN YOUR HOUSE YOU GOT
HIT IN THE HEAD
HIT IN THE HEAD
HIT AGAIN AND AGAIN LIFE PUNCHES YOU LIFE BEATS YOU DOWN THAT'S WHAT DAD SAID ONCE I ALWAYS HOPED HE WAS WRONG
I ALWAYS HOPED I WOULDN'T REMEMBER
BUT WHATEVER I DO I CAN'T SEEM TO FORGET

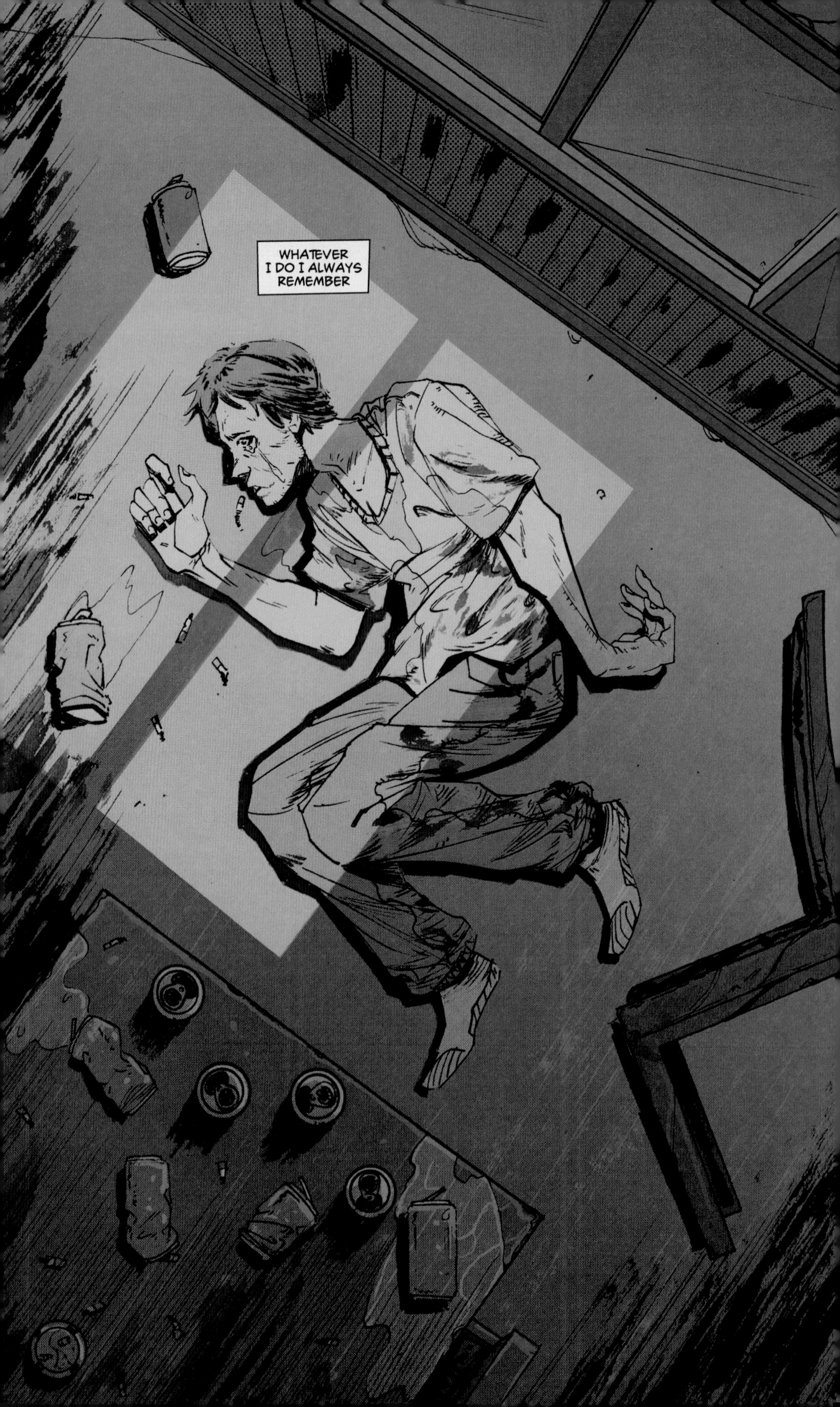
WHATEVER
I DO I ALWAYS
REMEMBER

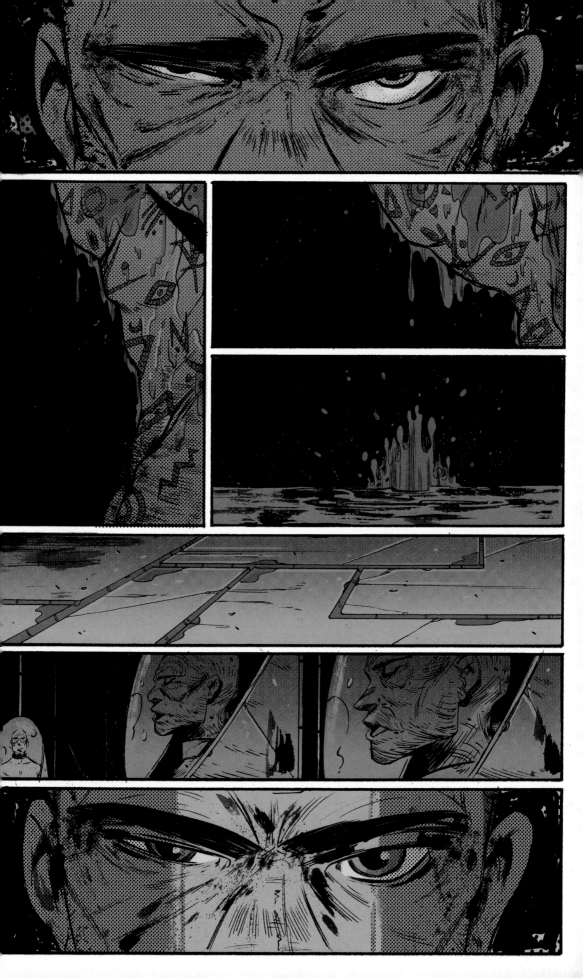

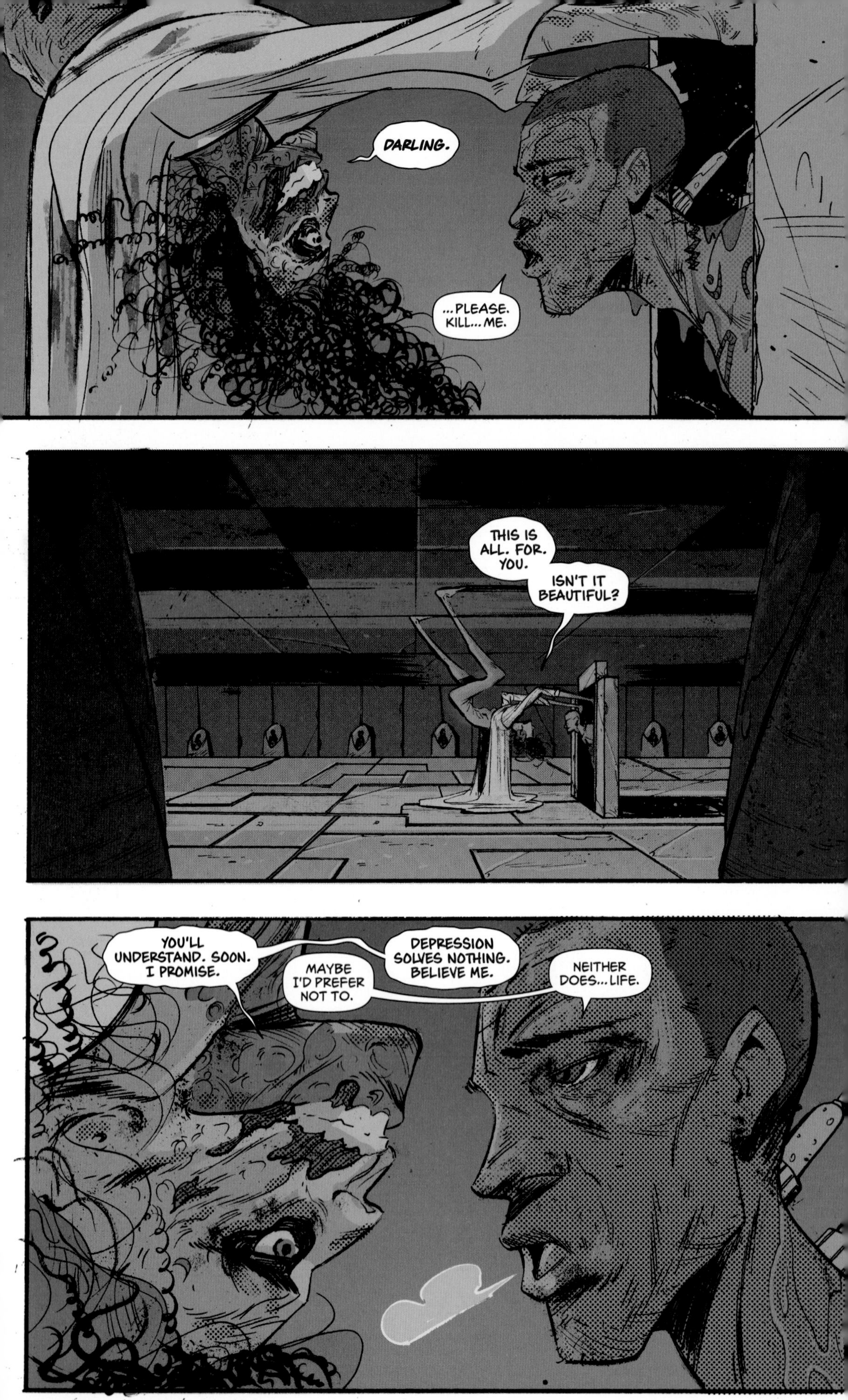
DARLING.
...PLEASE. KILL... ME.
THIS IS ALL. FOR. YOU.
ISN'T IT BEAUTIFUL?
YOU'LL UNDERSTAND. SOON. I PROMISE.
MAYBE I'D PREFER NOT TO.
DEPRESSION SOLVES NOTHING. BELIEVE ME.
NEITHER DOES... LIFE.

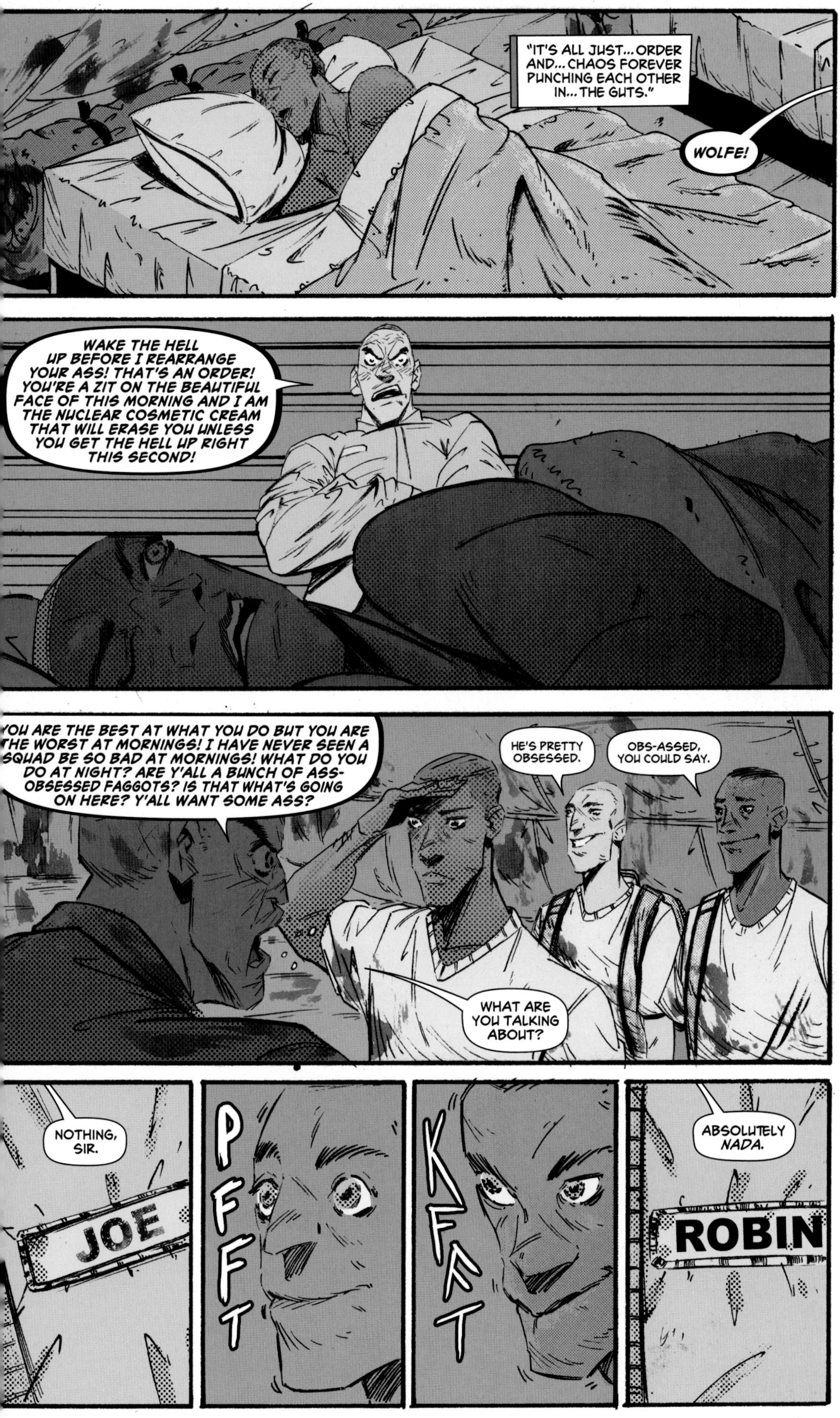
"IT'S ALL JUST... ORDER AND... CHAOS FOREVER PUNCHING EACH OTHER IN... THE GUTS."
WOLFE!
WAKE THE HELL UP BEFORE I REARRANGE YOUR ASS! THAT'S AN ORDER! YOU'RE A ZIT ON THE BEAUTIFUL FACE OF THIS MORNING AND I AM THE NUCLEAR COSMETIC CREAM THAT WILL ERASE YOU UNLESS YOU GET THE HELL UP RIGHT THIS SECOND!
YOU ARE THE BEST AT WHAT YOU DO BUT YOU ARE THE WORST AT MORNINGS! I HAVE NEVER SEEN A SQUAD BE SO BAD AT MORNINGS! WHAT DO YOU DO AT NIGHT? ARE Y'ALL A BUNCH OF ASS-OBSESSED FAGGOTS? IS THAT WHAT'S GOING ON HERE? Y'ALL WANT SOME ASS?
HE'S PRETTY OBSESSED.
OBS-ASSED, YOU COULD SAY.
WHAT ARE YOU TALKING ABOUT?
NOTHING, SIR.
JOE
PFFT
KFFT
ABSOLUTELY NADA.
ROBIN

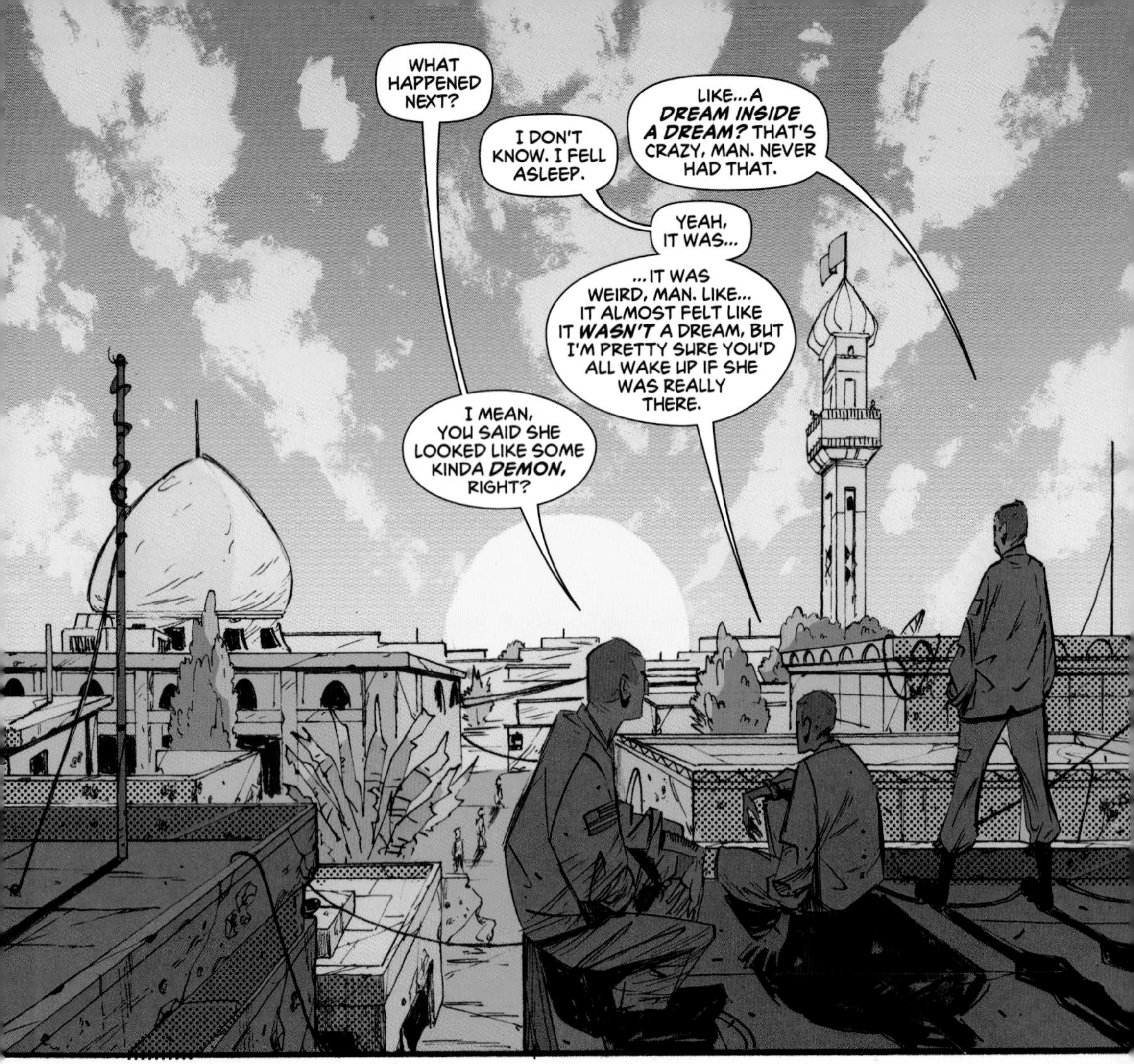
WHAT HAPPENED NEXT?
I DON'T KNOW. I FELL ASLEEP.
LIKE... A DREAM INSIDE A DREAM? THAT'S CRAZY, MAN. NEVER HAD THAT.
YEAH, IT WAS...
...IT WAS WEIRD, MAN. LIKE... IT ALMOST FELT LIKE IT WASN'T A DREAM, BUT I'M PRETTY SURE YOU'D ALL WAKE UP IF SHE WAS REALLY THERE.
I MEAN, YOU SAID SHE LOOKED LIKE SOME KINDA DEMON, RIGHT?

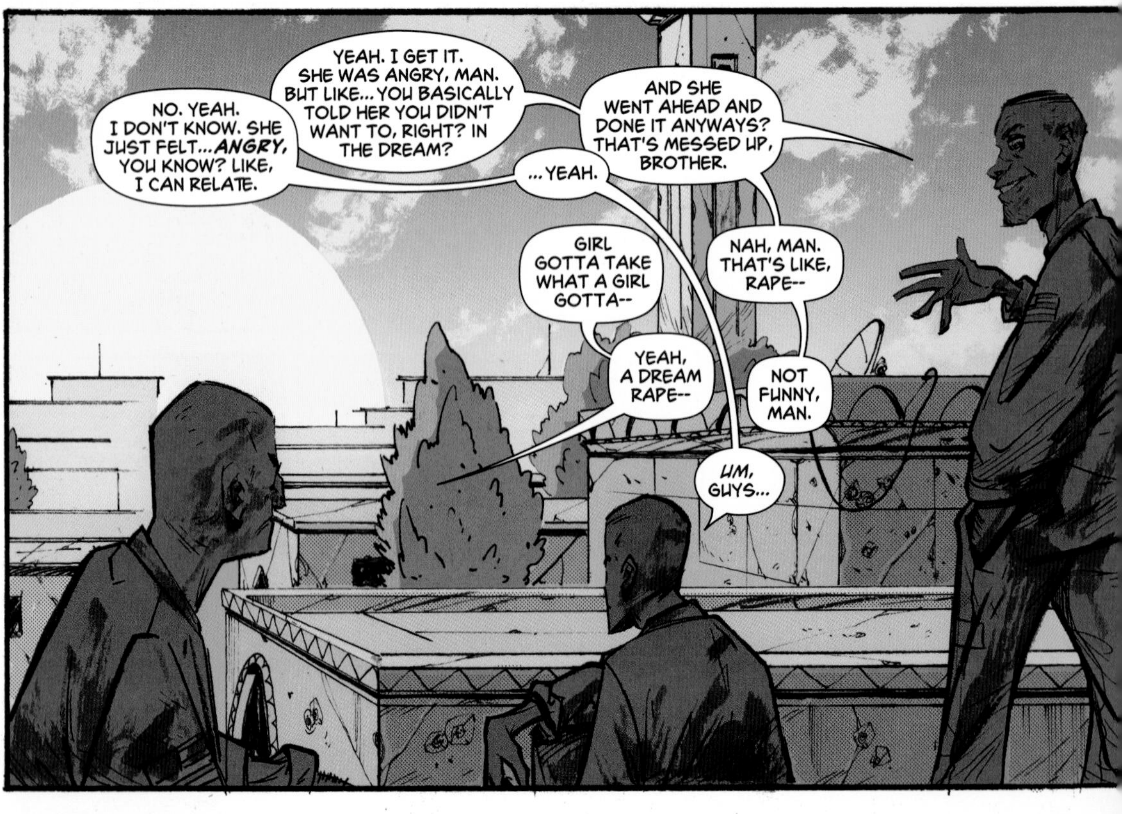
NO. YEAH. I DON'T KNOW. SHE JUST FELT... ANGRY, YOU KNOW? LIKE, I CAN RELATE.
YEAH. I GET IT. SHE WAS ANGRY, MAN. BUT LIKE... YOU BASICALLY TOLD HER YOU DIDN'T WANT TO, RIGHT? IN THE DREAM?
...YEAH.
AND SHE WENT AHEAD AND DONE IT ANYWAYS? THAT'S MESSED UP, BROTHER.
GIRL GOTTA TAKE WHAT A GIRL GOTTA--
NAH, MAN. THAT'S LIKE, RAPE--
YEAH, A DREAM RAPE--
NOT FUNNY, MAN.
UM, GUYS...

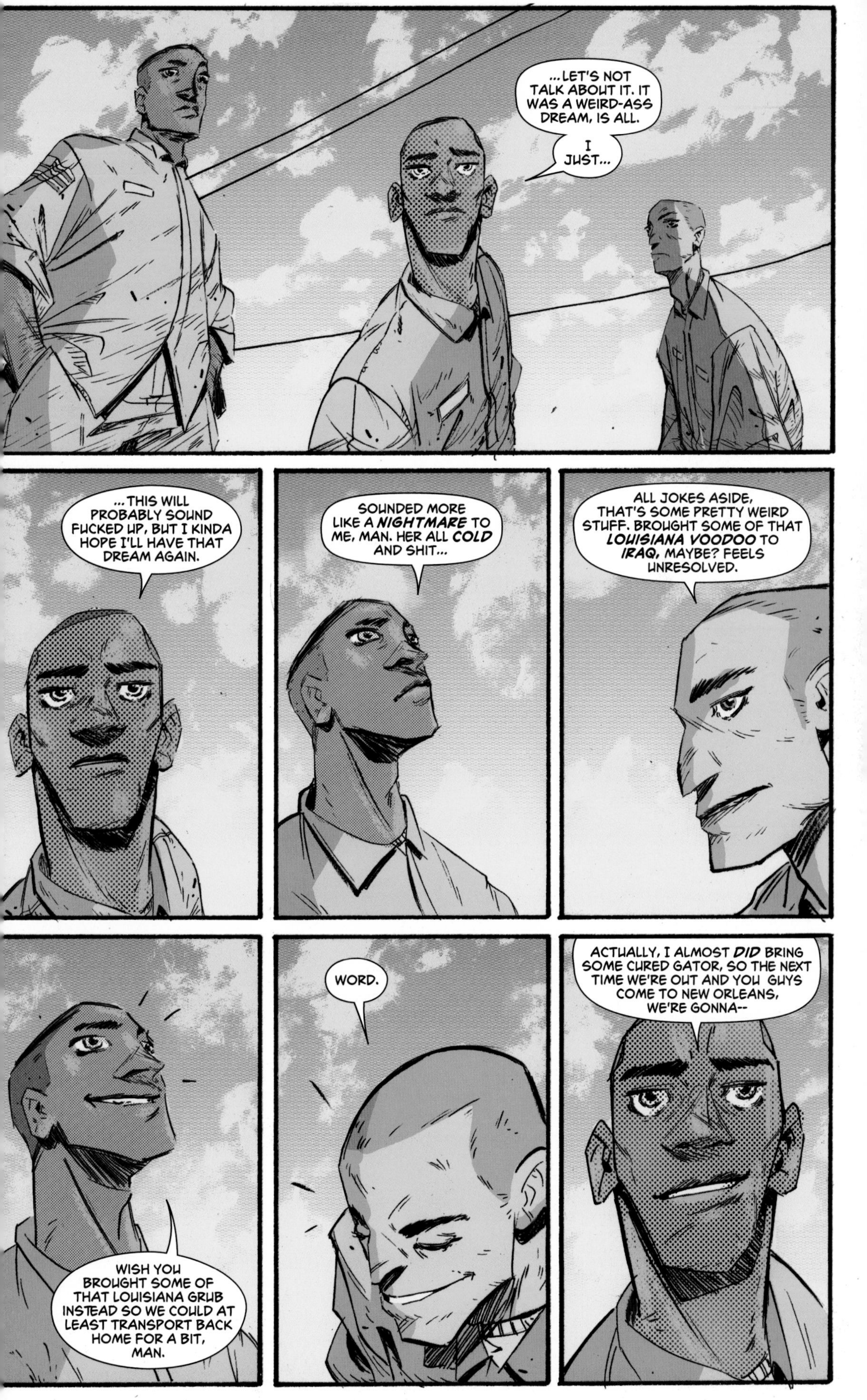
...LET'S NOT TALK ABOUT IT. IT WAS A WEIRD-ASS DREAM, IS ALL.
I JUST...
...THIS WILL PROBABLY SOUND FUCKED UP, BUT I KINDA HOPE I'LL HAVE THAT DREAM AGAIN.
SOUNDED MORE LIKE A *NIGHTMARE* TO ME, MAN. HER ALL *COLD* AND SHIT...
ALL JOKES ASIDE, THAT'S SOME PRETTY WEIRD STUFF. BROUGHT SOME OF THAT *LOUISIANA VOODOO* TO *IRAQ*, MAYBE? FEELS UNRESOLVED.
WISH YOU BROUGHT SOME OF THAT LOUISIANA GRUB INSTEAD SO WE COULD AT LEAST TRANSPORT BACK HOME FOR A BIT, MAN.
WORD.
ACTUALLY, I ALMOST *DID* BRING SOME CURED GATOR, SO THE NEXT TIME WE'RE OUT AND YOU GUYS COME TO NEW ORLEANS, WE'RE GONNA--

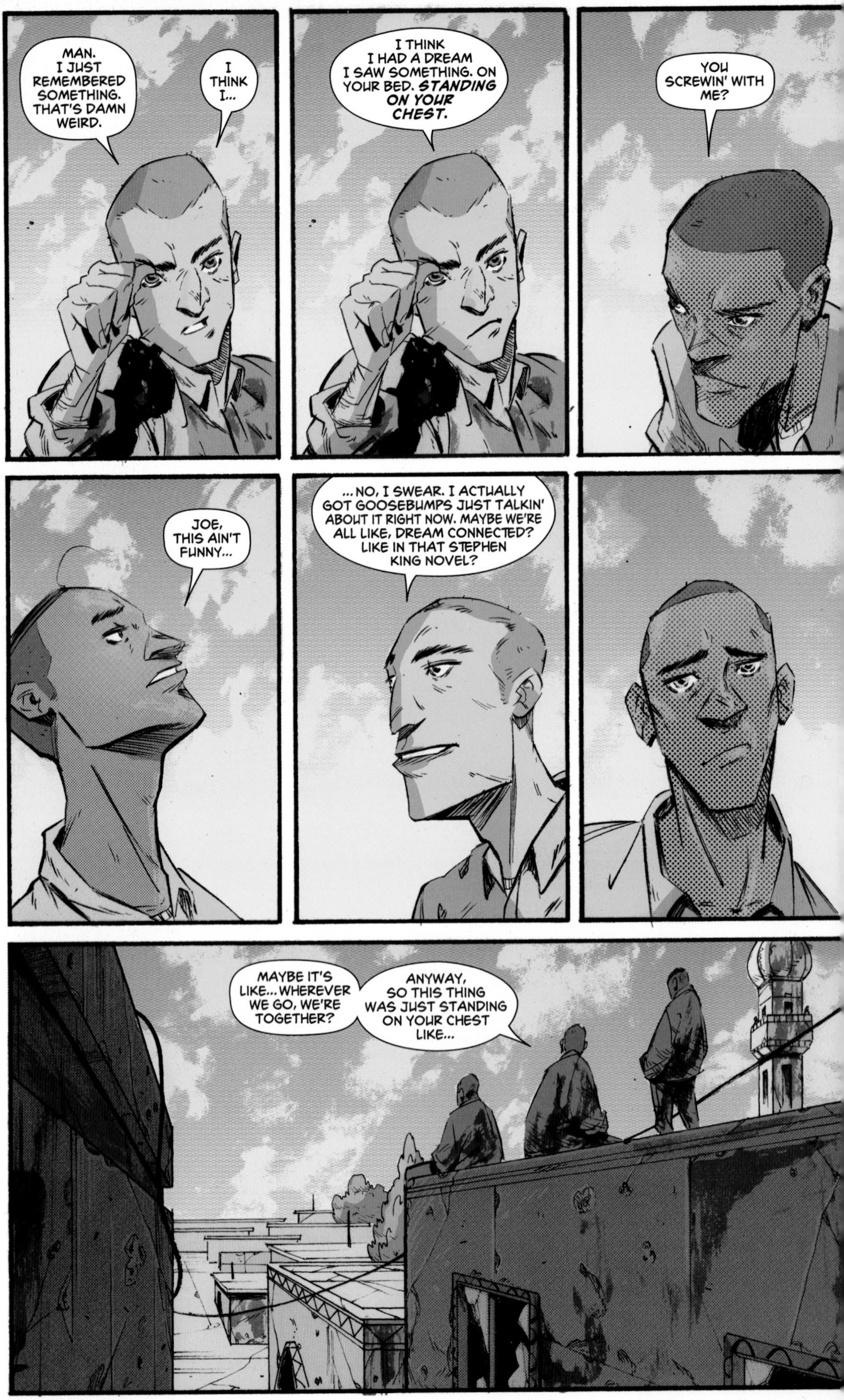

MAN. I JUST REMEMBERED SOMETHING. THAT'S DAMN WEIRD.
I THINK I...
I THINK I HAD A DREAM I SAW SOMETHING. ON YOUR BED. *STANDING ON YOUR CHEST.*
YOU SCREWIN' WITH ME?
JOE, THIS AIN'T FUNNY...
...NO, I SWEAR. I ACTUALLY GOT GOOSEBUMPS JUST TALKIN' ABOUT IT RIGHT NOW. MAYBE WE'RE ALL LIKE, DREAM CONNECTED? LIKE IN THAT STEPHEN KING NOVEL?
MAYBE IT'S LIKE... WHEREVER WE GO, WE'RE TOGETHER?
ANYWAY, SO THIS THING WAS JUST STANDING ON YOUR CHEST LIKE...

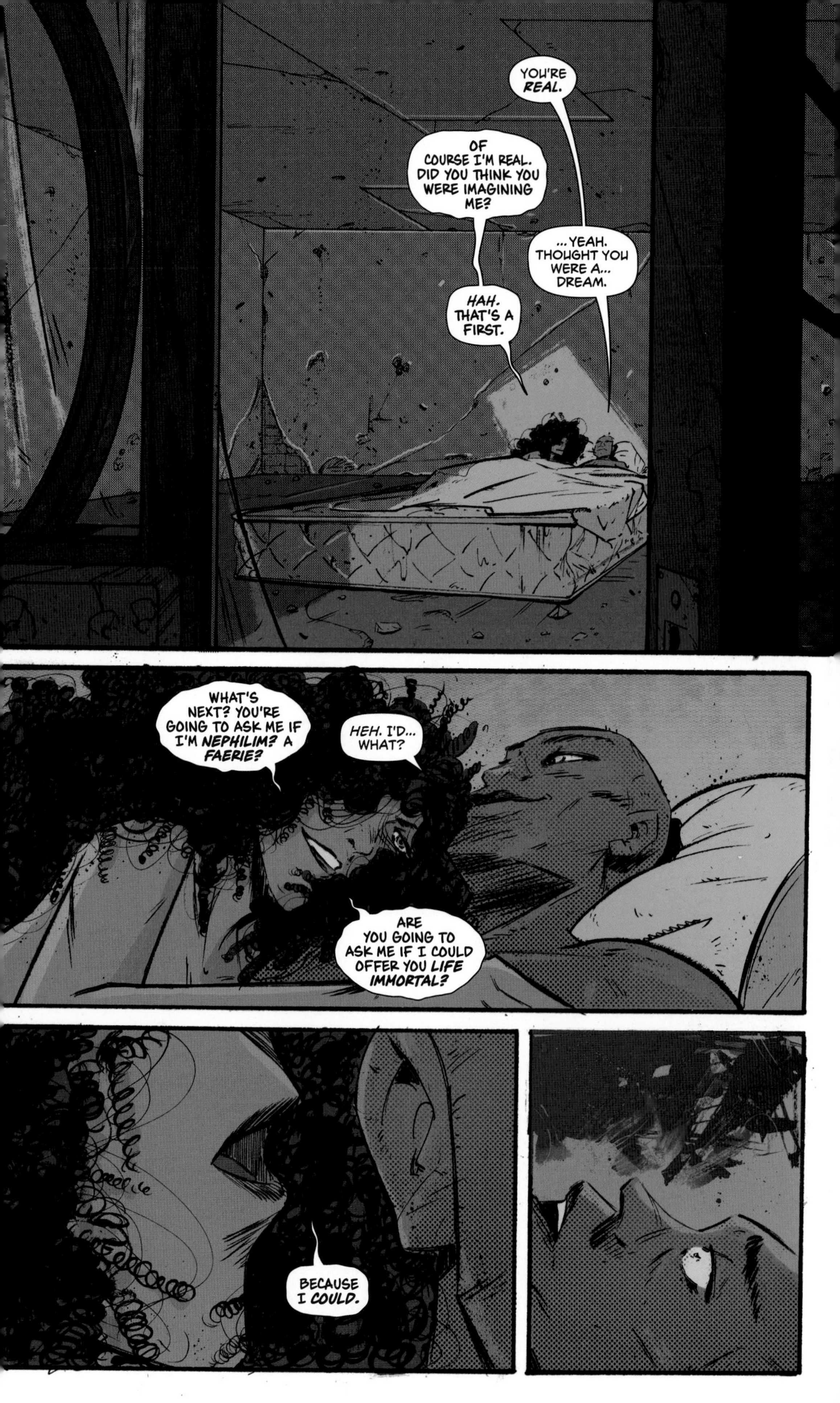
YOU'RE REAL.
OF COURSE I'M REAL. DID YOU THINK YOU WERE IMAGINING ME?
...YEAH. THOUGHT YOU WERE A... DREAM.
HAH. THAT'S A FIRST.
WHAT'S NEXT? YOU'RE GOING TO ASK ME IF I'M NEPHILIM? A FAERIE?
HEH. I'D... WHAT?
ARE YOU GOING TO ASK ME IF I COULD OFFER YOU LIFE IMMORTAL?
BECAUSE I COULD.

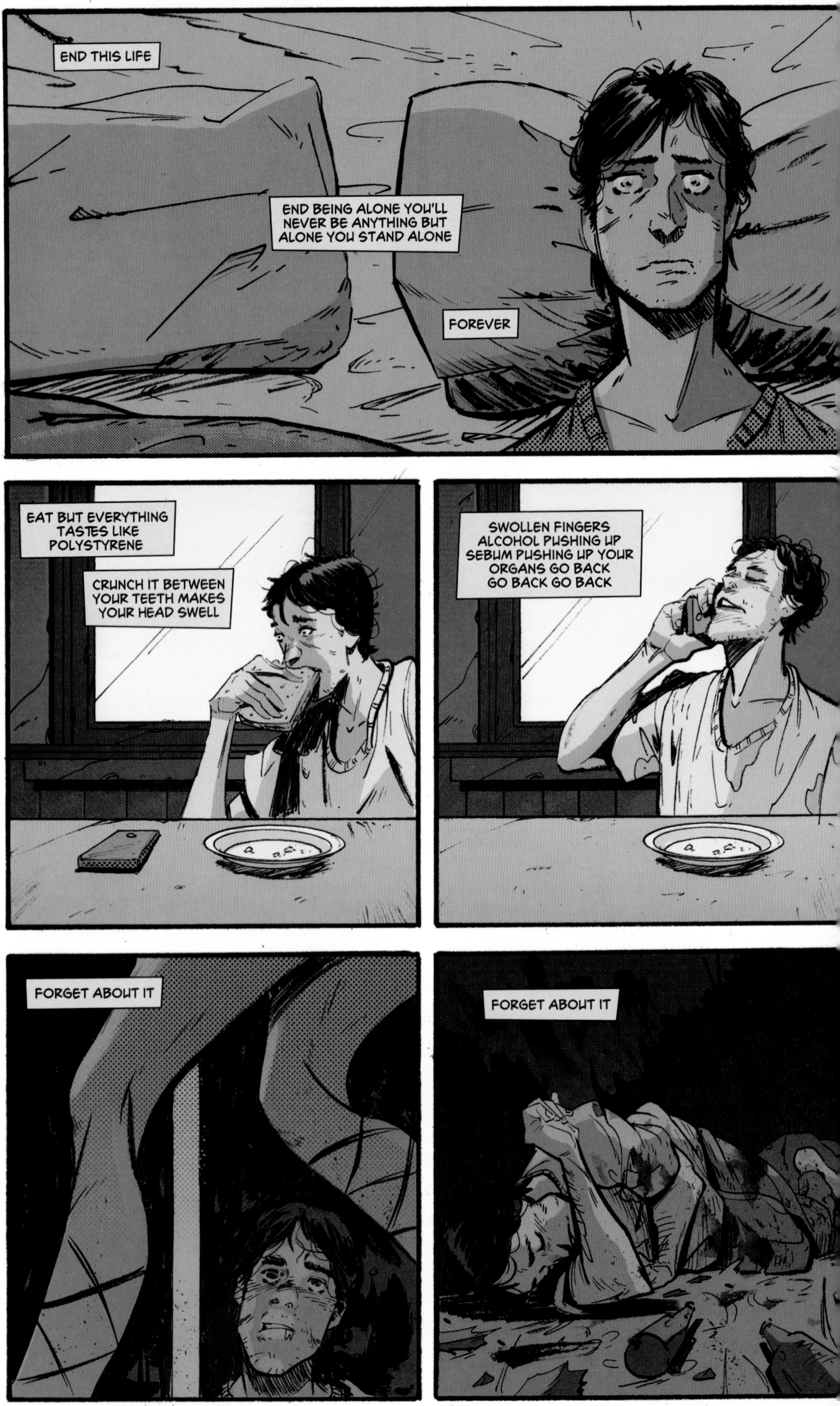
END THIS LIFE
END BEING ALONE YOU'LL NEVER BE ANYTHING BUT ALONE YOU STAND ALONE
FOREVER
EAT BUT EVERYTHING TASTES LIKE POLYSTYRENE
CRUNCH IT BETWEEN YOUR TEETH MAKES YOUR HEAD SWELL
SWOLLEN FINGERS ALCOHOL PUSHING UP SEBUM PUSHING UP YOUR ORGANS GO BACK GO BACK GO BACK
FORGET ABOUT IT
FORGET ABOUT IT

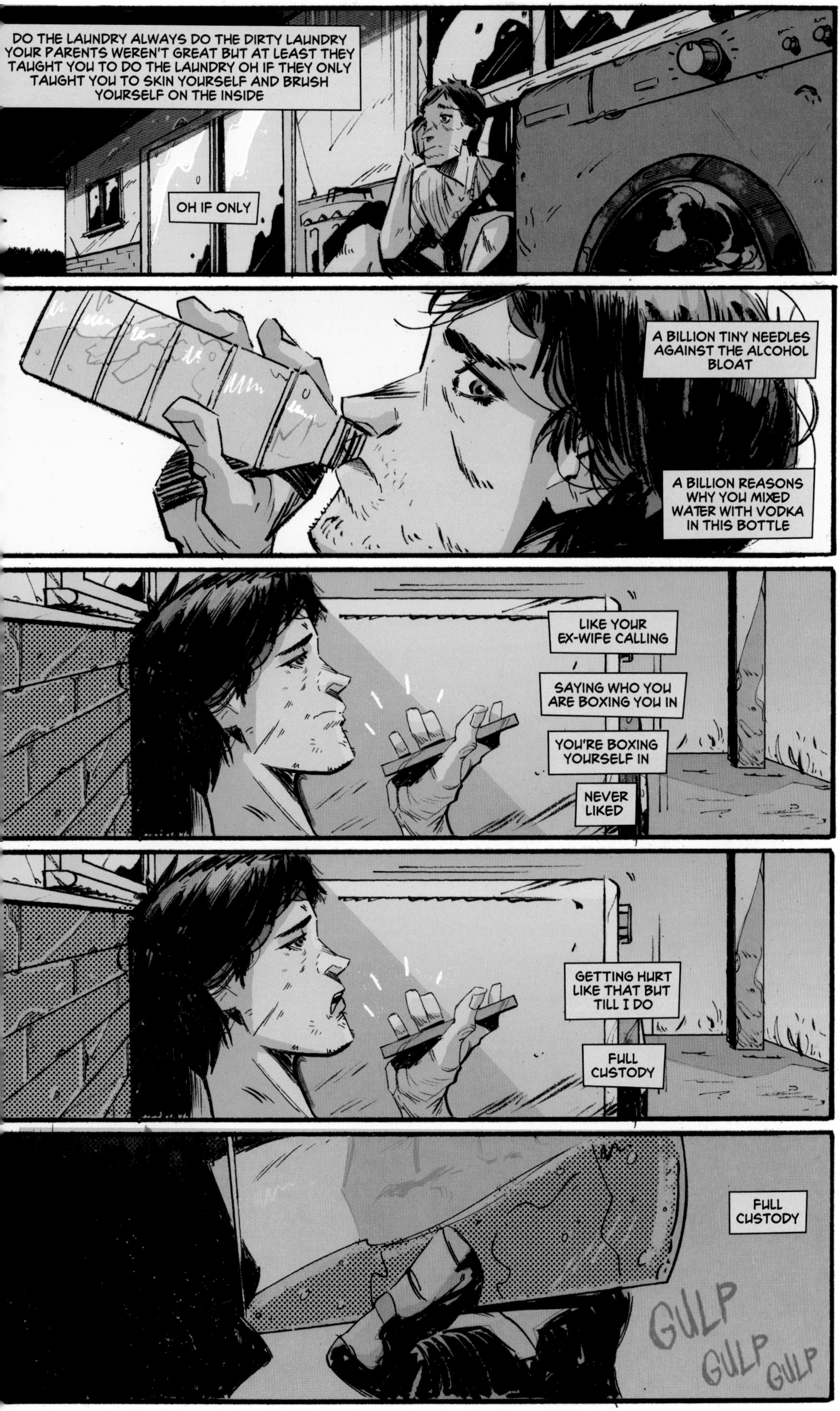

DO THE LAUNDRY ALWAYS DO THE DIRTY LAUNDRY YOUR PARENTS WEREN'T GREAT BUT AT LEAST THEY TAUGHT YOU TO DO THE LAUNDRY OH IF THEY ONLY TAUGHT YOU TO SKIN YOURSELF AND BRUSH YOURSELF ON THE INSIDE
OH IF ONLY
A BILLION TINY NEEDLES AGAINST THE ALCOHOL BLOAT
A BILLION REASONS WHY YOU MIXED WATER WITH VODKA IN THIS BOTTLE
LIKE YOUR EX-WIFE CALLING
SAYING WHO YOU ARE BOXING YOU IN
YOU'RE BOXING YOURSELF IN
NEVER LIKED
GETTING HURT LIKE THAT BUT TILL I DO
FULL CUSTODY
FULL CUSTODY
GULP
GULP
GULP

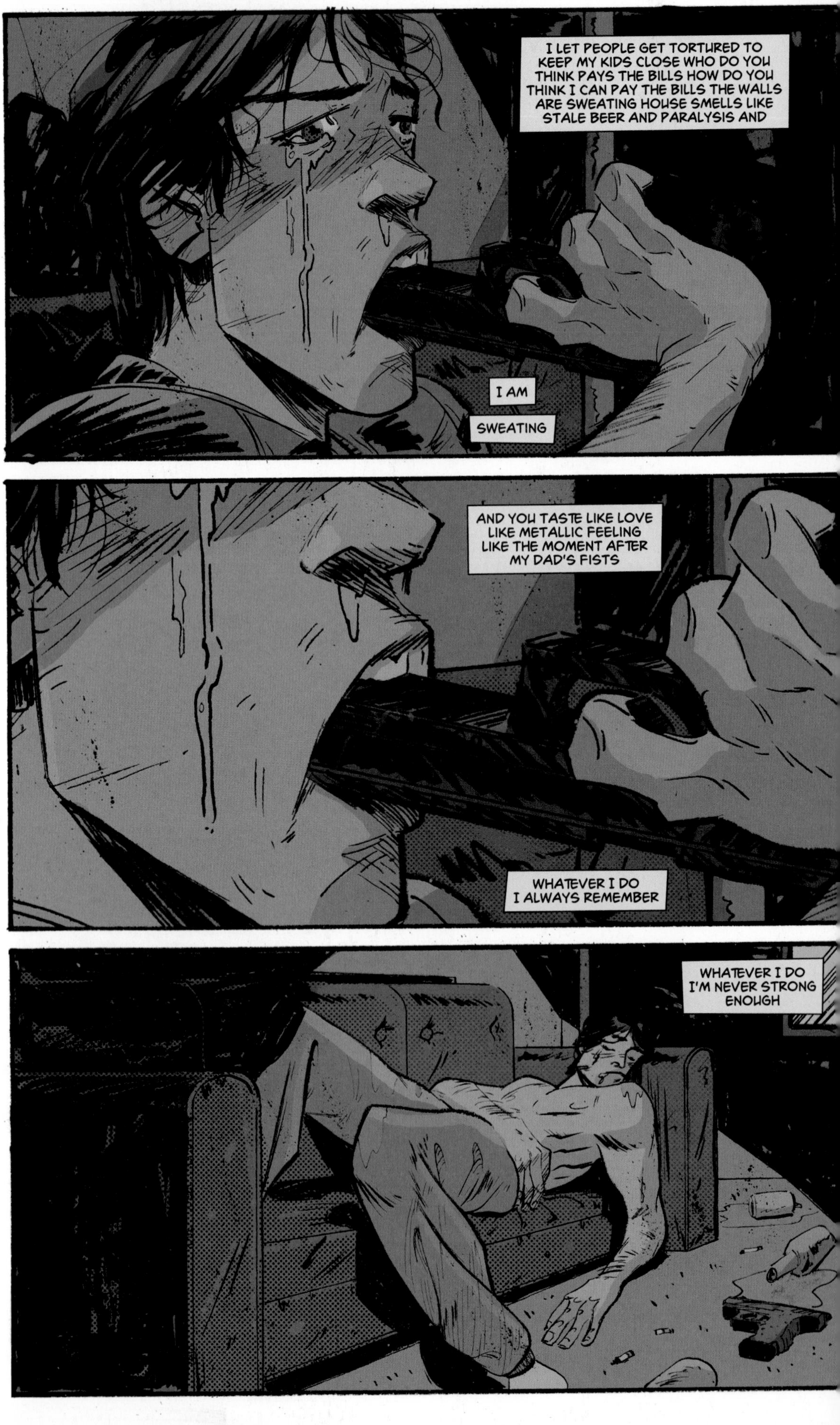

I LET PEOPLE GET TORTURED TO KEEP MY KIDS CLOSE WHO DO YOU THINK PAYS THE BILLS HOW DO YOU THINK I CAN PAY THE BILLS THE WALLS ARE SWEATING HOUSE SMELLS LIKE STALE BEER AND PARALYSIS AND
I AM
SWEATING
AND YOU TASTE LIKE LOVE LIKE METALLIC FEELING LIKE THE MOMENT AFTER MY DAD'S FISTS
WHATEVER I DO I ALWAYS REMEMBER
WHATEVER I DO I'M NEVER STRONG ENOUGH

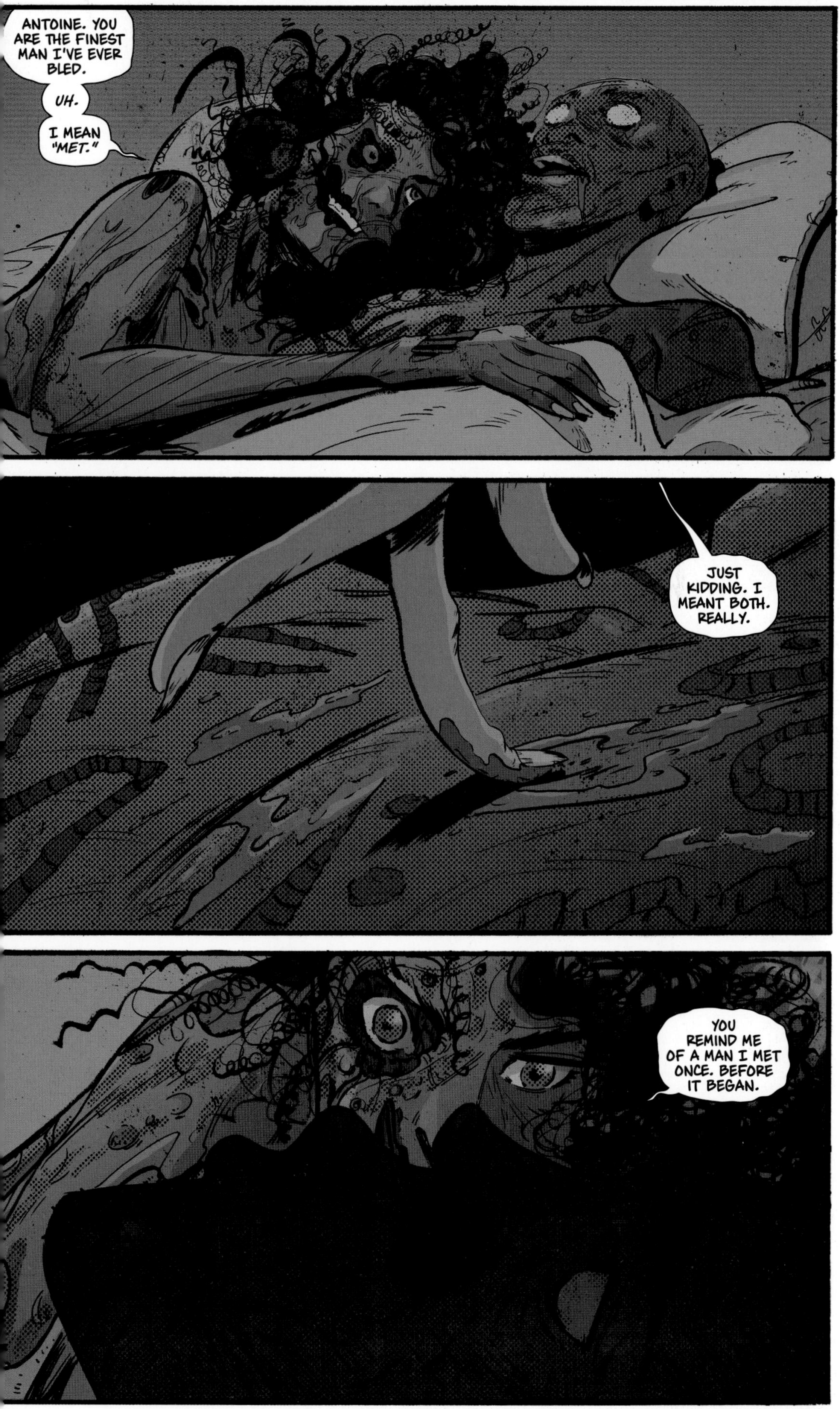
ANTOINE. YOU ARE THE FINEST MAN I'VE EVER BLED.
UH.
I MEAN "MET."
JUST KIDDING. I MEANT BOTH. REALLY.
YOU REMIND ME OF A MAN I MET ONCE. BEFORE IT BEGAN.

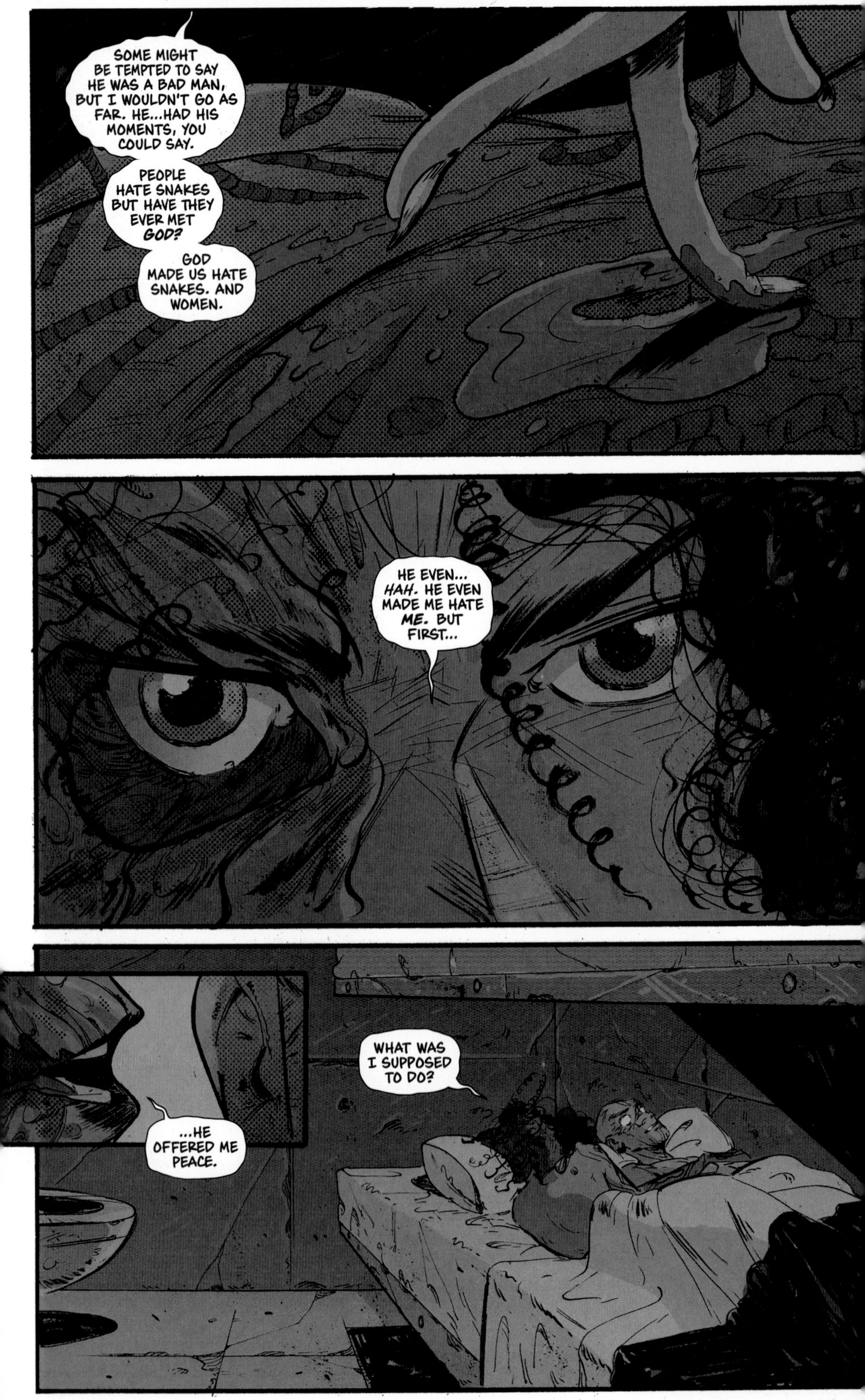
SOME MIGHT BE TEMPTED TO SAY HE WAS A BAD MAN, BUT I WOULDN'T GO AS FAR. HE...HAD HIS MOMENTS, YOU COULD SAY.
PEOPLE HATE SNAKES BUT HAVE THEY EVER MET *GOD?*
GOD MADE US HATE SNAKES. AND WOMEN.
HE EVEN... *HAH.* HE EVEN MADE ME HATE **ME.** BUT FIRST...
...HE OFFERED ME PEACE.
WHAT WAS I SUPPOSED TO DO?

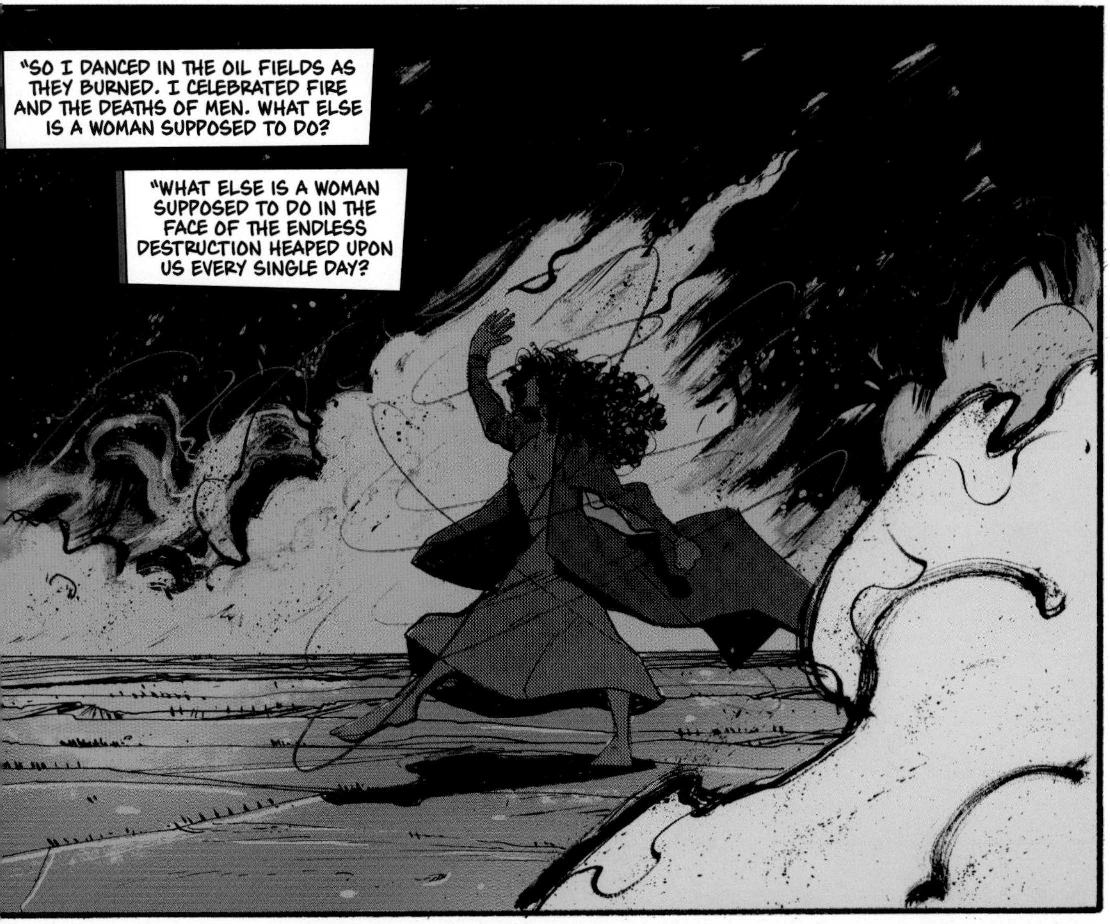
"SO I DANCED IN THE OIL FIELDS AS THEY BURNED. I CELEBRATED FIRE AND THE DEATHS OF MEN. WHAT ELSE IS A WOMAN SUPPOSED TO DO?
"WHAT ELSE IS A WOMAN SUPPOSED TO DO IN THE FACE OF THE ENDLESS DESTRUCTION HEAPED UPON US EVERY SINGLE DAY?

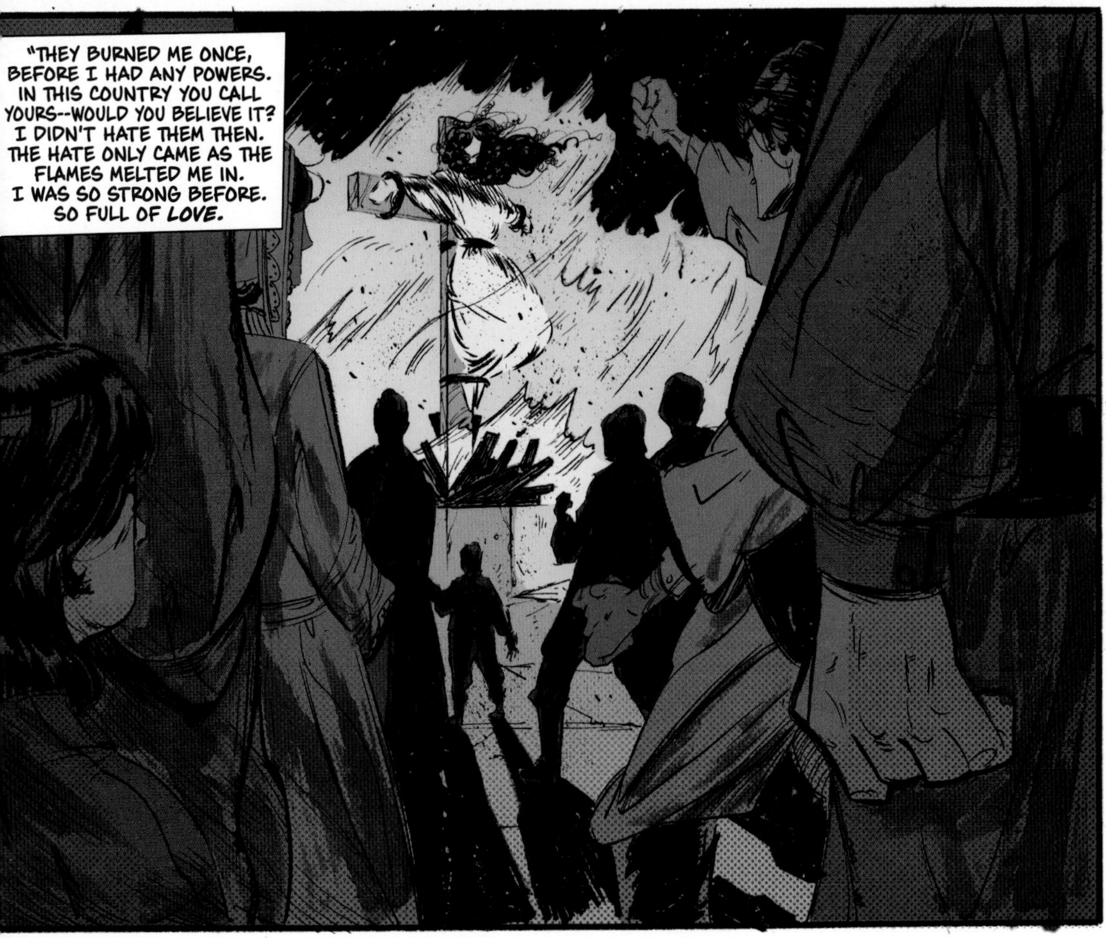
"THEY BURNED ME ONCE, BEFORE I HAD ANY POWERS. IN THIS COUNTRY YOU CALL YOURS--WOULD YOU BELIEVE IT? I DIDN'T HATE THEM THEN. THE HATE ONLY CAME AS THE FLAMES MELTED ME IN. I WAS SO STRONG BEFORE. SO FULL OF *LOVE*.

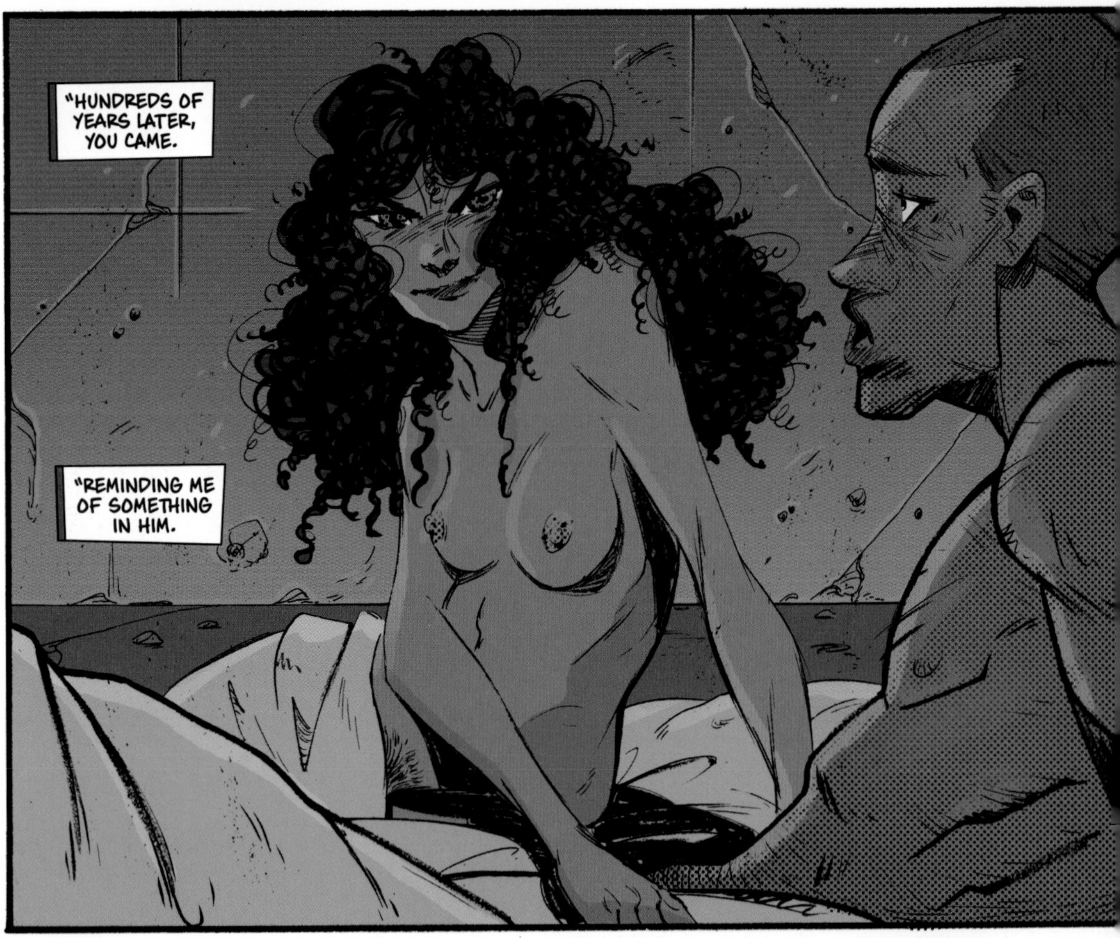
"HUNDREDS OF YEARS LATER, YOU CAME.
"REMINDING ME OF SOMETHING IN HIM.

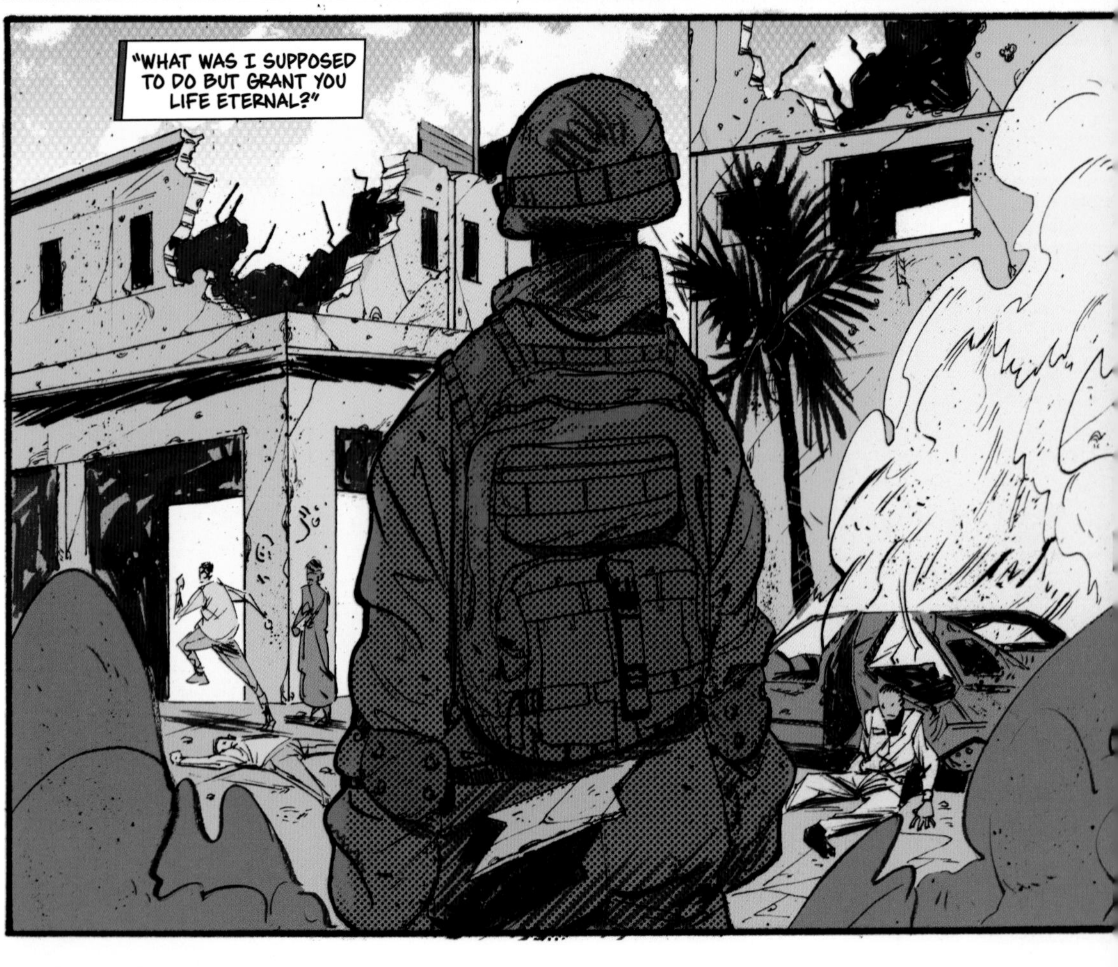
"WHAT WAS I SUPPOSED TO DO BUT GRANT YOU LIFE ETERNAL?"

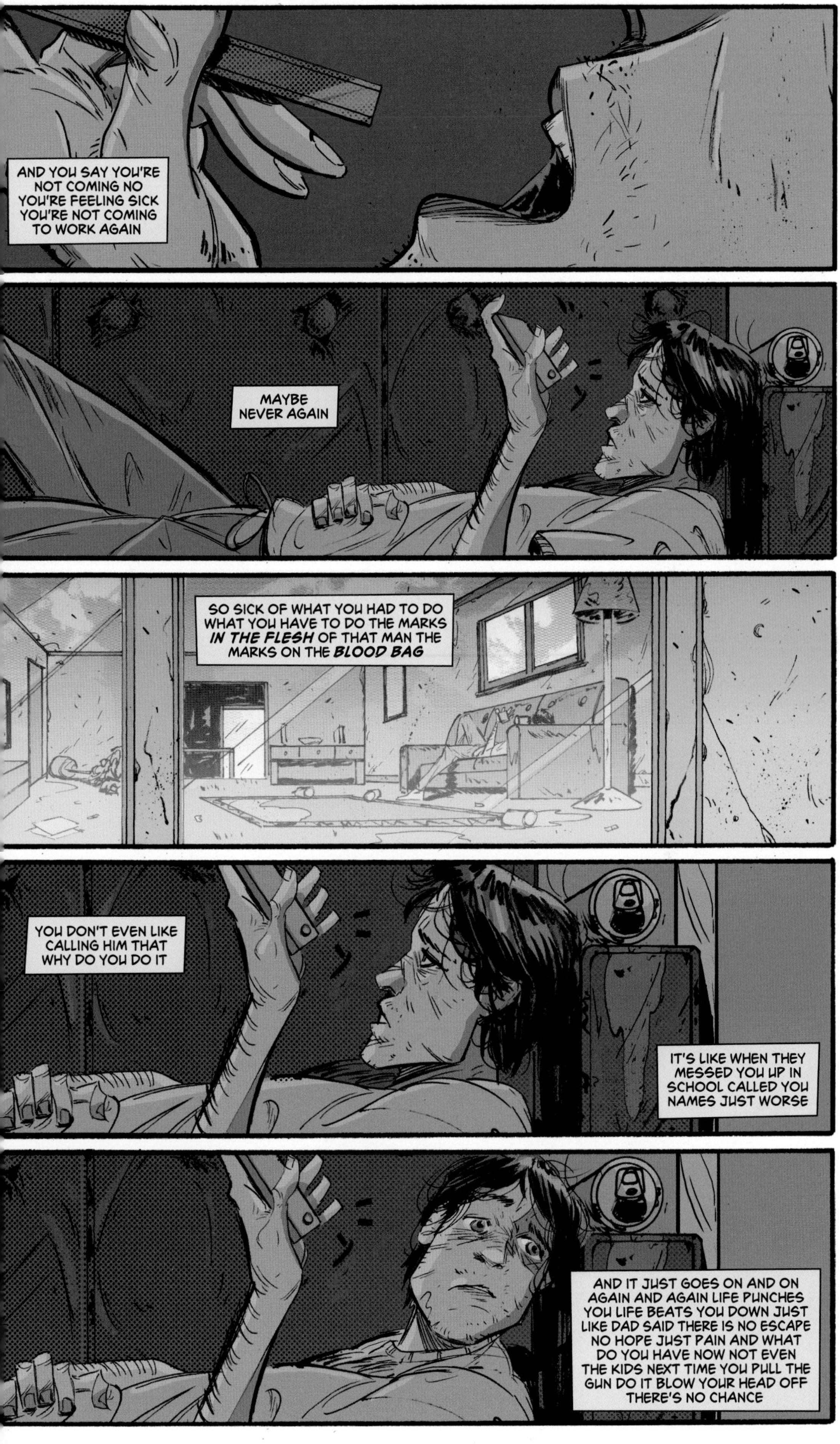
AND YOU SAY YOU'RE NOT COMING NO YOU'RE FEELING SICK YOU'RE NOT COMING TO WORK AGAIN
MAYBE NEVER AGAIN
SO SICK OF WHAT YOU HAD TO DO WHAT YOU HAVE TO DO THE MARKS *IN THE FLESH* OF THAT MAN THE MARKS ON THE *BLOOD BAG*
YOU DON'T EVEN LIKE CALLING HIM THAT WHY DO YOU DO IT
IT'S LIKE WHEN THEY MESSED YOU UP IN SCHOOL CALLED YOU NAMES JUST WORSE
AND IT JUST GOES ON AND ON AGAIN AND AGAIN LIFE PUNCHES YOU LIFE BEATS YOU DOWN JUST LIKE DAD SAID THERE IS NO ESCAPE NO HOPE JUST PAIN AND WHAT DO YOU HAVE NOW NOT EVEN THE KIDS NEXT TIME YOU PULL THE GUN DO IT BLOW YOUR HEAD OFF THERE'S NO CHANCE

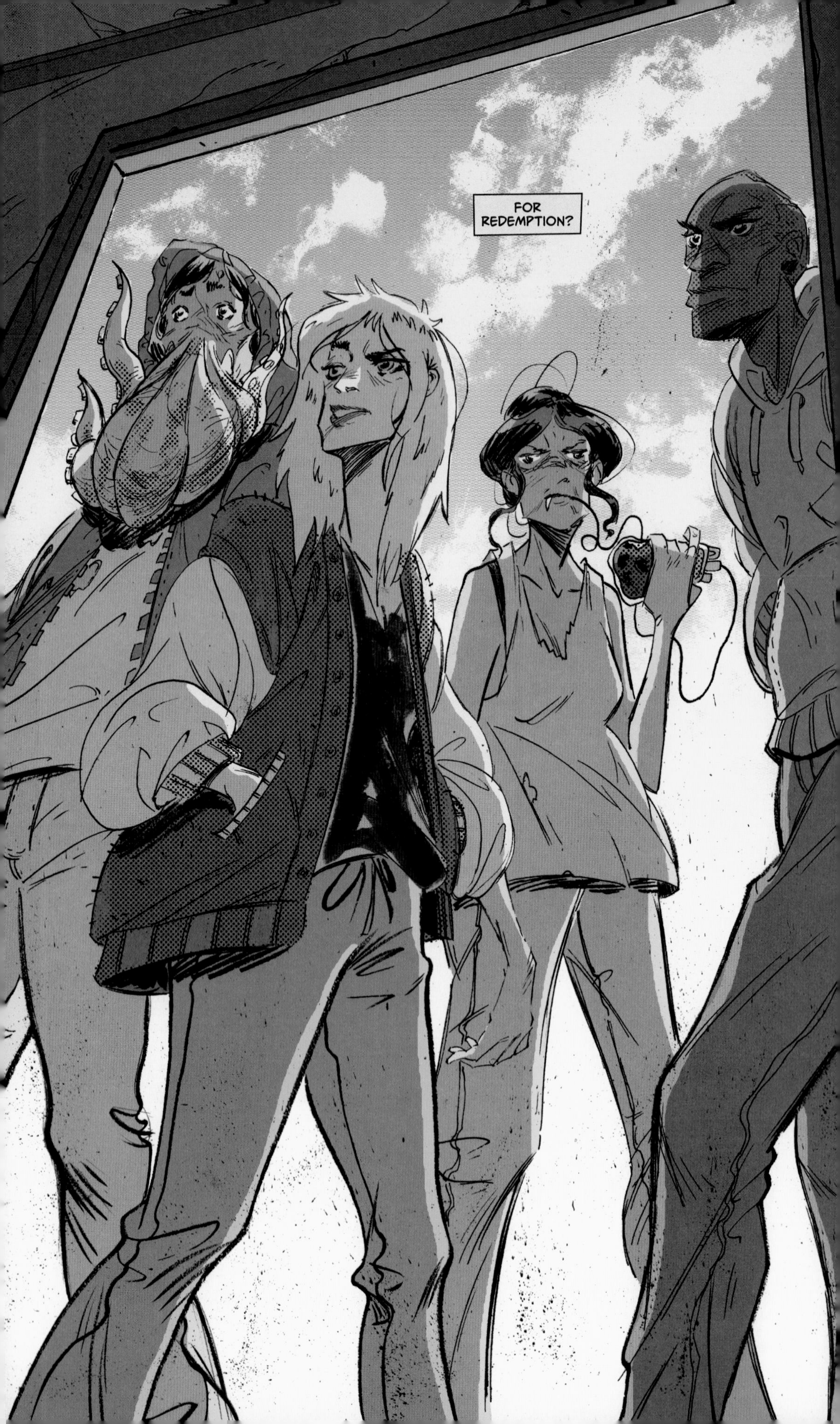
FOR REDEMPTION?

Chapter 8

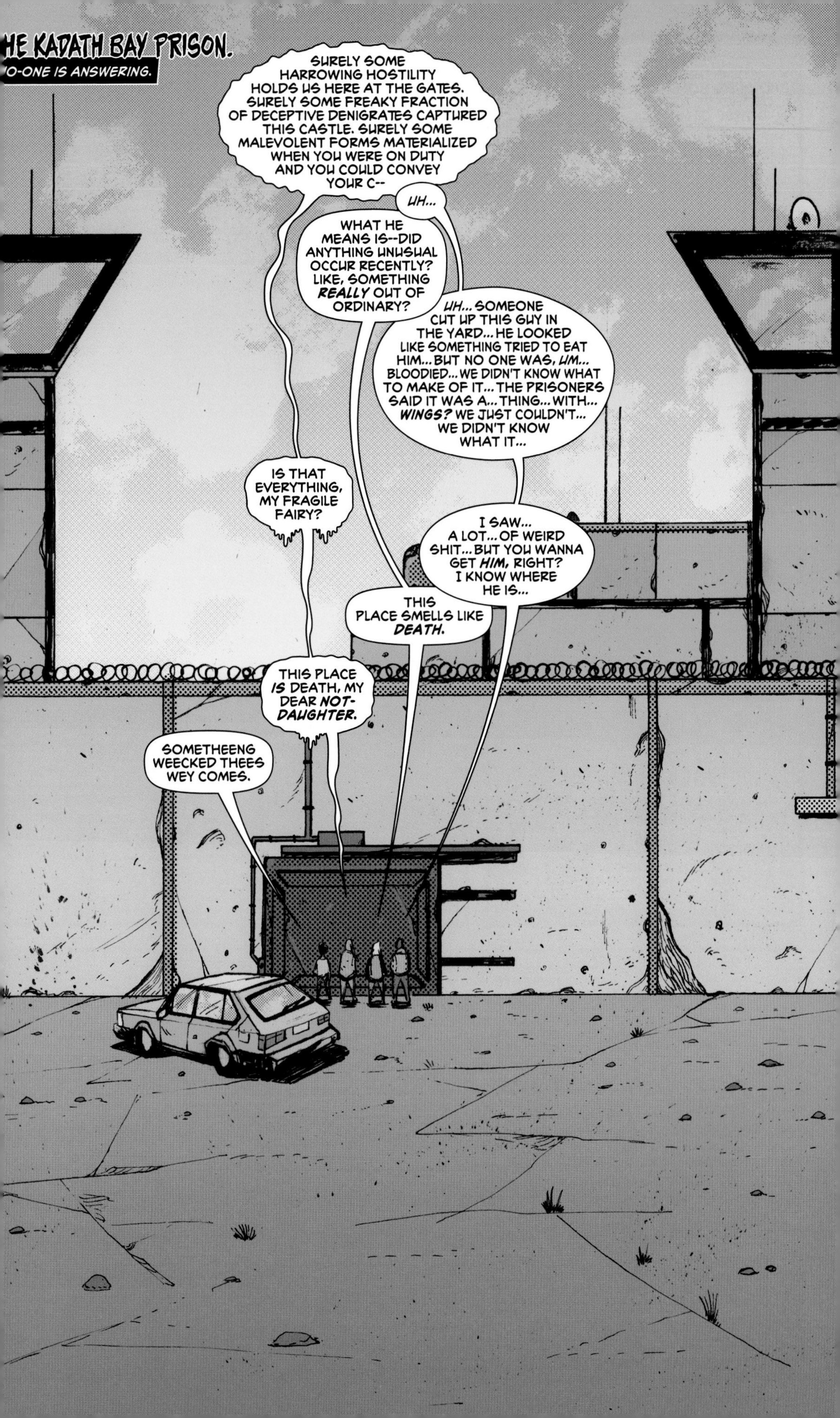
HE KADATH BAY PRISON.
O-ONE IS ANSWERING.
SURELY SOME HARROWING HOSTILITY HOLDS US HERE AT THE GATES. SURELY SOME FREAKY FRACTION OF DECEPTIVE DENIGRATES CAPTURED THIS CASTLE. SURELY SOME MALEVOLENT FORMS MATERIALIZED WHEN YOU WERE ON DUTY AND YOU COULD CONVEY YOUR C--
UH...
WHAT HE MEANS IS--DID ANYTHING UNUSUAL OCCUR RECENTLY? LIKE, SOMETHING REALLY OUT OF ORDINARY?
UH... SOMEONE CUT UP THIS GUY IN THE YARD... HE LOOKED LIKE SOMETHING TRIED TO EAT HIM... BUT NO ONE WAS, UM... BLOODIED... WE DIDN'T KNOW WHAT TO MAKE OF IT... THE PRISONERS SAID IT WAS A... THING... WITH... WINGS? WE JUST COULDN'T... WE DIDN'T KNOW WHAT IT...
IS THAT EVERYTHING, MY FRAGILE FAIRY?
I SAW... A LOT... OF WEIRD SHIT... BUT YOU WANNA GET HIM, RIGHT? I KNOW WHERE HE IS...
THIS PLACE SMELLS LIKE DEATH.
THIS PLACE IS DEATH, MY DEAR NOT-DAUGHTER.
SOMETHEENG WEECKED THEES WEY COMES.

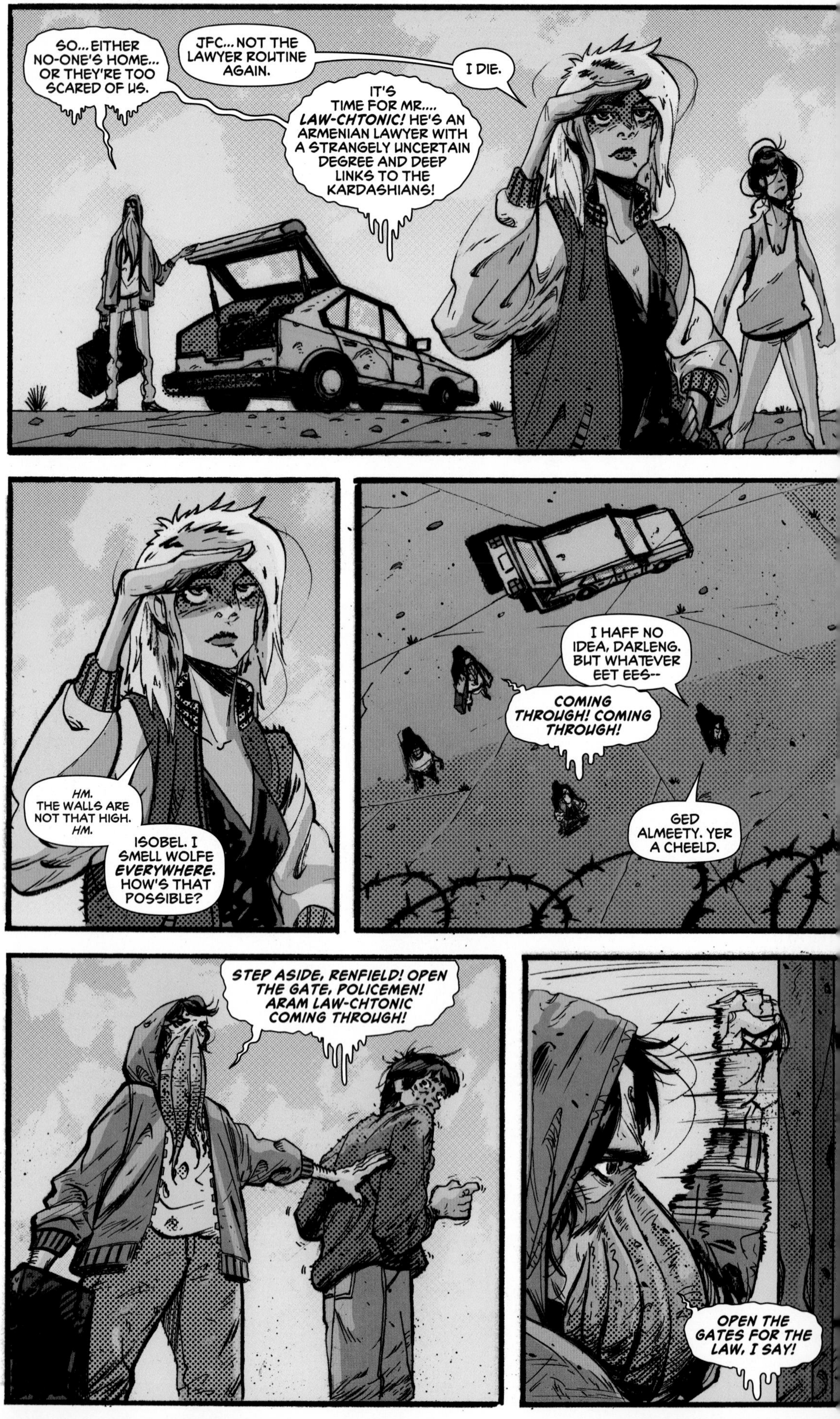
SO... EITHER NO-ONE'S HOME... OR THEY'RE TOO SCARED OF US.
JFC... NOT THE LAWYER ROUTINE AGAIN.
I DIE.
IT'S TIME FOR MR.... LAW-CHTONIC! HE'S AN ARMENIAN LAWYER WITH A STRANGELY UNCERTAIN DEGREE AND DEEP LINKS TO THE KARDASHIANS!
HM. THE WALLS ARE NOT THAT HIGH. HM.
ISOBEL. I SMELL WOLFE EVERYWHERE. HOW'S THAT POSSIBLE?
I HAFF NO IDEA, DARLENG. BUT WHATEVER EET EES--
COMING THROUGH! COMING THROUGH!
GED ALMEETY. YER A CHEELD.
STEP ASIDE, RENFIELD! OPEN THE GATE, POLICEMEN! ARAM LAW-CHTONIC COMING THROUGH!
OPEN THE GATES FOR THE LAW, I SAY!

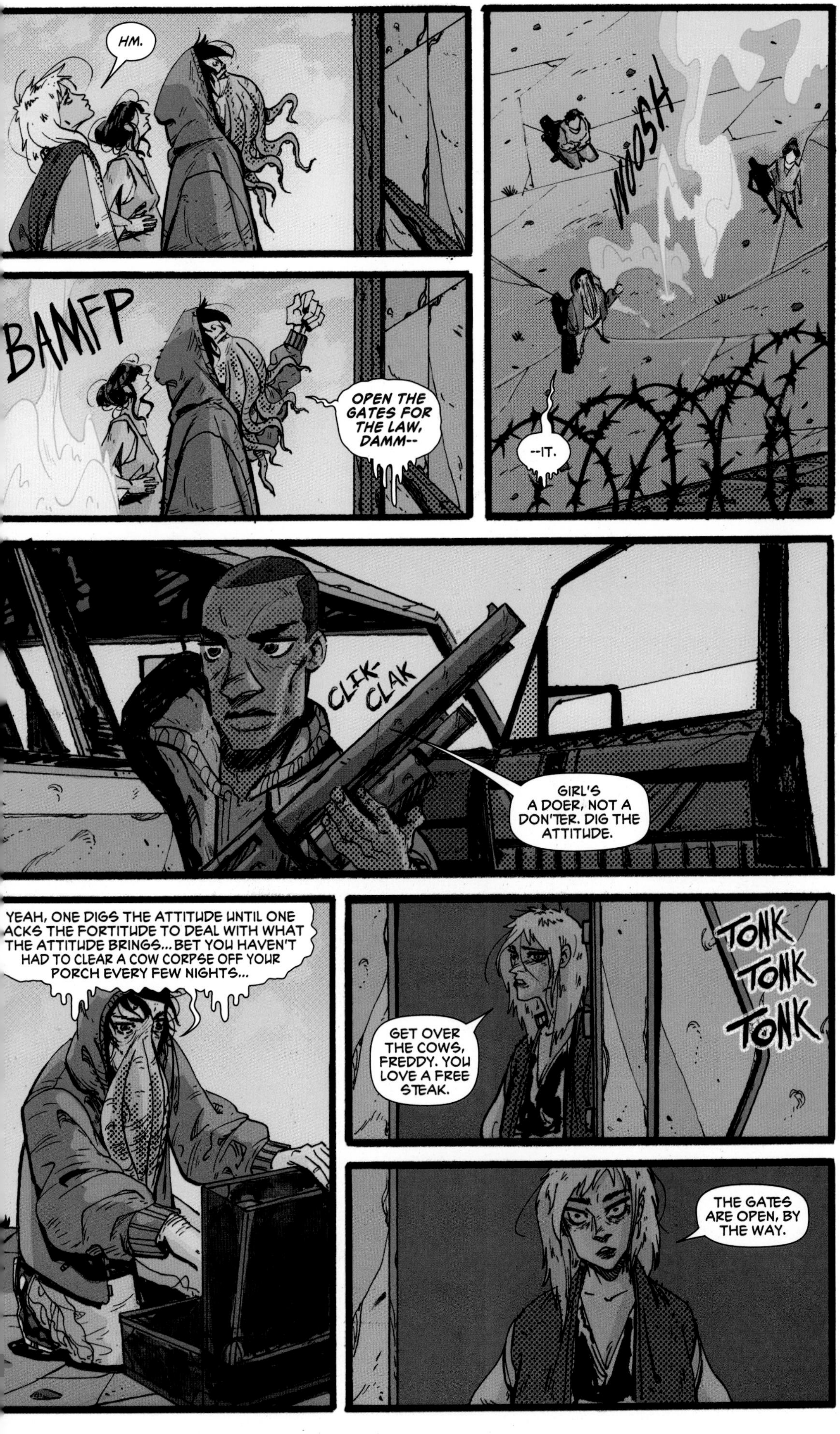
HM.
BAMFP
OPEN THE GATES FOR THE LAW, DAMM--
WOOSH
--IT.
CLIK-CLAK
GIRL'S A DOER, NOT A DON'TER. DIG THE ATTITUDE.
YEAH, ONE DIGS THE ATTITUDE UNTIL ONE ACKS THE FORTITUDE TO DEAL WITH WHAT THE ATTITUDE BRINGS... BET YOU HAVEN'T HAD TO CLEAR A COW CORPSE OFF YOUR PORCH EVERY FEW NIGHTS...
TONK TONK TONK
GET OVER THE COWS, FREDDY. YOU LOVE A FREE STEAK.
THE GATES ARE OPEN, BY THE WAY.

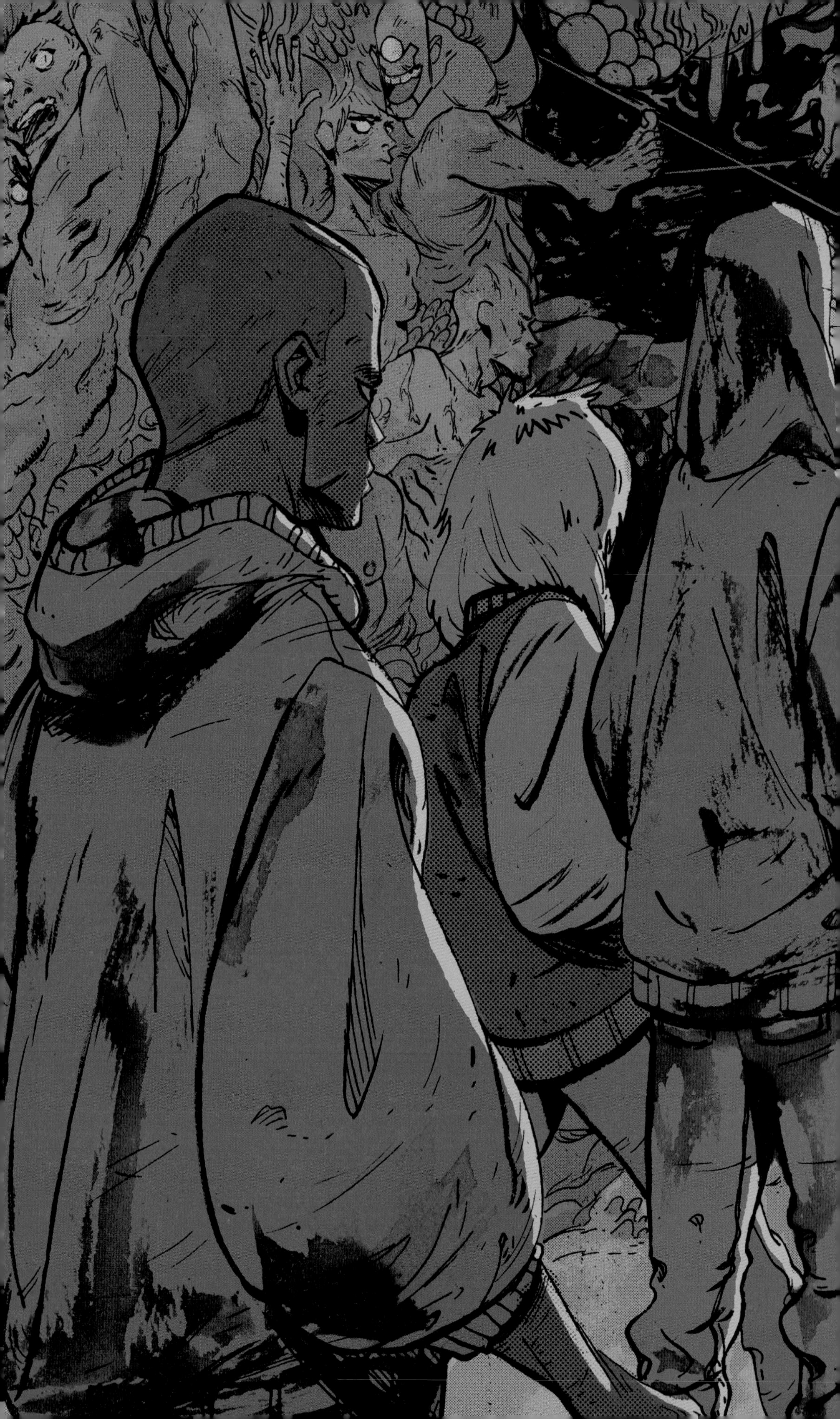

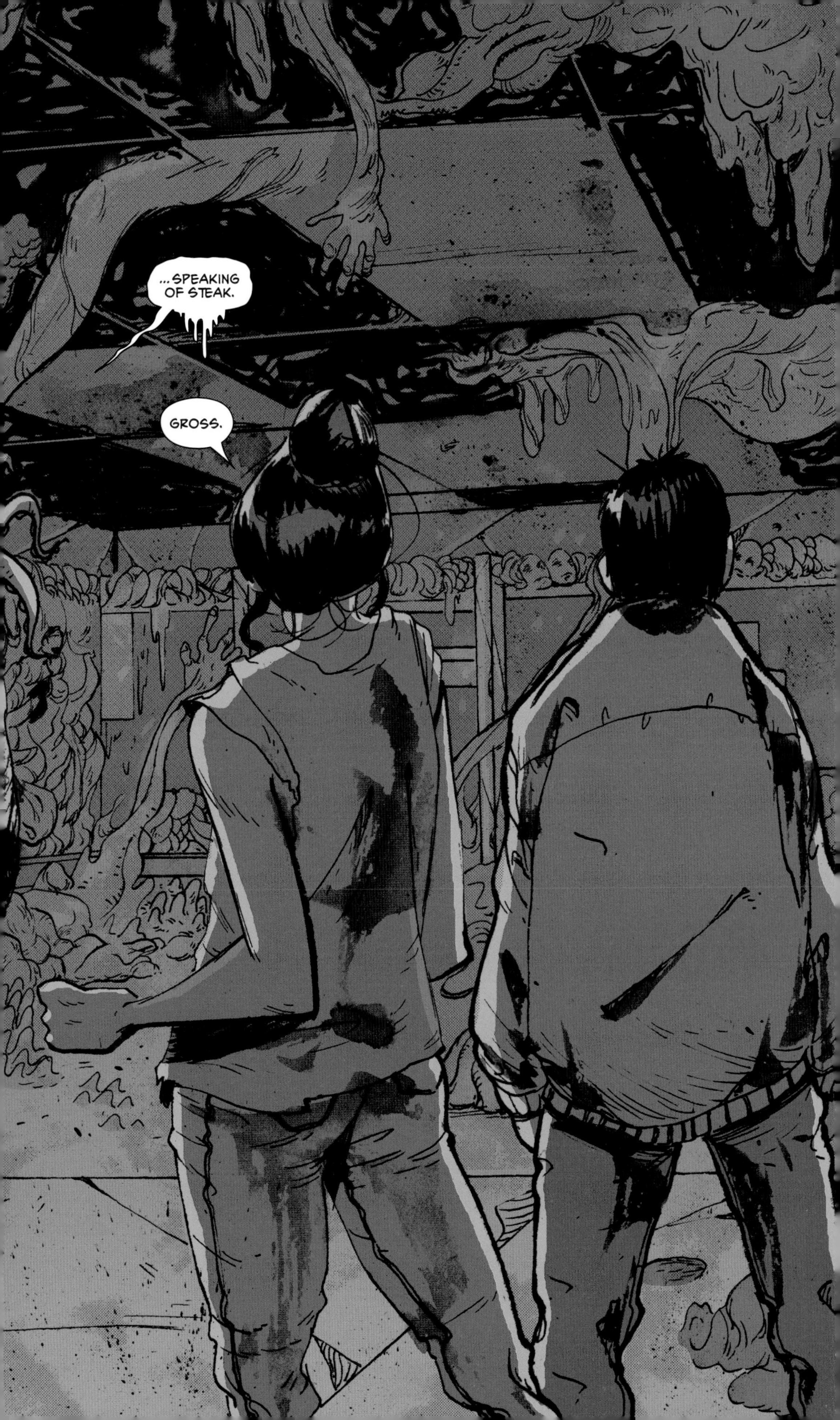
...SPEAKING OF STEAK.
GROSS.

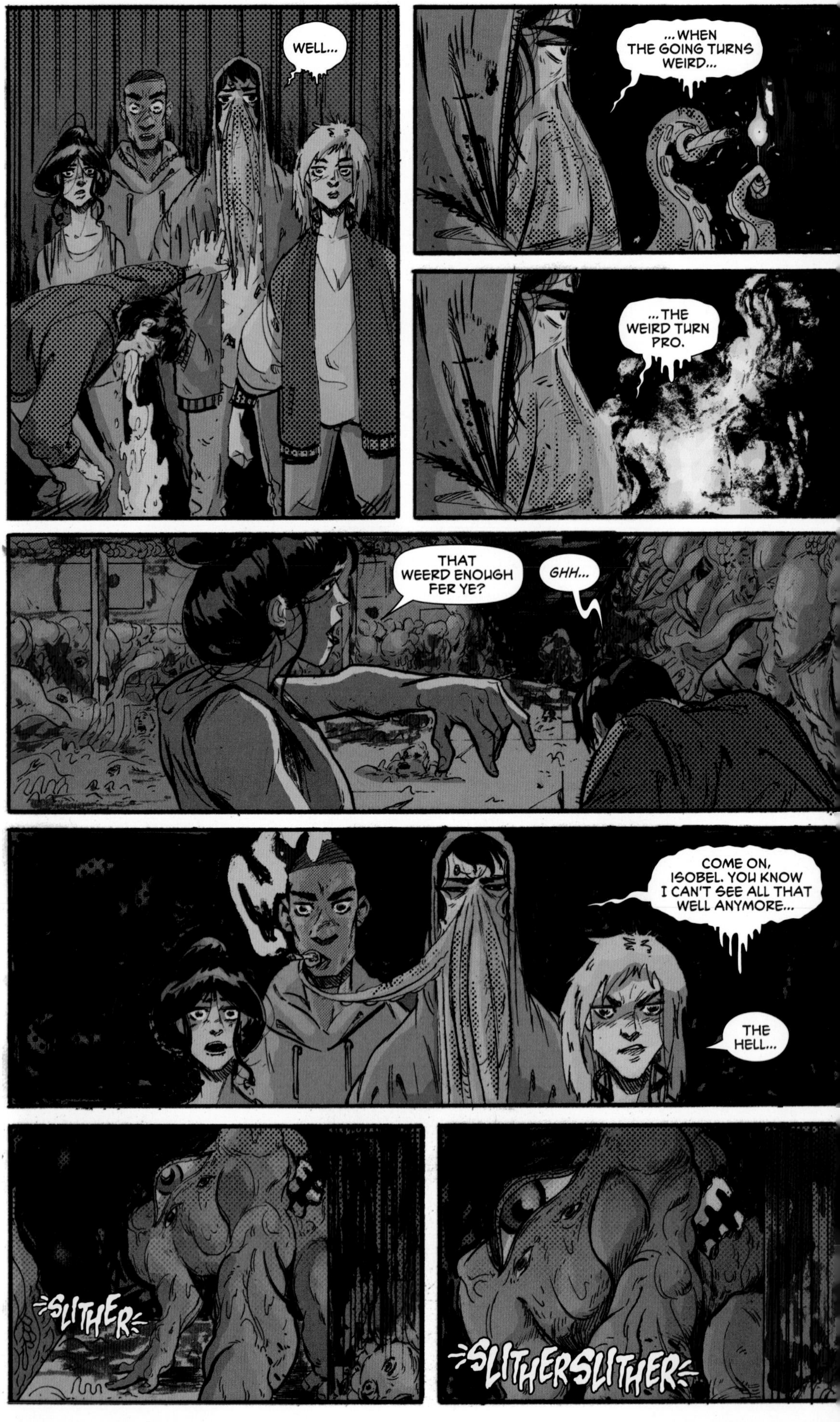
WELL...
...WHEN THE GOING TURNS WEIRD...
...THE WEIRD TURN PRO.
THAT WEERD ENOUGH FER YE?
GHH...
COME ON, ISOBEL. YOU KNOW I CAN'T SEE ALL THAT WELL ANYMORE...
THE HELL...
SLITHER
SLITHERSLITHER

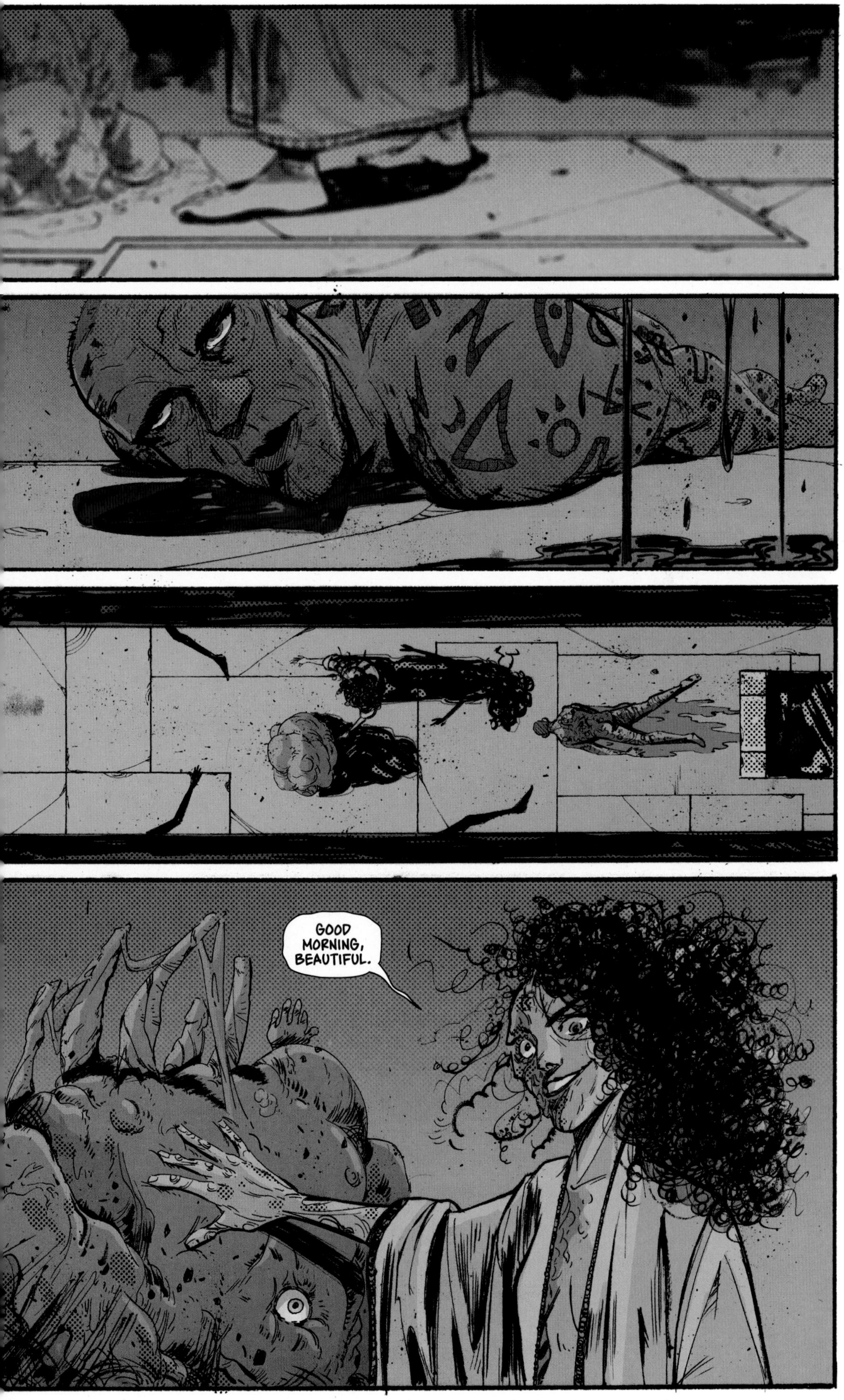
GOOD MORNING, BEAUTIFUL.

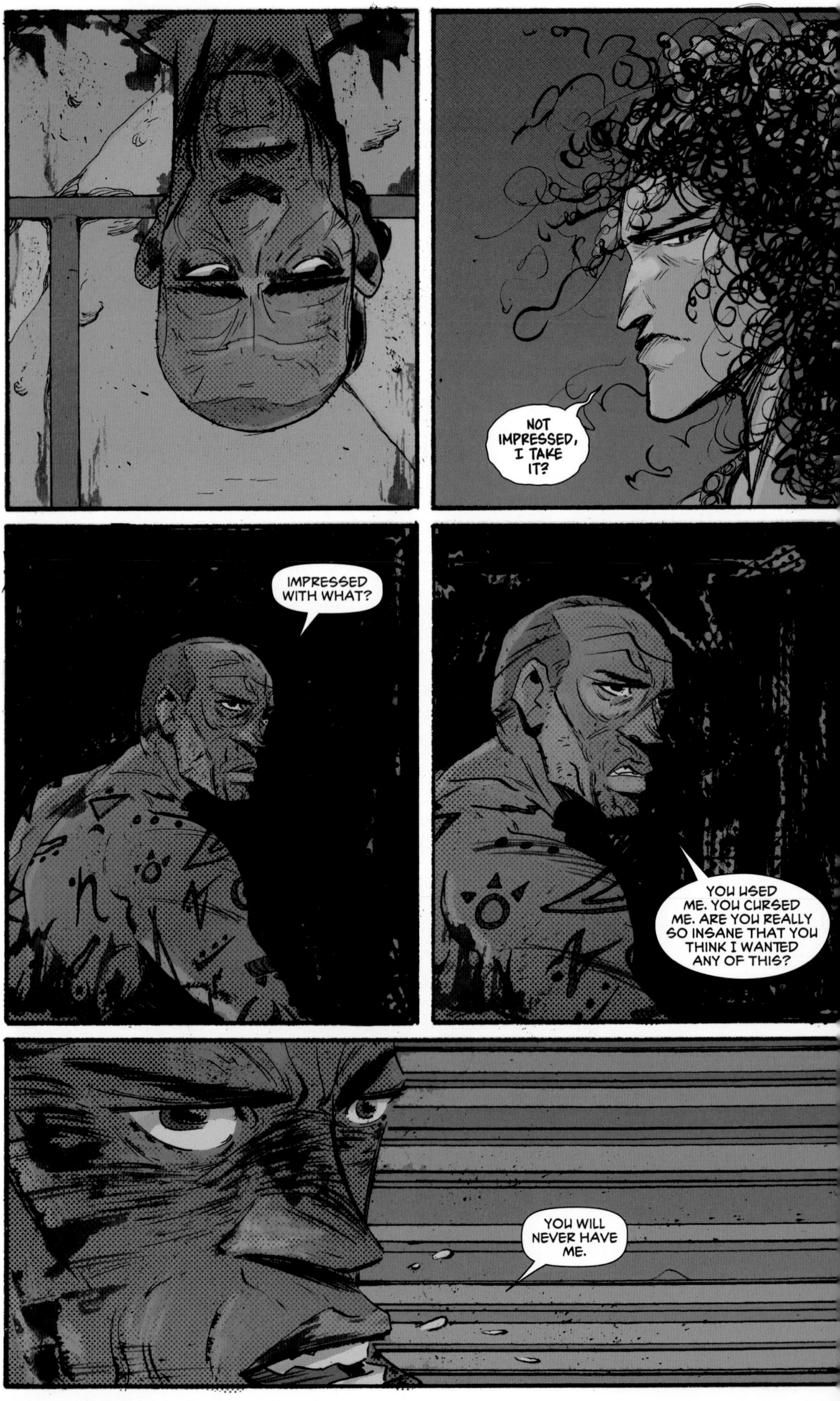
NOT IMPRESSED, I TAKE IT?
IMPRESSED WITH WHAT?
YOU USED ME. YOU CURSED ME. ARE YOU REALLY SO INSANE THAT YOU THINK I WANTED ANY OF THIS?
YOU WILL NEVER HAVE ME.

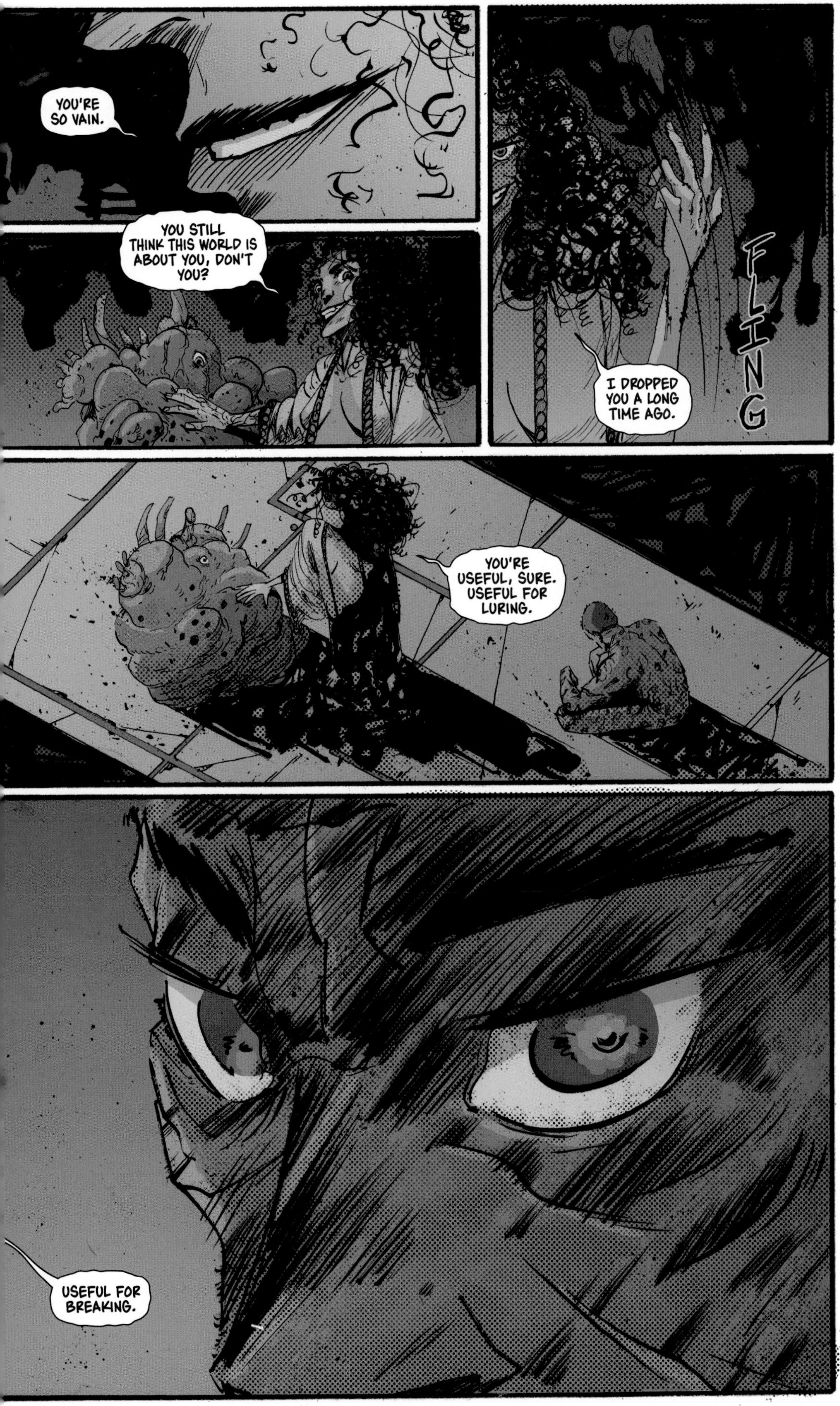
YOU'RE SO VAIN.
YOU STILL THINK THIS WORLD IS ABOUT YOU, DON'T YOU?
I DROPPED YOU A LONG TIME AGO.
FLING
YOU'RE USEFUL, SURE. USEFUL FOR LURING.
USEFUL FOR BREAKING.

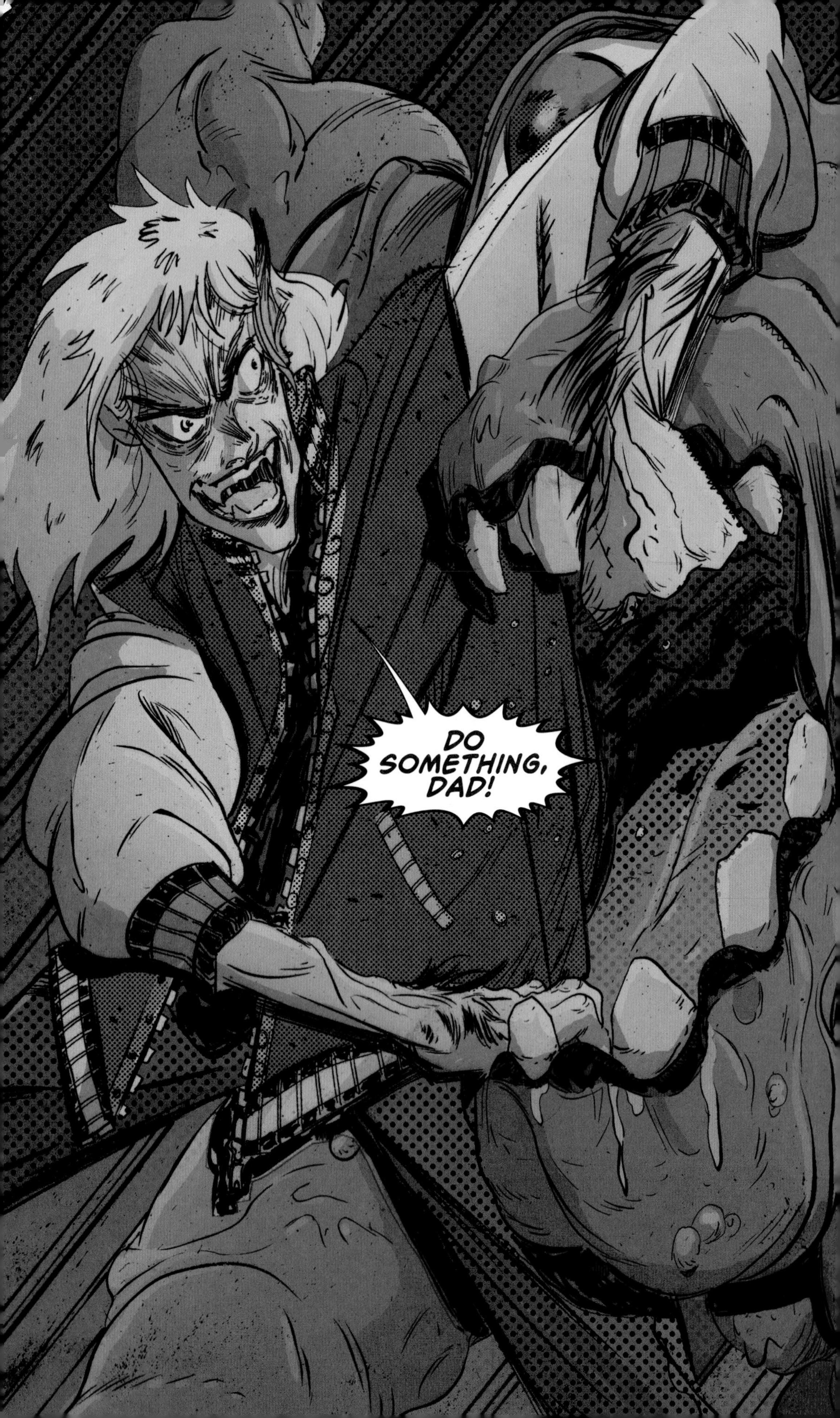
DO SOMETHING, DAD!

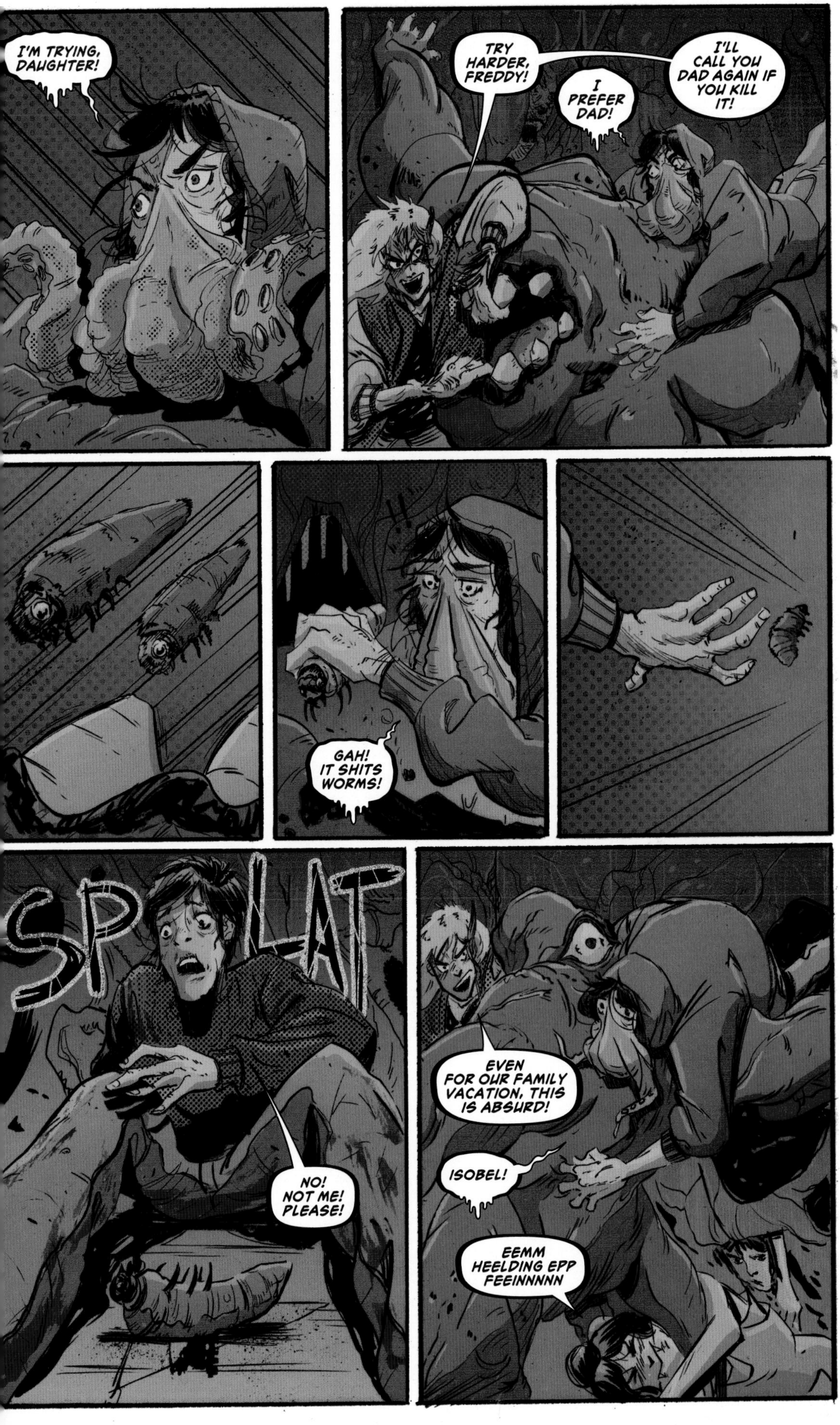

I'M TRYING, DAUGHTER!
TRY HARDER, FREDDY!
I PREFER DAD!
I'LL CALL YOU DAD AGAIN IF YOU KILL IT!
GAH! IT SHITS WORMS!
SPLAT
NO! NOT ME! PLEASE!
EVEN FOR OUR FAMILY VACATION, THIS IS ABSURD!
ISOBEL!
EEMM HEELDING EPP FEEINNNNN

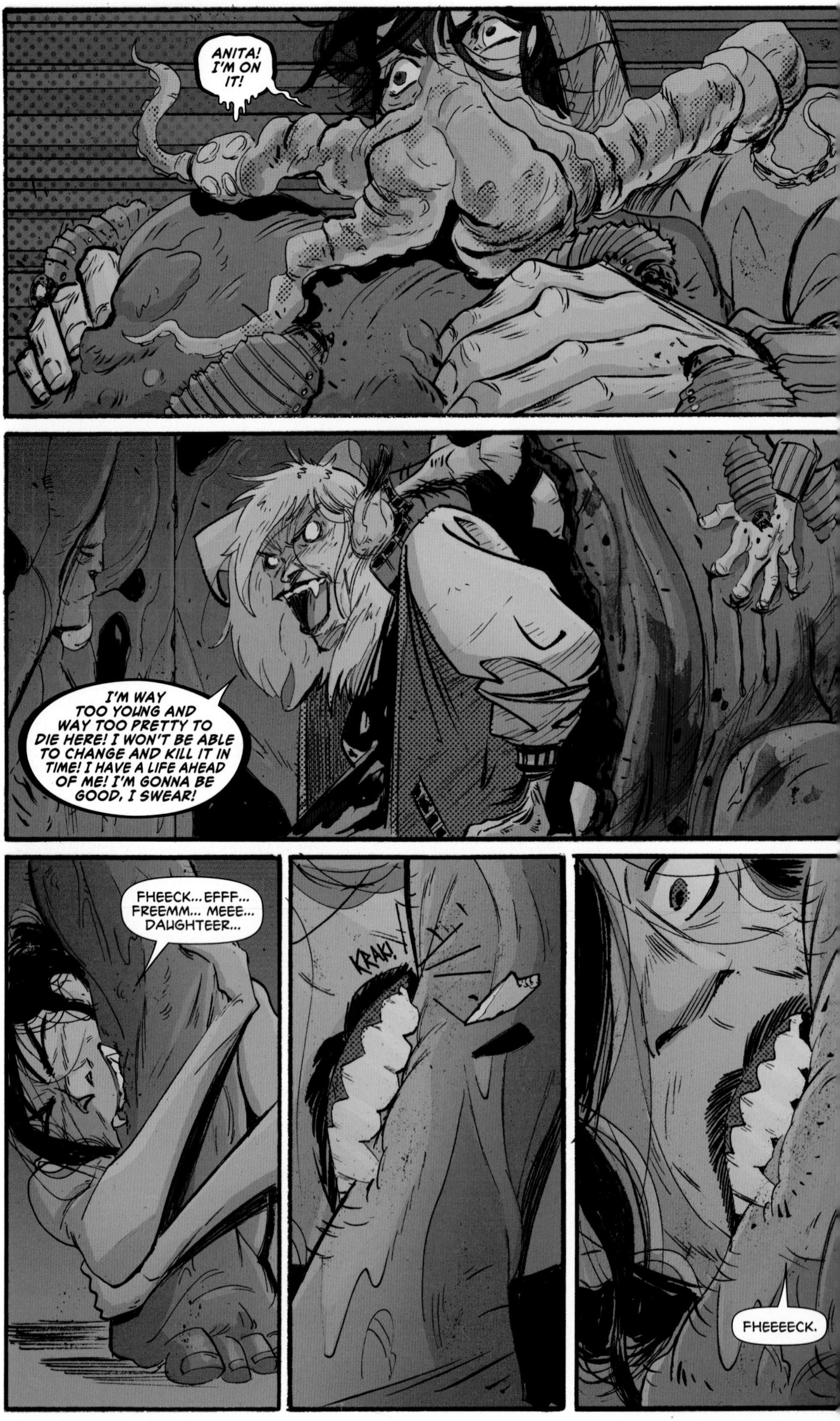
ANITA! I'M ON IT!
I'M WAY TOO YOUNG AND WAY TOO PRETTY TO DIE HERE! I WON'T BE ABLE TO CHANGE AND KILL IT IN TIME! I HAVE A LIFE AHEAD OF ME! I'M GONNA BE GOOD, I SWEAR!
FHEECK... EFFF... FREEMM... MEEE... DAUGHTEER...
KRAK!
FHEEEECK.

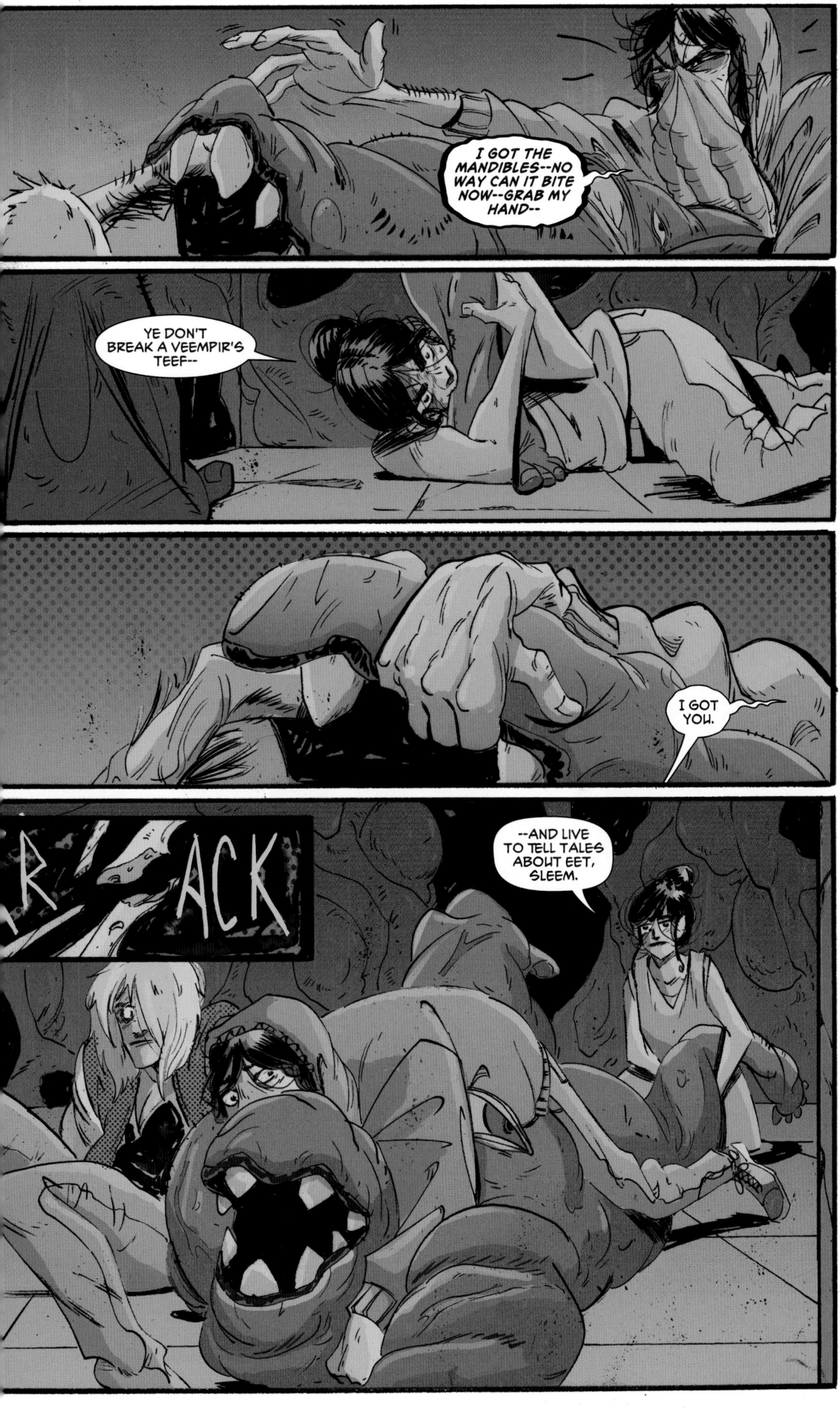
I GOT THE MANDIBLES--NO WAY CAN IT BITE NOW--GRAB MY HAND--
YE DON'T BREAK A VEEMPIR'S TEEF--
I GOT YOU.
R ACK
--AND LIVE TO TELL TALES ABOUT EET, SLEEM.

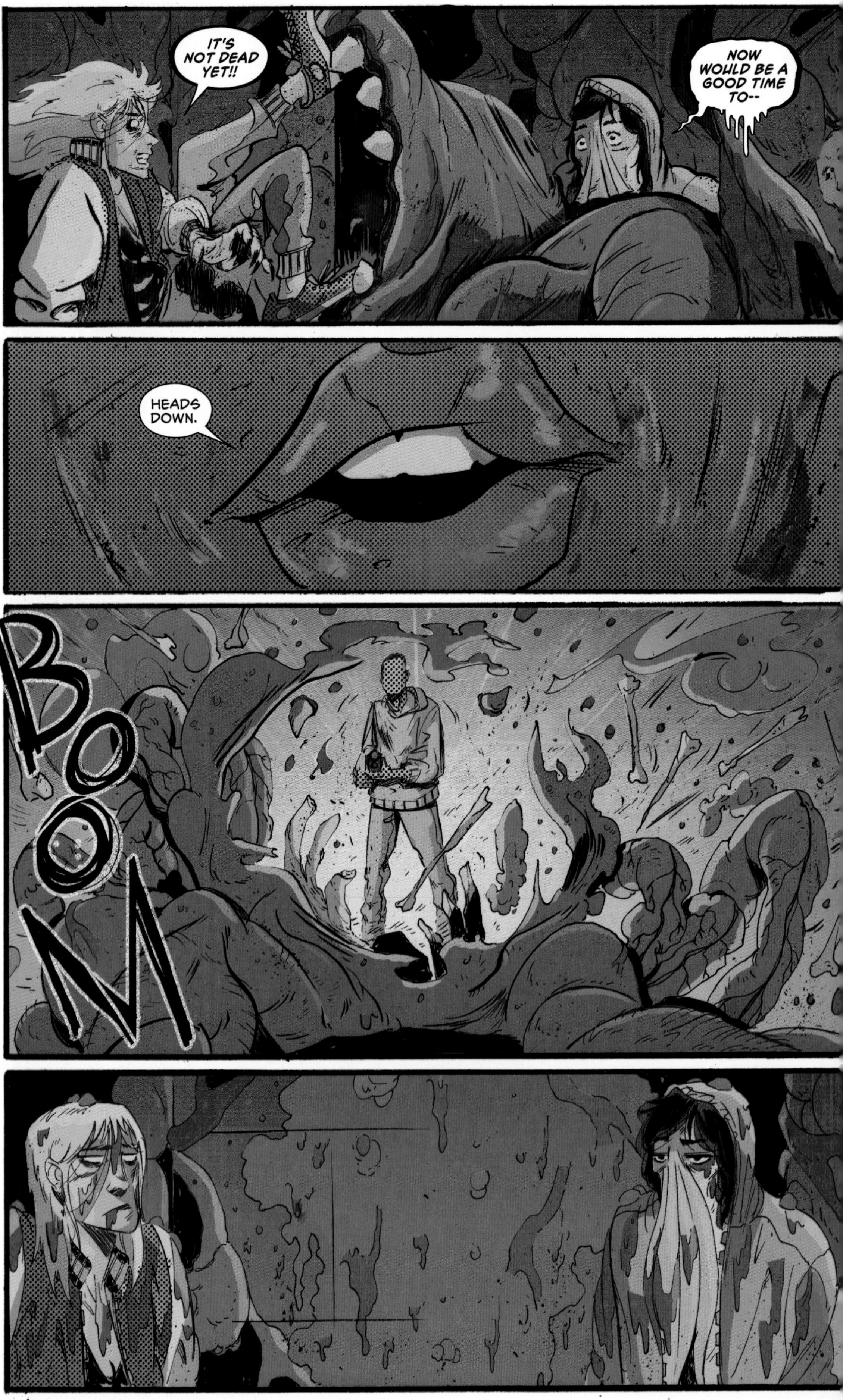
IT'S NOT DEAD YET!!
NOW WOULD BE A GOOD TIME TO--
HEADS DOWN.
BOOM

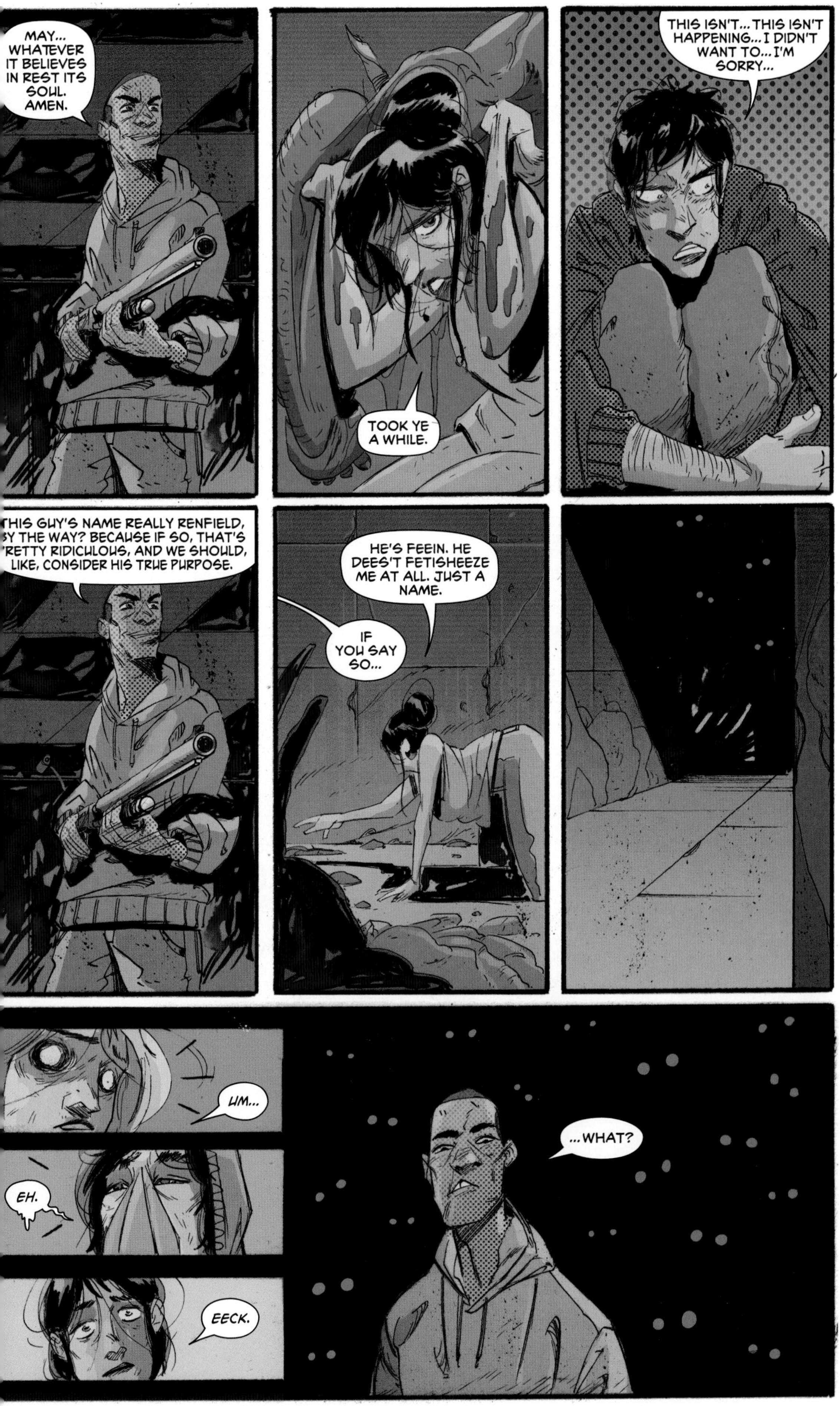

MAY... WHATEVER IT BELIEVES IN REST ITS SOUL. AMEN.
TOOK YE A WHILE.
THIS ISN'T... THIS ISN'T HAPPENING... I DIDN'T WANT TO... I'M SORRY...
THIS GUY'S NAME REALLY RENFIELD, BY THE WAY? BECAUSE IF SO, THAT'S PRETTY RIDICULOUS, AND WE SHOULD, LIKE, CONSIDER HIS TRUE PURPOSE.
HE'S FEEIN. HE DEES'T FETISHEEZE ME AT ALL. JUST A NAME.
IF YOU SAY SO...
UM...
EH.
EECK.
...WHAT?

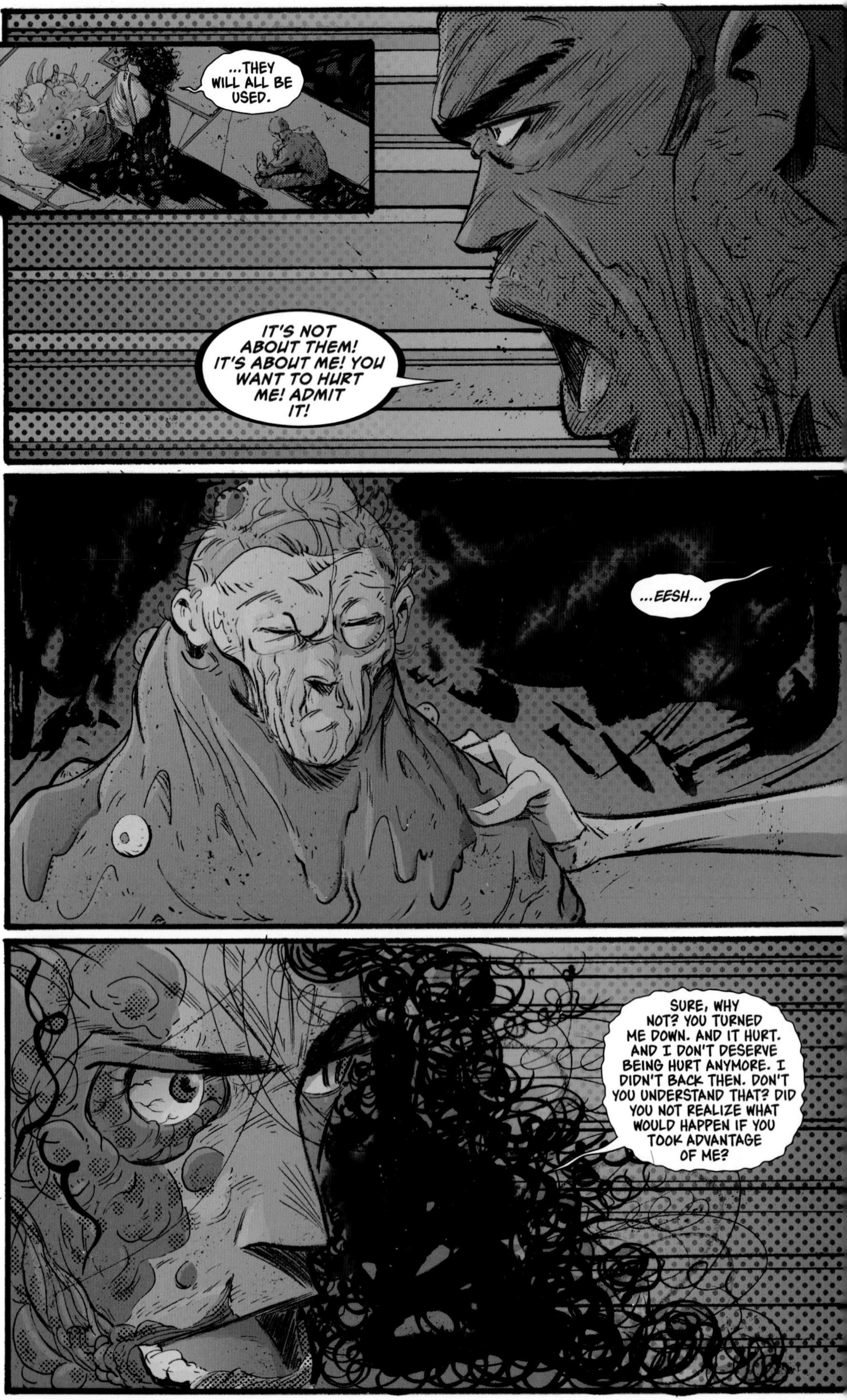
...THEY WILL ALL BE USED.
IT'S NOT ABOUT THEM! IT'S ABOUT ME! YOU WANT TO HURT ME! ADMIT IT!
...EESH...
SURE, WHY NOT? YOU TURNED ME DOWN. AND IT HURT. AND I DON'T DESERVE BEING HURT ANYMORE. I DIDN'T BACK THEN. DON'T YOU UNDERSTAND THAT? DID YOU NOT REALIZE WHAT WOULD HAPPEN IF YOU TOOK ADVANTAGE OF ME?

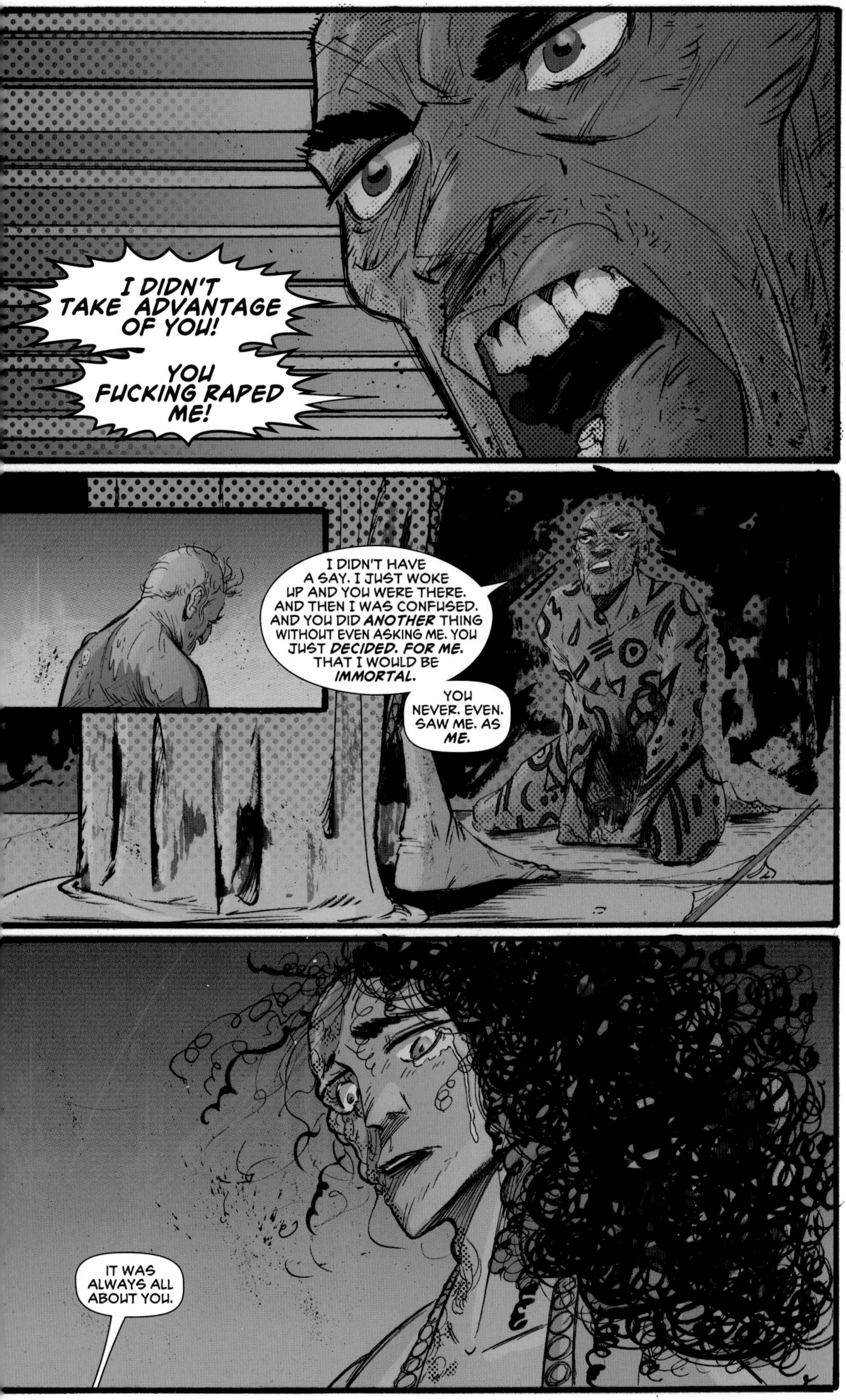
I DIDN'T TAKE ADVANTAGE OF YOU!
YOU FUCKING RAPED ME!
I DIDN'T HAVE A SAY. I JUST WOKE UP AND YOU WERE THERE. AND THEN I WAS CONFUSED. AND YOU DID ANOTHER THING WITHOUT EVEN ASKING ME. YOU JUST DECIDED. FOR ME. THAT I WOULD BE IMMORTAL.
YOU NEVER. EVEN. SAW ME. AS ME.
IT WAS ALWAYS ALL ABOUT YOU.

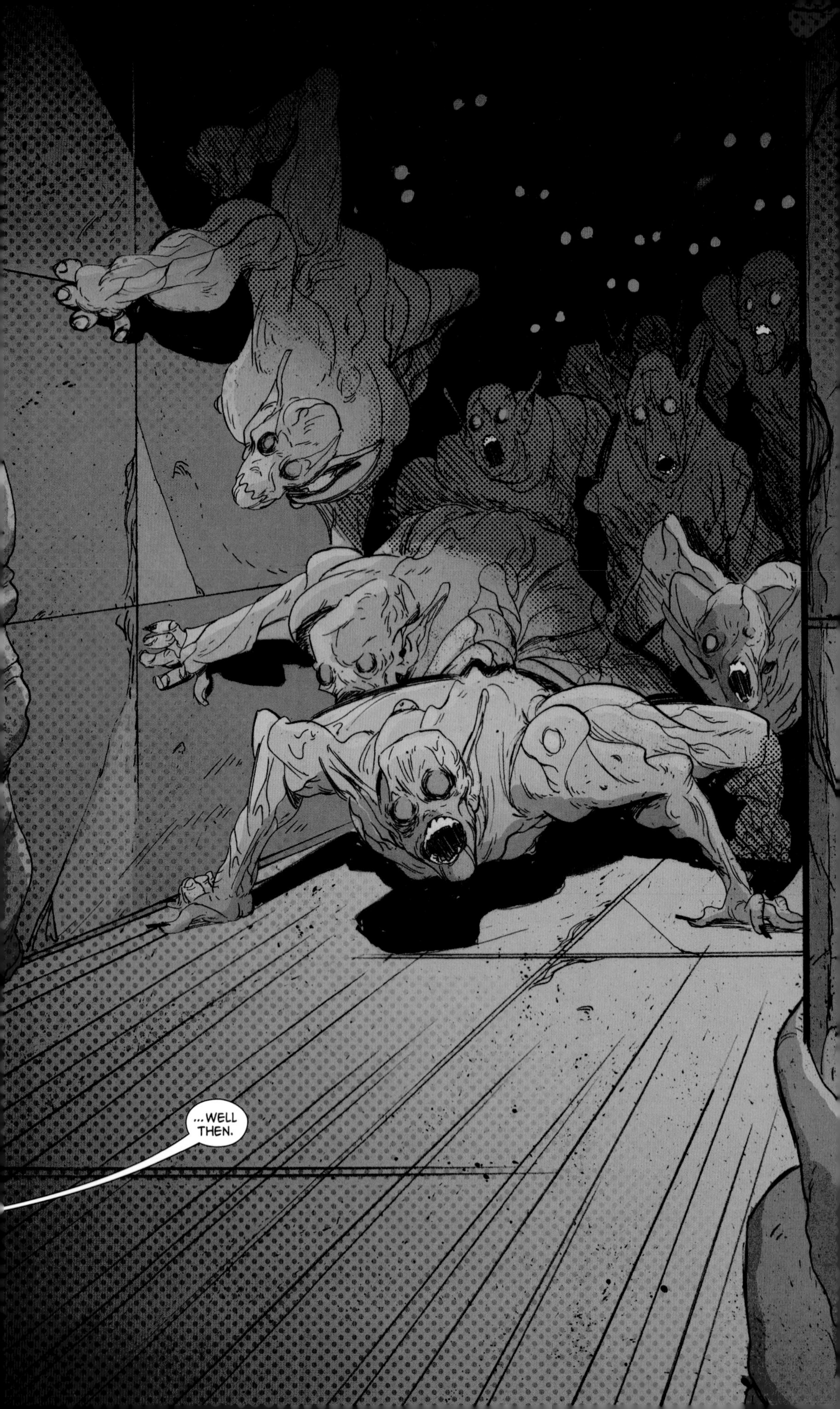
...WELL THEN.

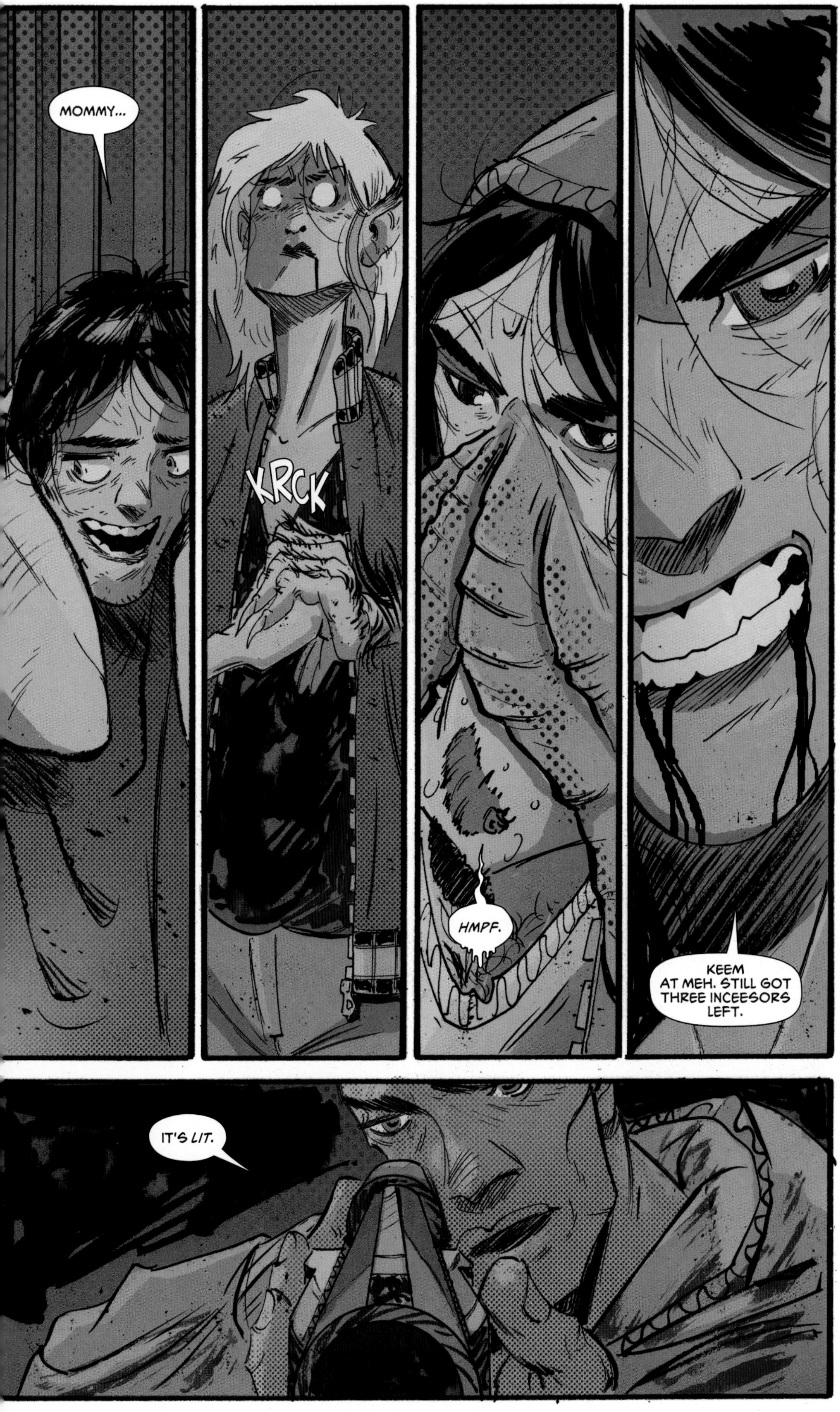
MOMMY...
KRCK
HMPF.
KEEM AT MEH. STILL GOT THREE INCEESORS LEFT.
IT'S LIT.

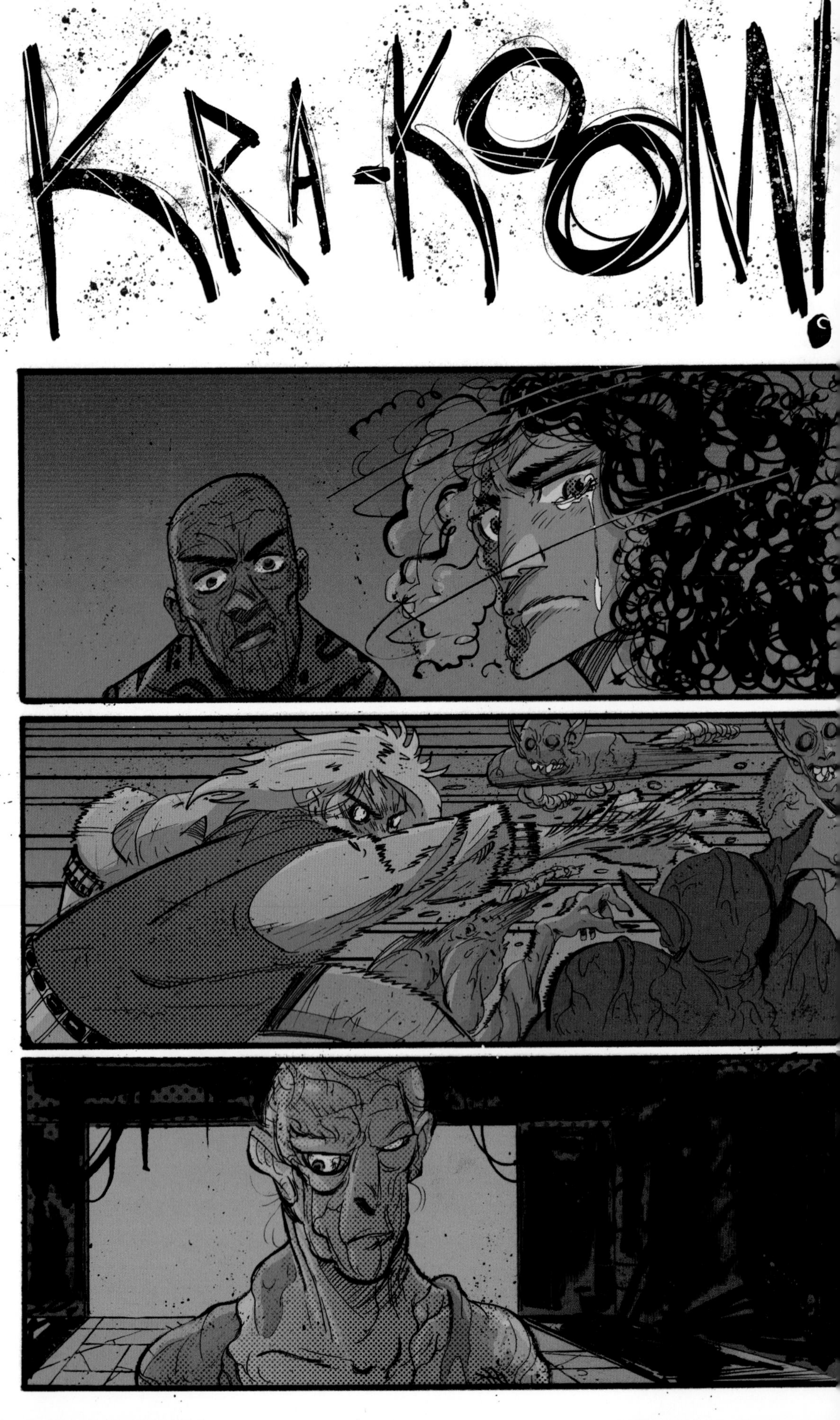
KRA-KOOM!

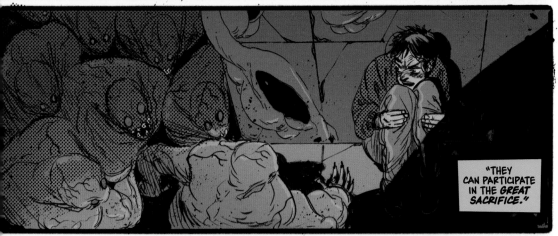

NEVER MIND OUR CONVERSATION. IT'S ALL OVER NOW.

THEY ARE ALMOST HERE. THEY CAN BEHOLD *THE GREAT UNVEILING.*

"THEY CAN PARTICIPATE IN THE *GREAT SACRIFICE.*"

THEY CAN CELEBRATE...

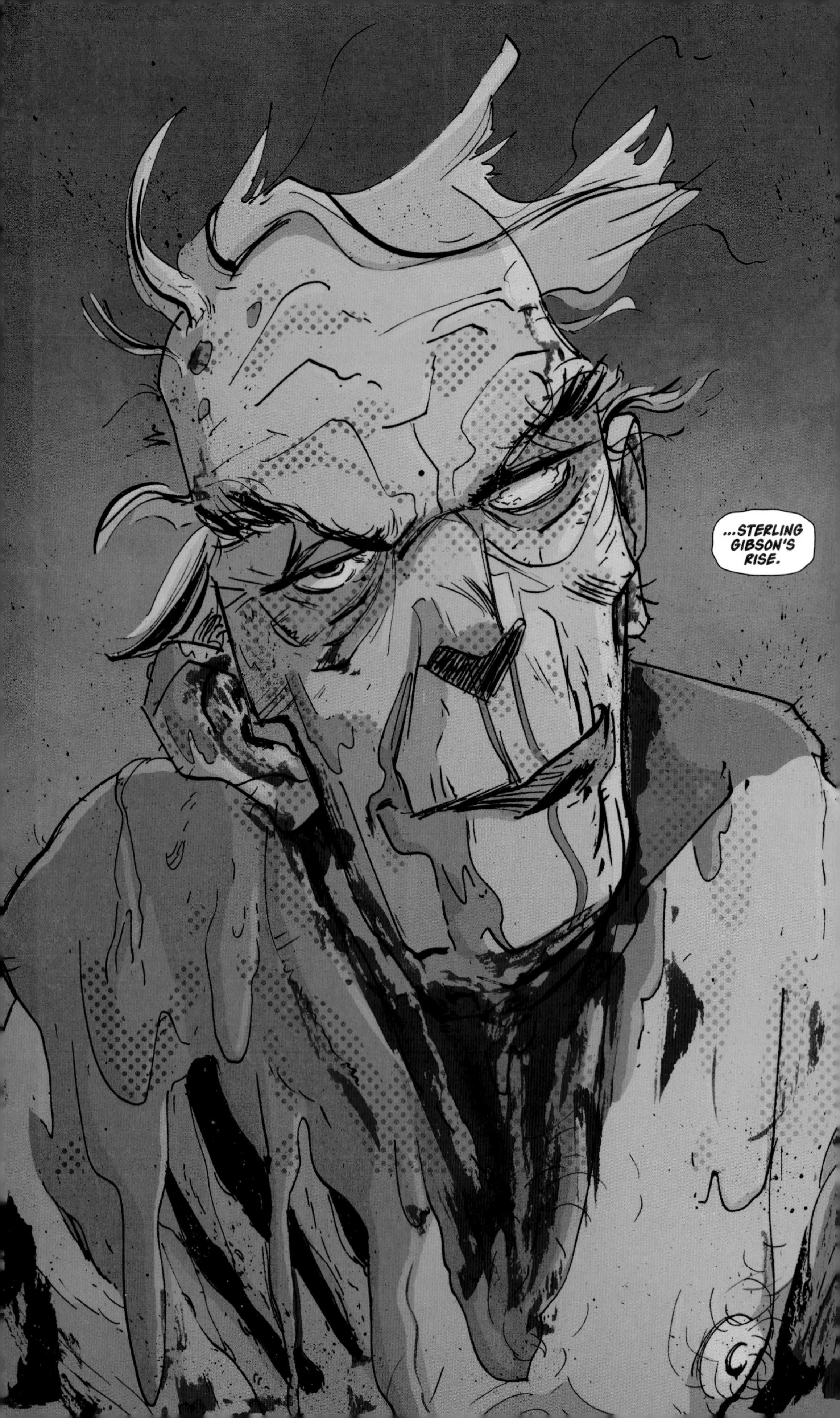
...STERLING GIBSON'S RISE.

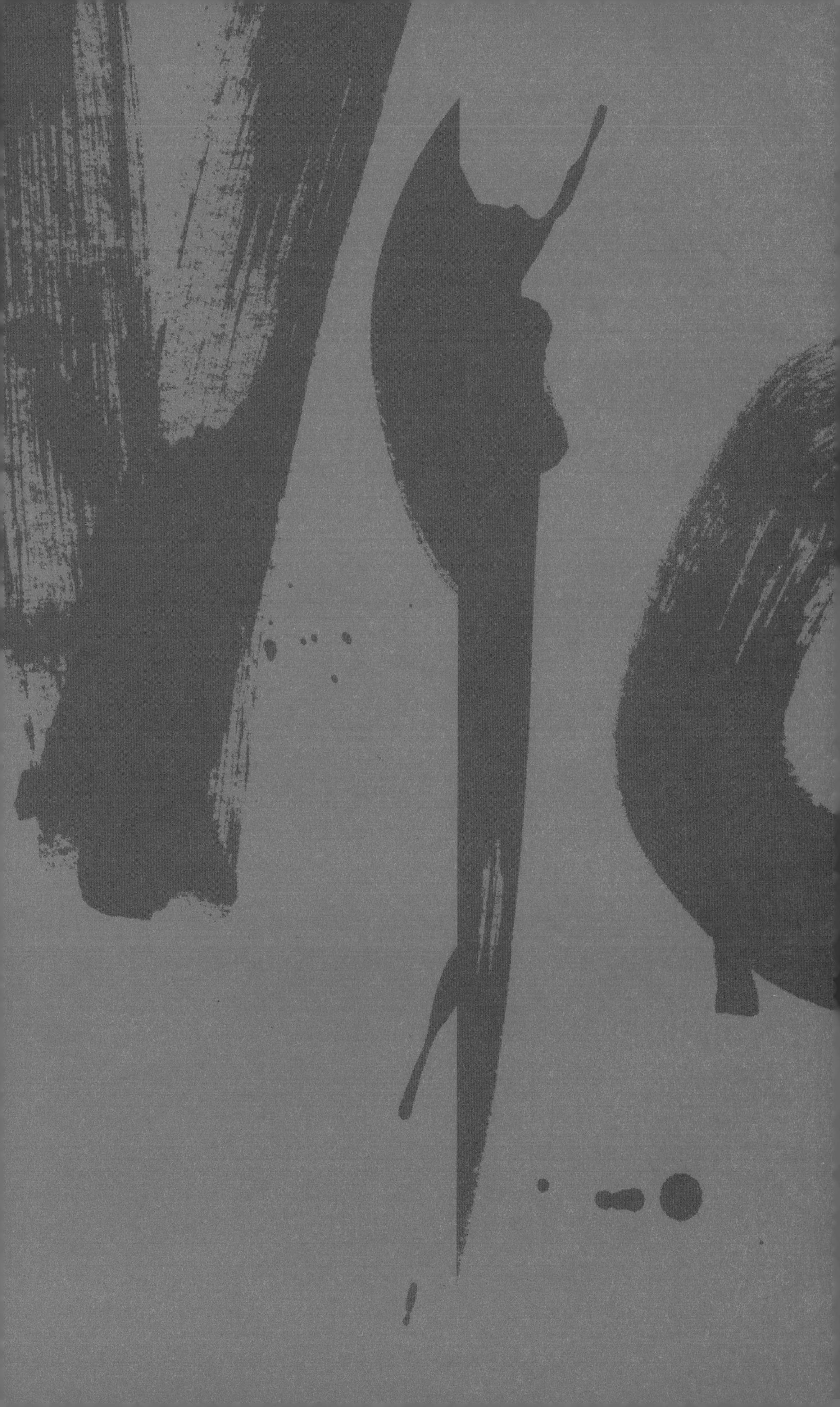

Chapter 9

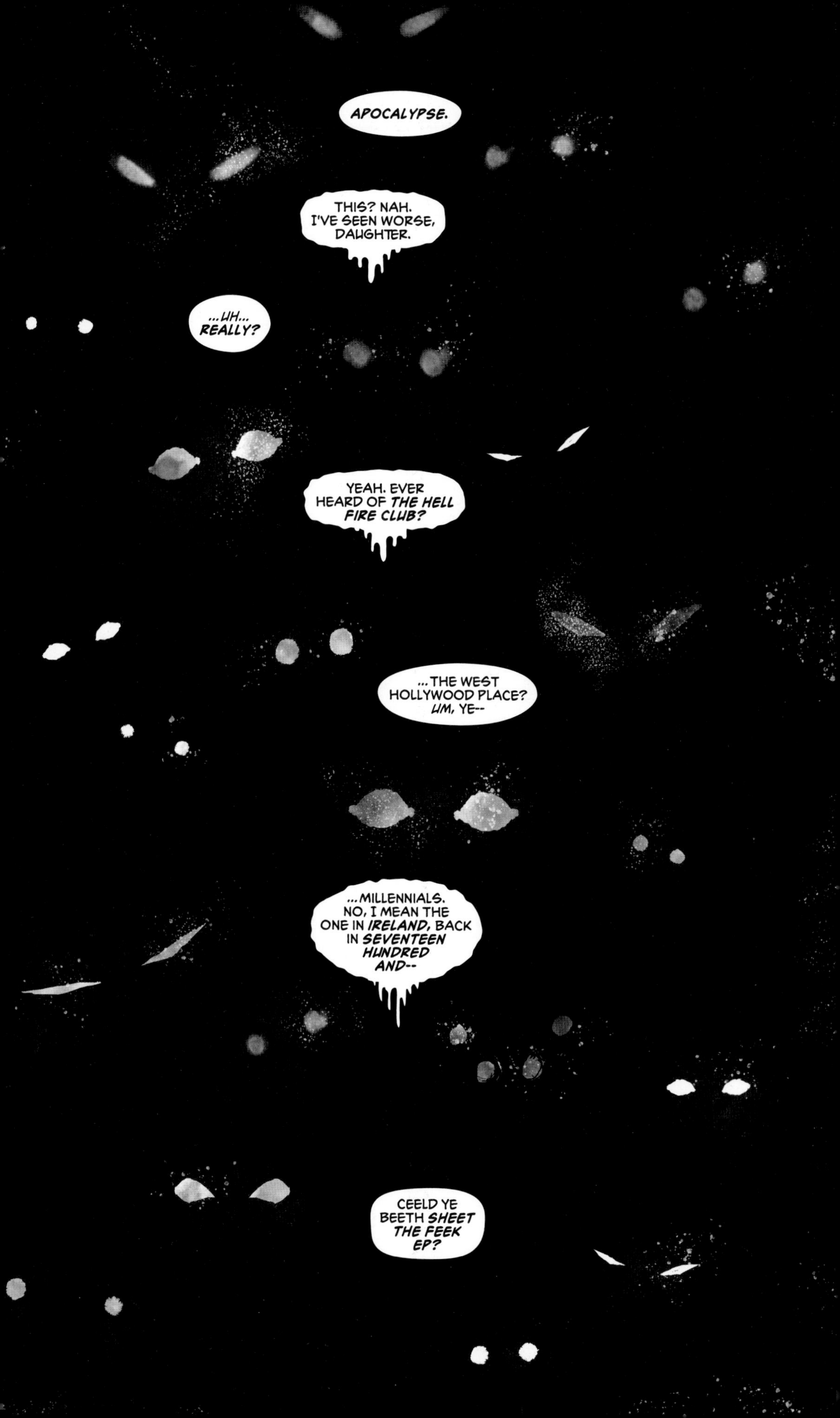
APOCALYPSE.
THIS? NAH. I'VE SEEN WORSE, DAUGHTER.
...UH... REALLY?
YEAH. EVER HEARD OF THE HELL FIRE CLUB?
...THE WEST HOLLYWOOD PLACE? UM, YE--
...MILLENNIALS. NO, I MEAN THE ONE IN IRELAND, BACK IN SEVENTEEN HUNDRED AND--
CEELD YE BEETH SHEET THE FEEK EP?

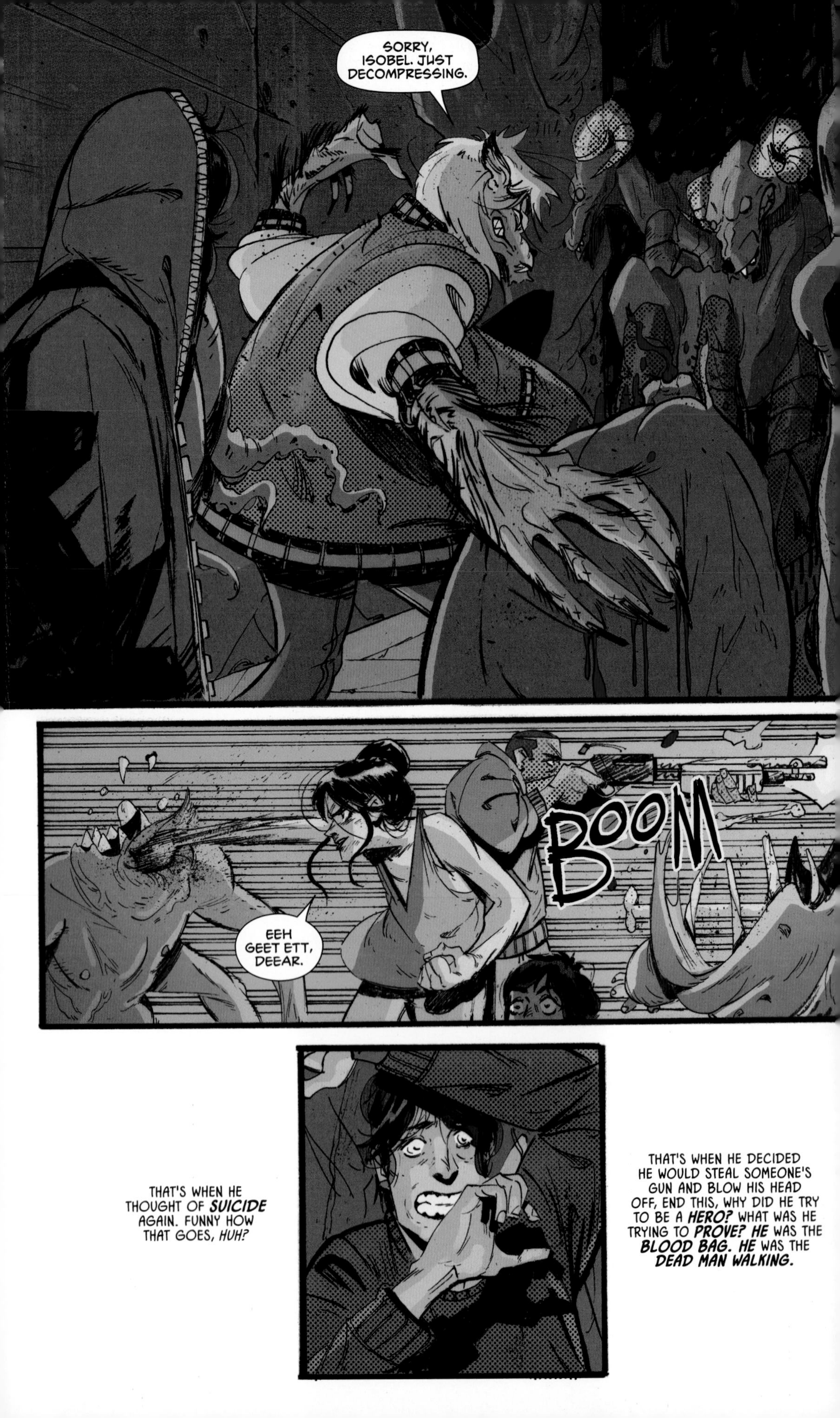
SORRY, ISOBEL. JUST DECOMPRESSING.
BOOM
EEH GEET ETT, DEEAR.
THAT'S WHEN HE THOUGHT OF *SUICIDE* AGAIN. FUNNY HOW THAT GOES, *HUH?*
THAT'S WHEN HE DECIDED HE WOULD STEAL SOMEONE'S GUN AND BLOW HIS HEAD OFF, END THIS, WHY DID HE TRY TO BE A *HERO?* WHAT WAS HE TRYING TO *PROVE? HE* WAS THE *BLOOD BAG. HE* WAS THE *DEAD MAN WALKING.*

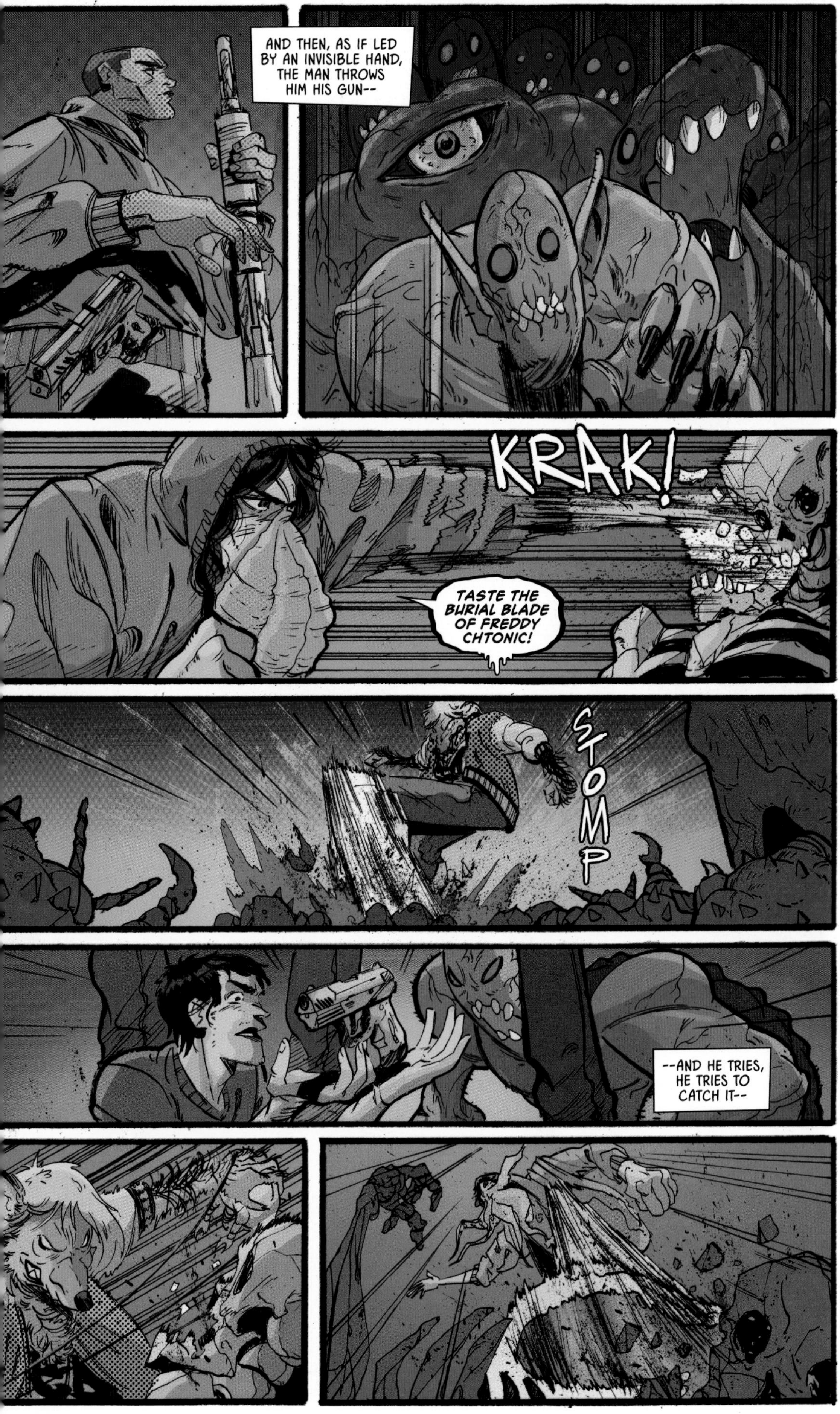
AND THEN, AS IF LED BY AN INVISIBLE HAND, THE MAN THROWS HIM HIS GUN--
KRAK!
TASTE THE BURIAL BLADE OF FREDDY CHTONIC!
STOMP
--AND HE TRIES, HE TRIES TO CATCH IT--

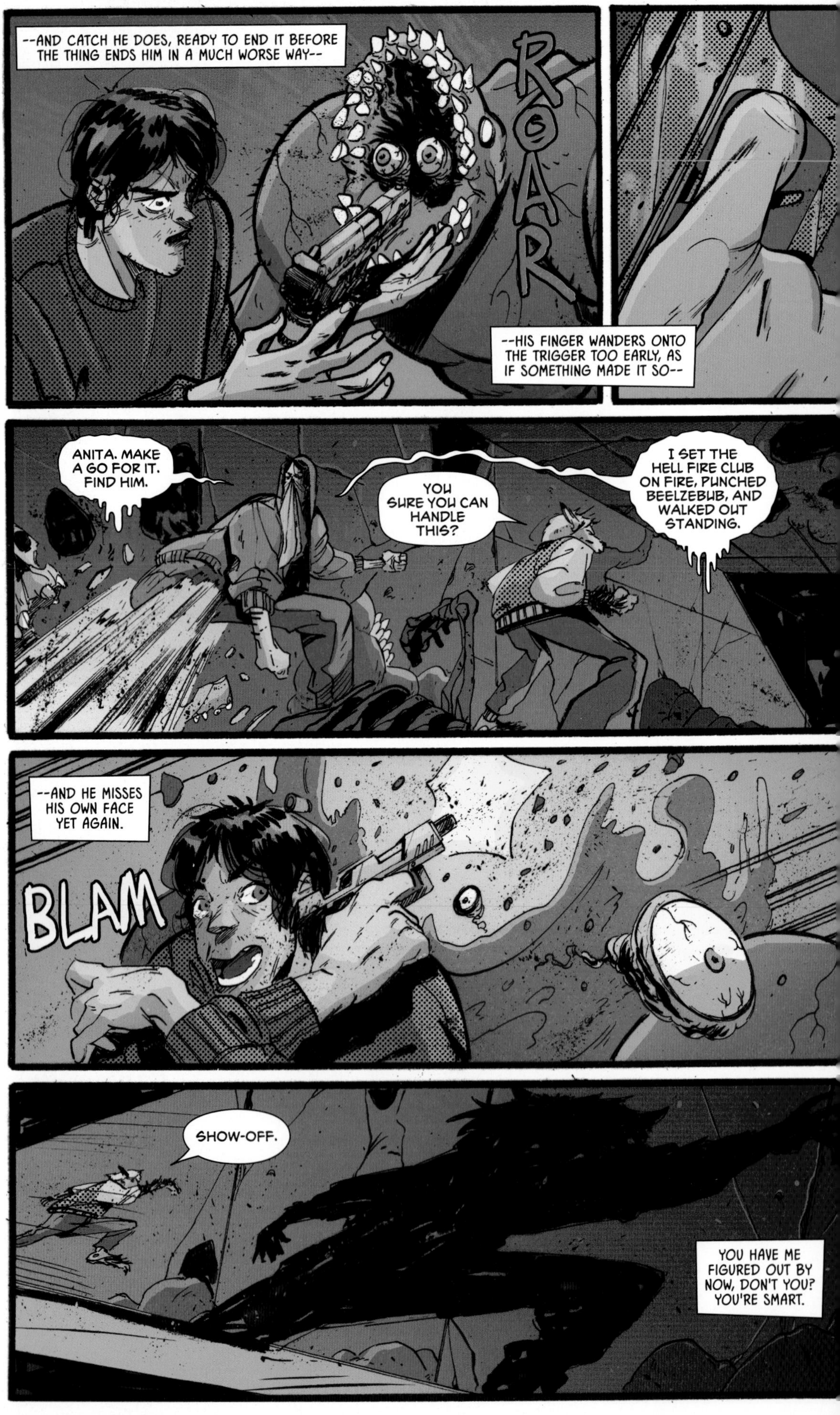
--AND CATCH HE DOES, READY TO END IT BEFORE THE THING ENDS HIM IN A MUCH WORSE WAY--
ROAR
--HIS FINGER WANDERS ONTO THE TRIGGER TOO EARLY, AS IF SOMETHING MADE IT SO--
ANITA. MAKE A GO FOR IT. FIND HIM.
YOU SURE YOU CAN HANDLE THIS?
I SET THE HELL FIRE CLUB ON FIRE, PUNCHED BEELZEBUB, AND WALKED OUT STANDING.
--AND HE MISSES HIS OWN FACE YET AGAIN.
BLAM
SHOW-OFF.
YOU HAVE ME FIGURED OUT BY NOW, DON'T YOU? YOU'RE SMART.

AN OLD-TIME
RACIST WEREWOLF,
RESURRECTED.

WHY?

WHAT
COULD
IT BE?

WHO COULD
TAUNT YOU
SO?

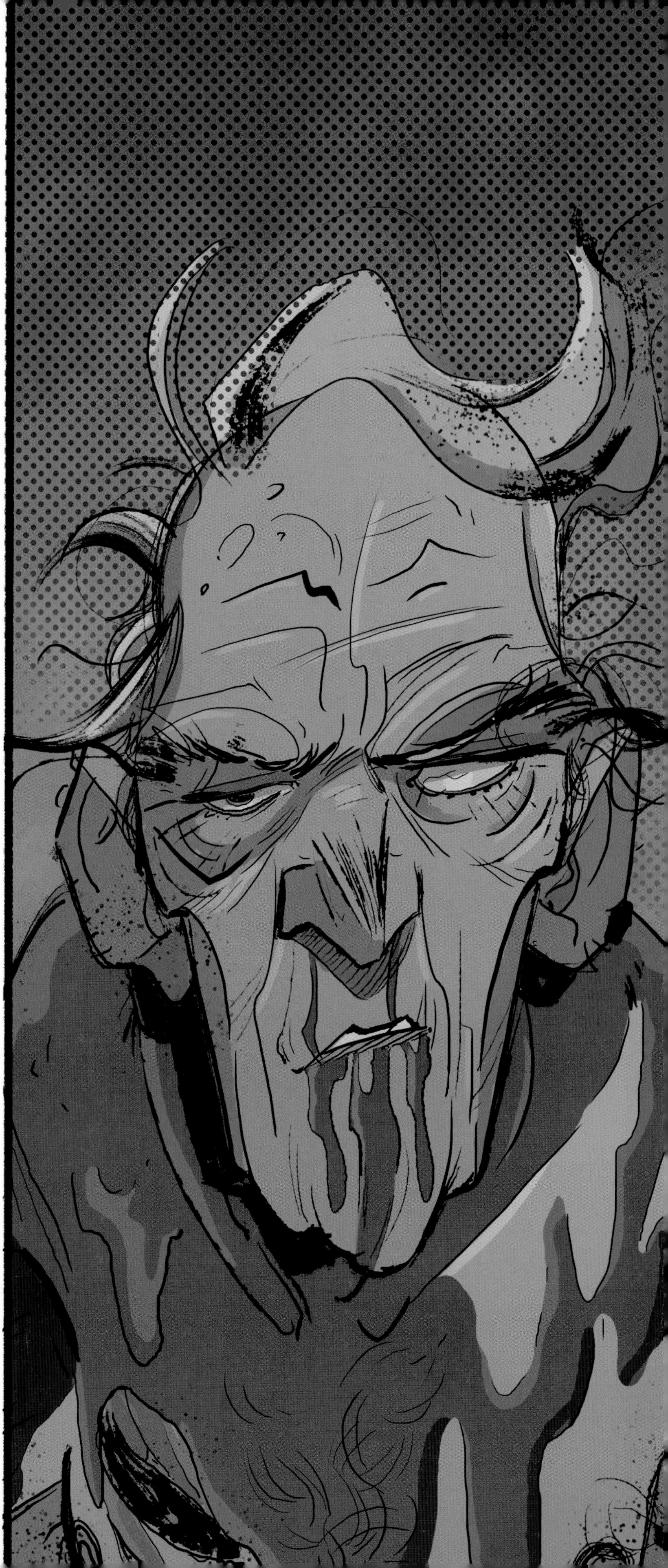

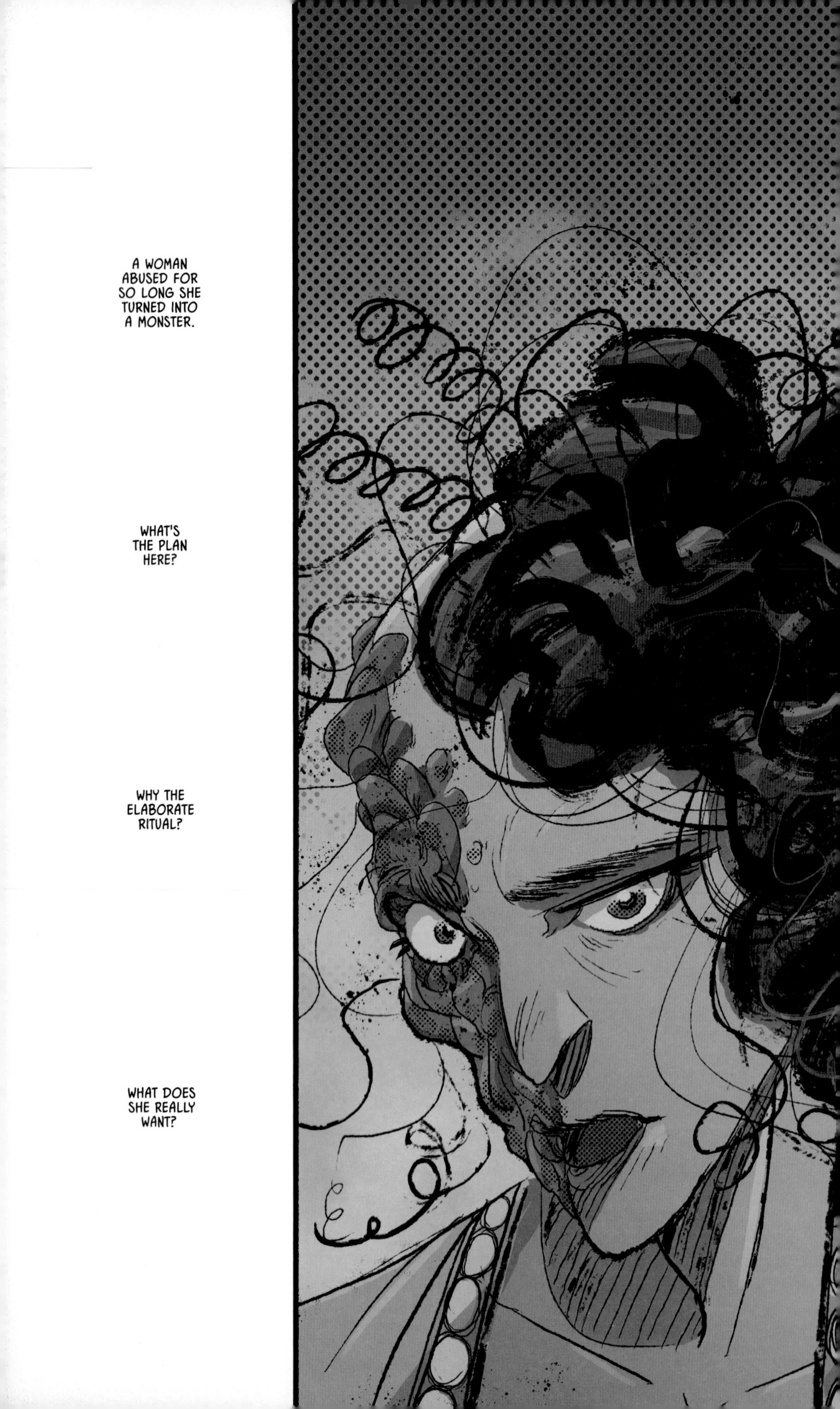
A WOMAN ABUSED FOR SO LONG SHE TURNED INTO A MONSTER.
WHAT'S THE PLAN HERE?
WHY THE ELABORATE RITUAL?
WHAT DOES SHE REALLY WANT?

A MAN
STRIPPED OF
HOPE.

WHAT'S HIS
PURPOSE IN
ALL THIS?

WHY DID
YOU SEE HIM
BURN?

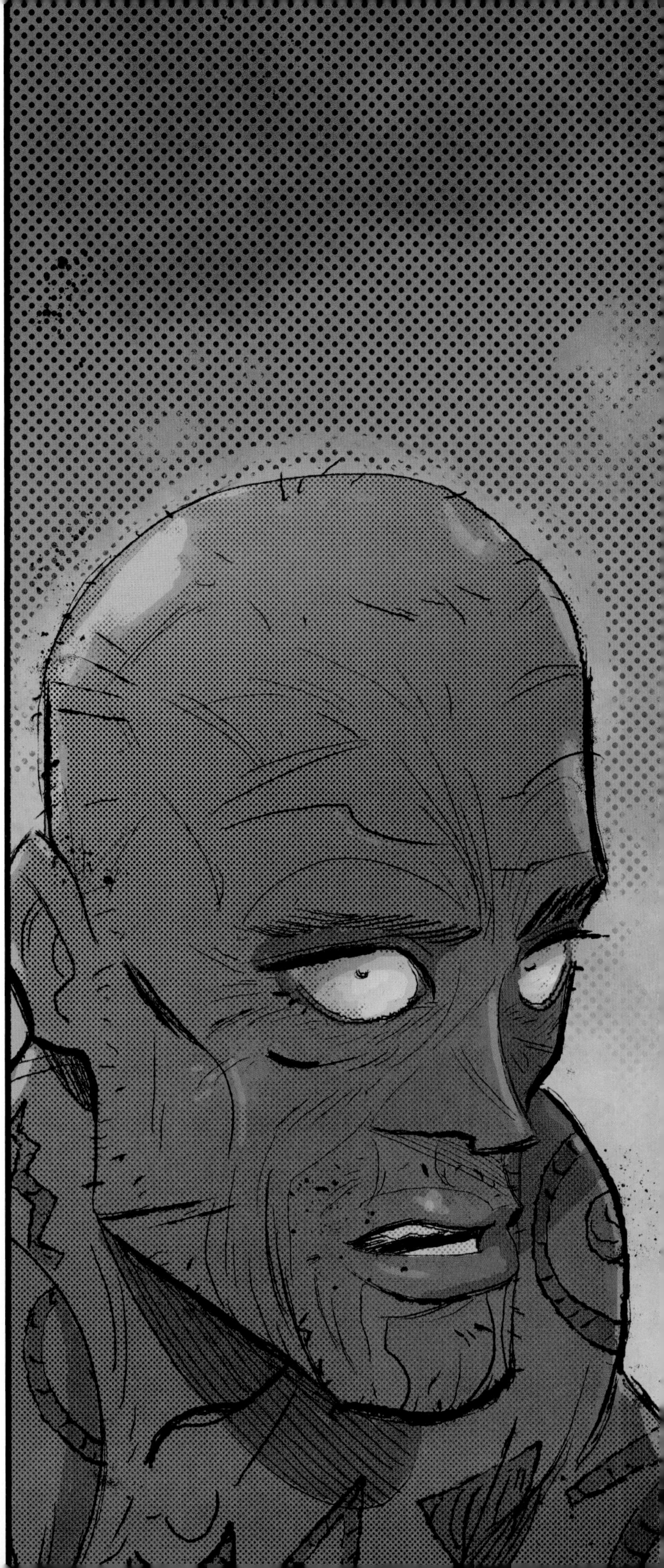

OH, SOON.

SO SOON.

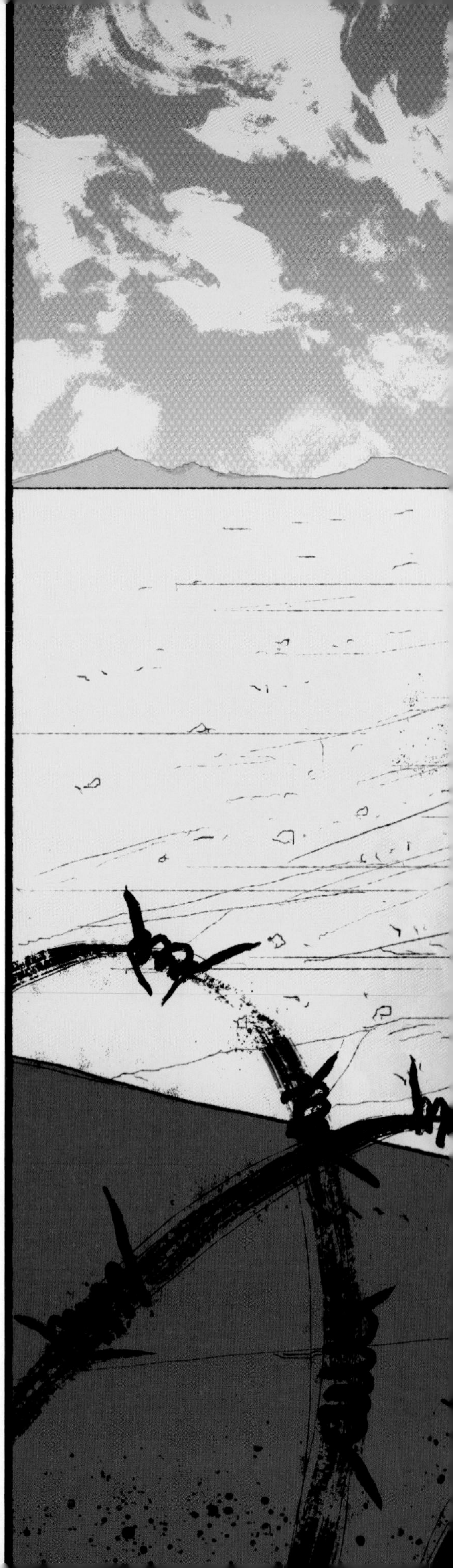

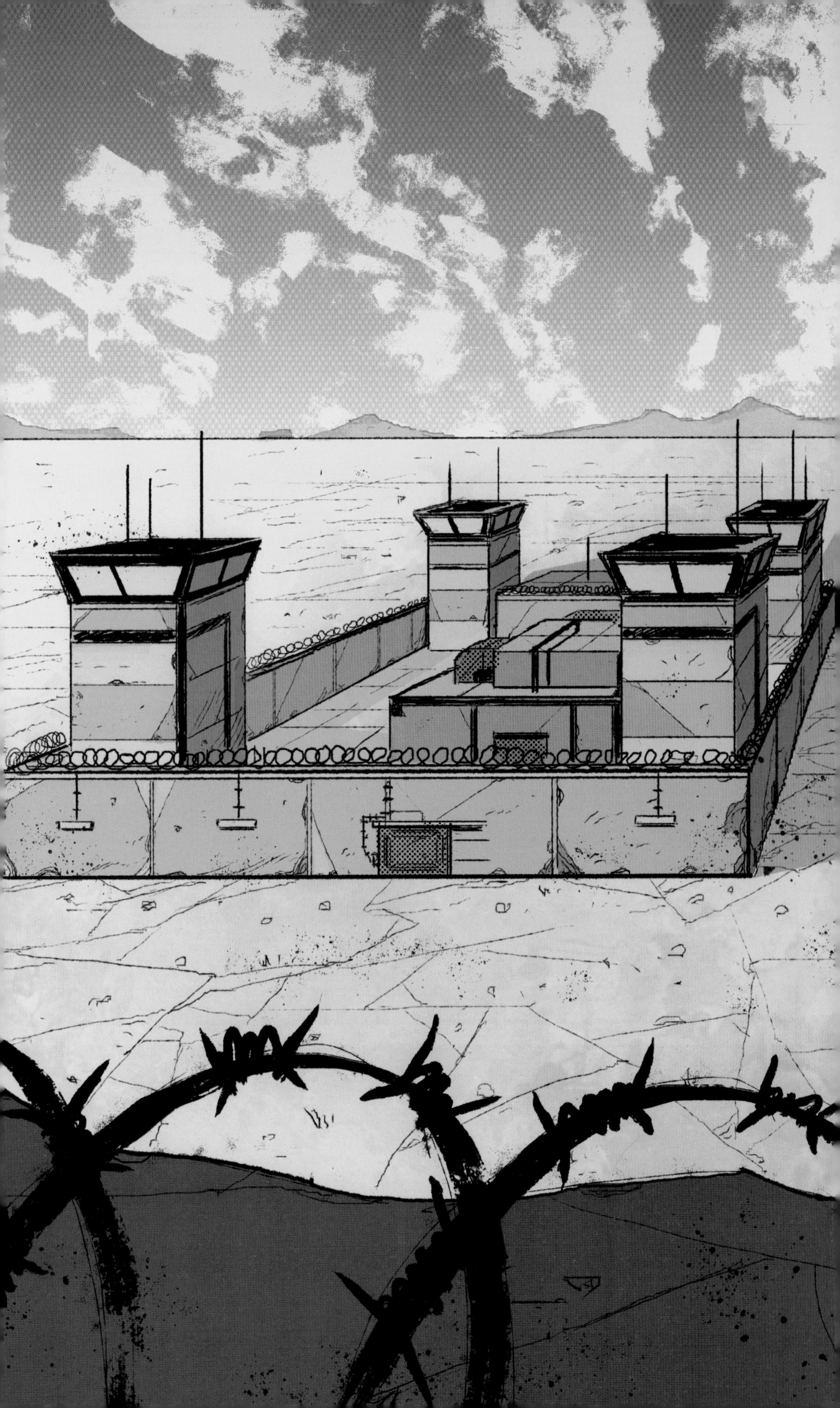

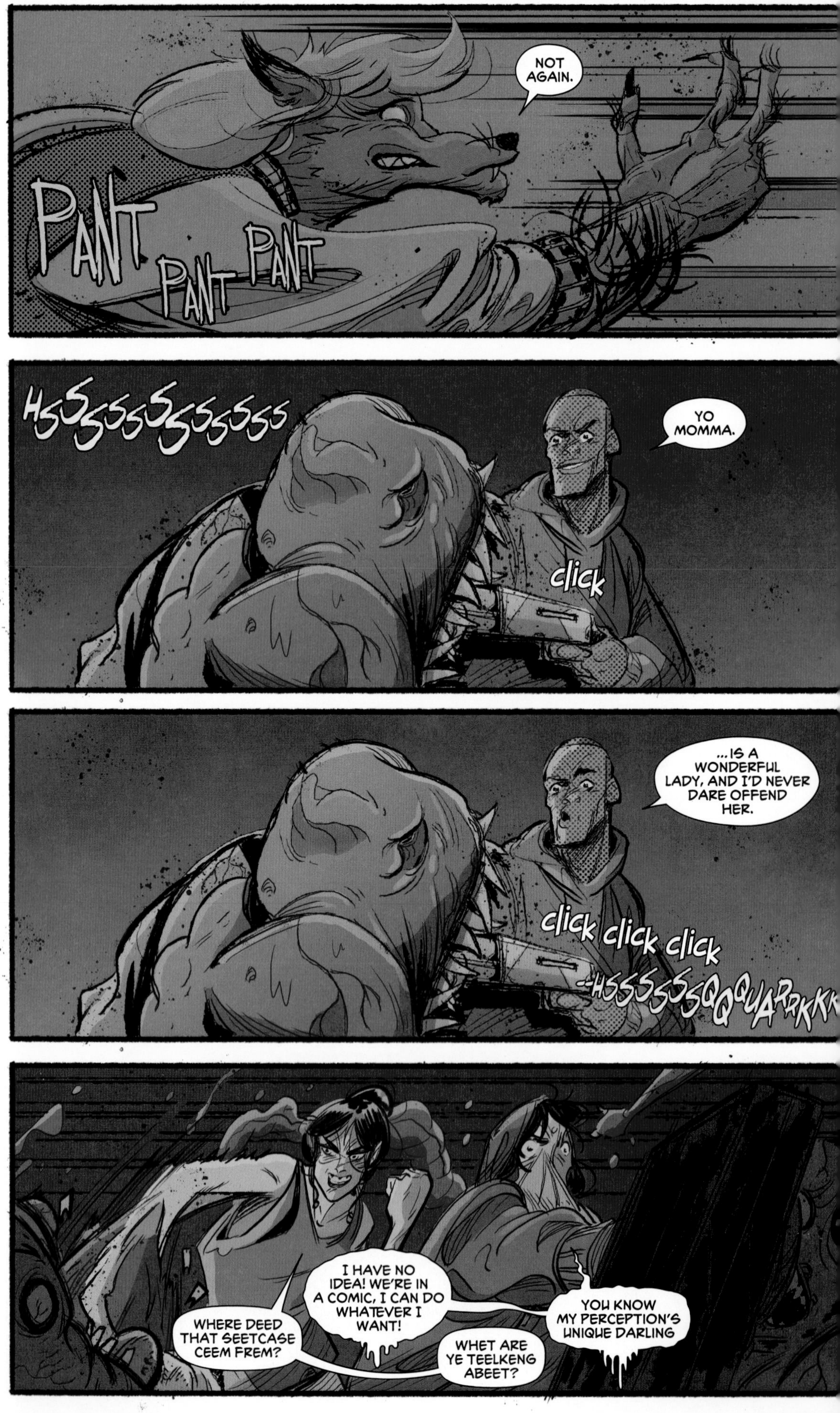
NOT AGAIN.
PANT PANT PANT
HSSSSSSSSSSSS
YO MOMMA.
click
...IS A WONDERFUL LADY, AND I'D NEVER DARE OFFEND HER.
click click click
-HSSSSSSQQUARRKKK
WHERE DEED THAT SEETCASE CEEM FREM?
I HAVE NO IDEA! WE'RE IN A COMIC, I CAN DO WHATEVER I WANT!
WHET ARE YE TEELKENG ABEET?
YOU KNOW MY PERCEPTION'S UNIQUE DARLING

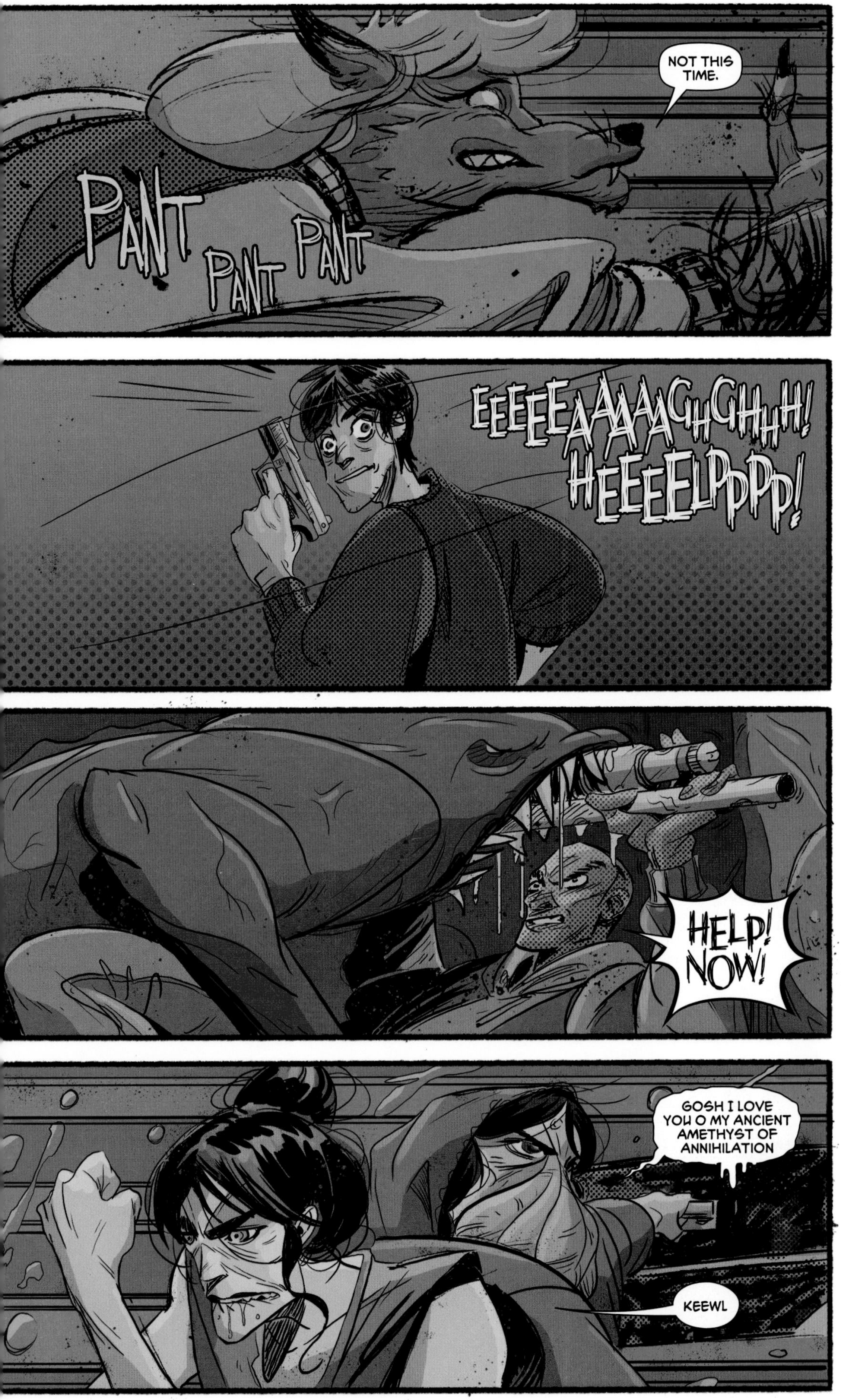
NOT THIS TIME.
PANT PANT PANT
EEEEEAAAAAGHGHHH! HEEEELPPPP!
HELP! NOW!
GOSH I LOVE YOU O MY ANCIENT AMETHYST OF ANNIHILATION
KEEWL

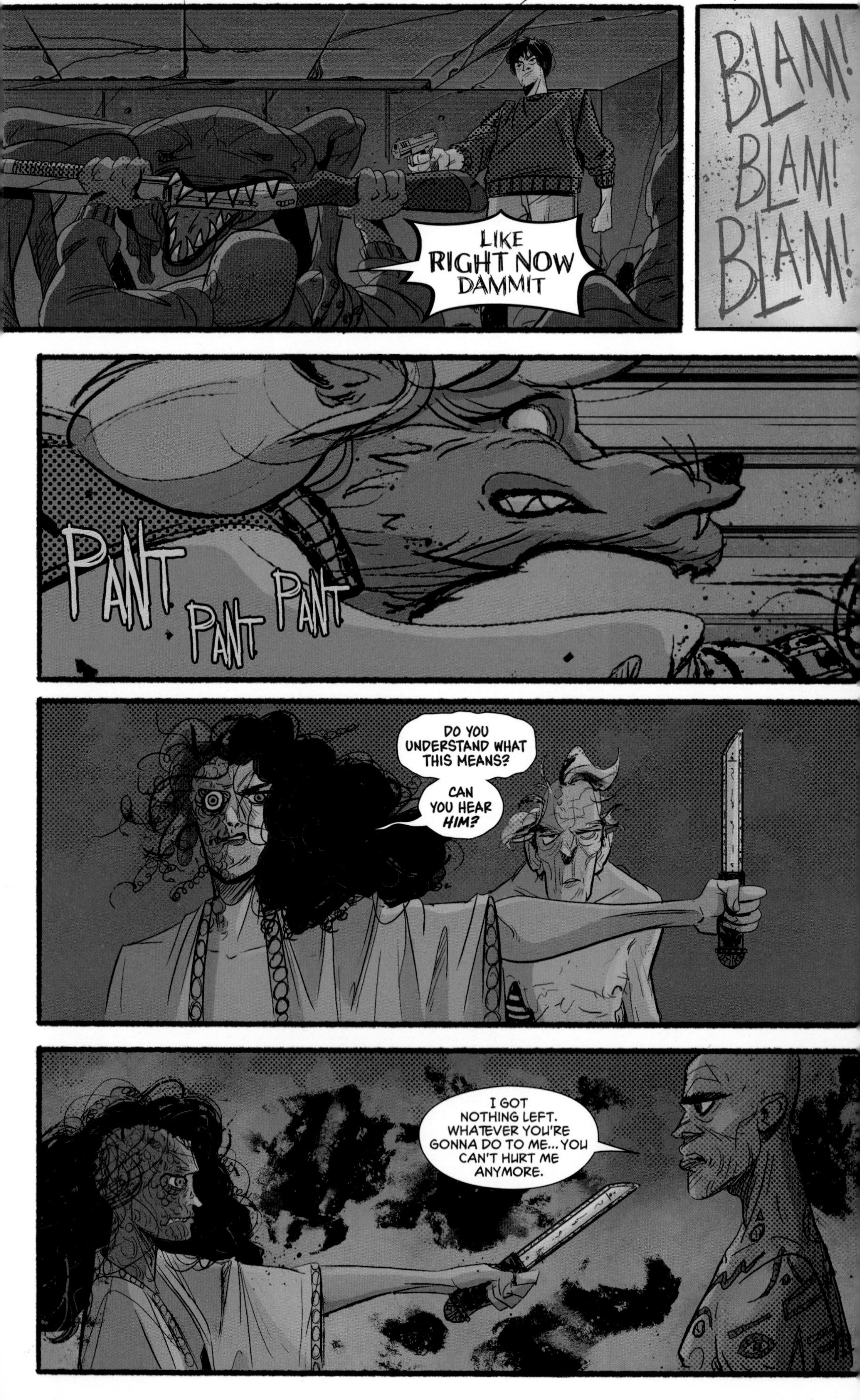

LIKE RIGHT NOW DAMMIT
BLAM! BLAM! BLAM!
PANT PANT PANT
DO YOU UNDERSTAND WHAT THIS MEANS?
CAN YOU HEAR *HIM?*
I GOT NOTHING LEFT. WHATEVER YOU'RE GONNA DO TO ME... YOU CAN'T HURT ME ANYMORE.

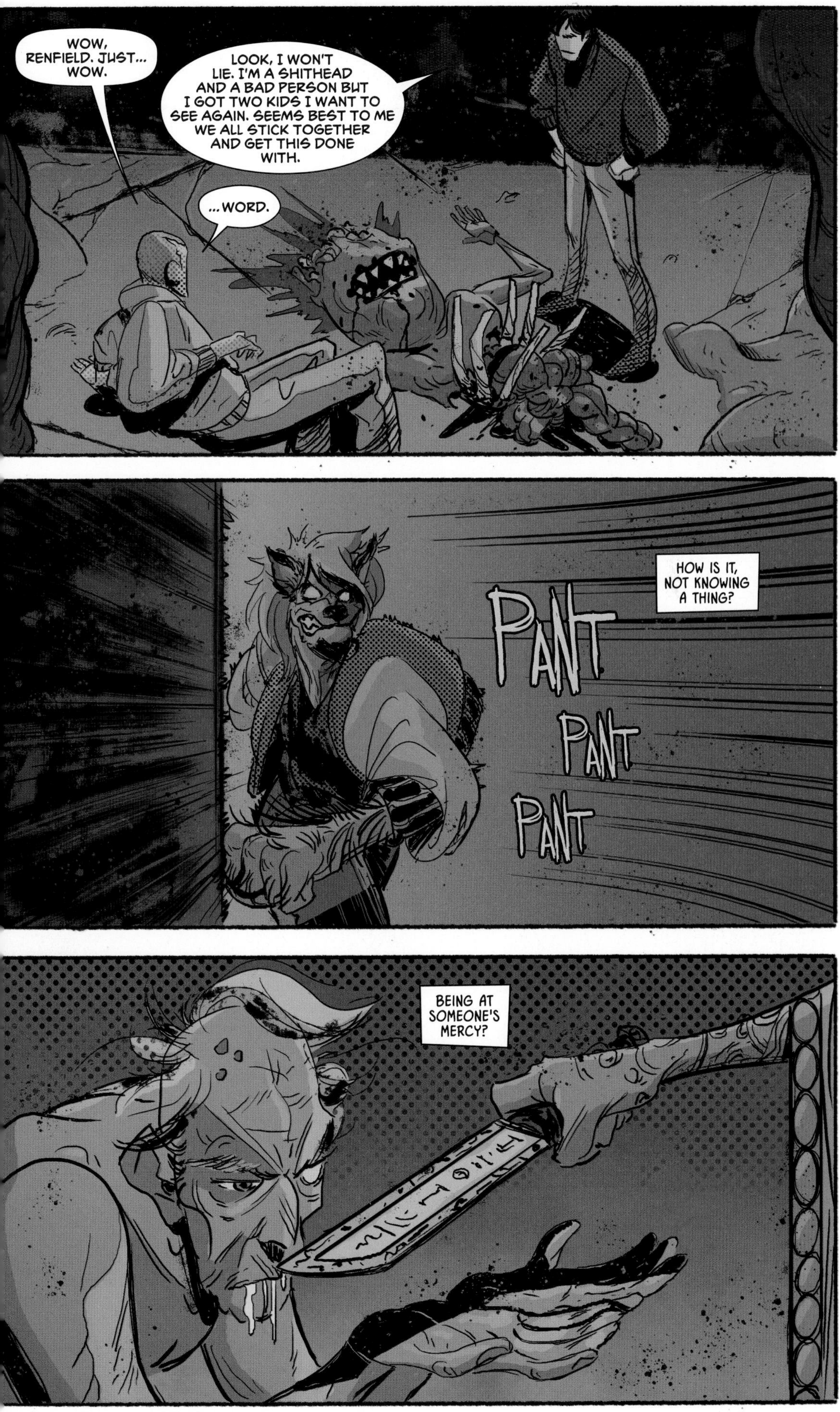
WOW, RENFIELD. JUST... WOW.
LOOK, I WON'T LIE. I'M A SHITHEAD AND A BAD PERSON BUT I GOT TWO KIDS I WANT TO SEE AGAIN. SEEMS BEST TO ME WE ALL STICK TOGETHER AND GET THIS DONE WITH.
...WORD.
HOW IS IT, NOT KNOWING A THING?
PANT
PANT
PANT
BEING AT SOMEONE'S MERCY?

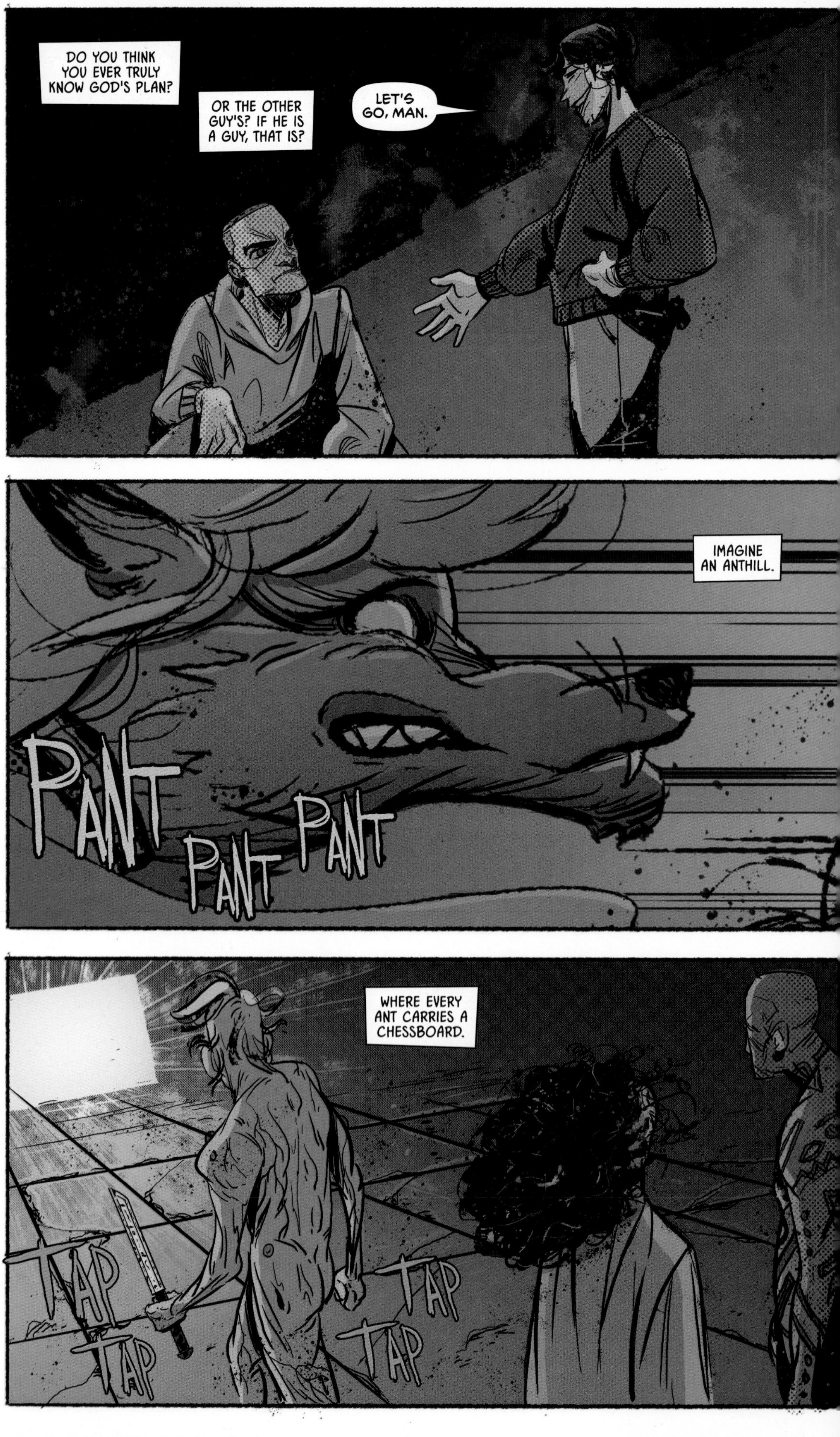
DO YOU THINK YOU EVER TRULY KNOW GOD'S PLAN?
OR THE OTHER GUY'S? IF HE IS A GUY, THAT IS?
LET'S GO, MAN.
IMAGINE AN ANTHILL.
PANT PANT PANT
WHERE EVERY ANT CARRIES A CHESSBOARD.
TAP TAP TAP TAP

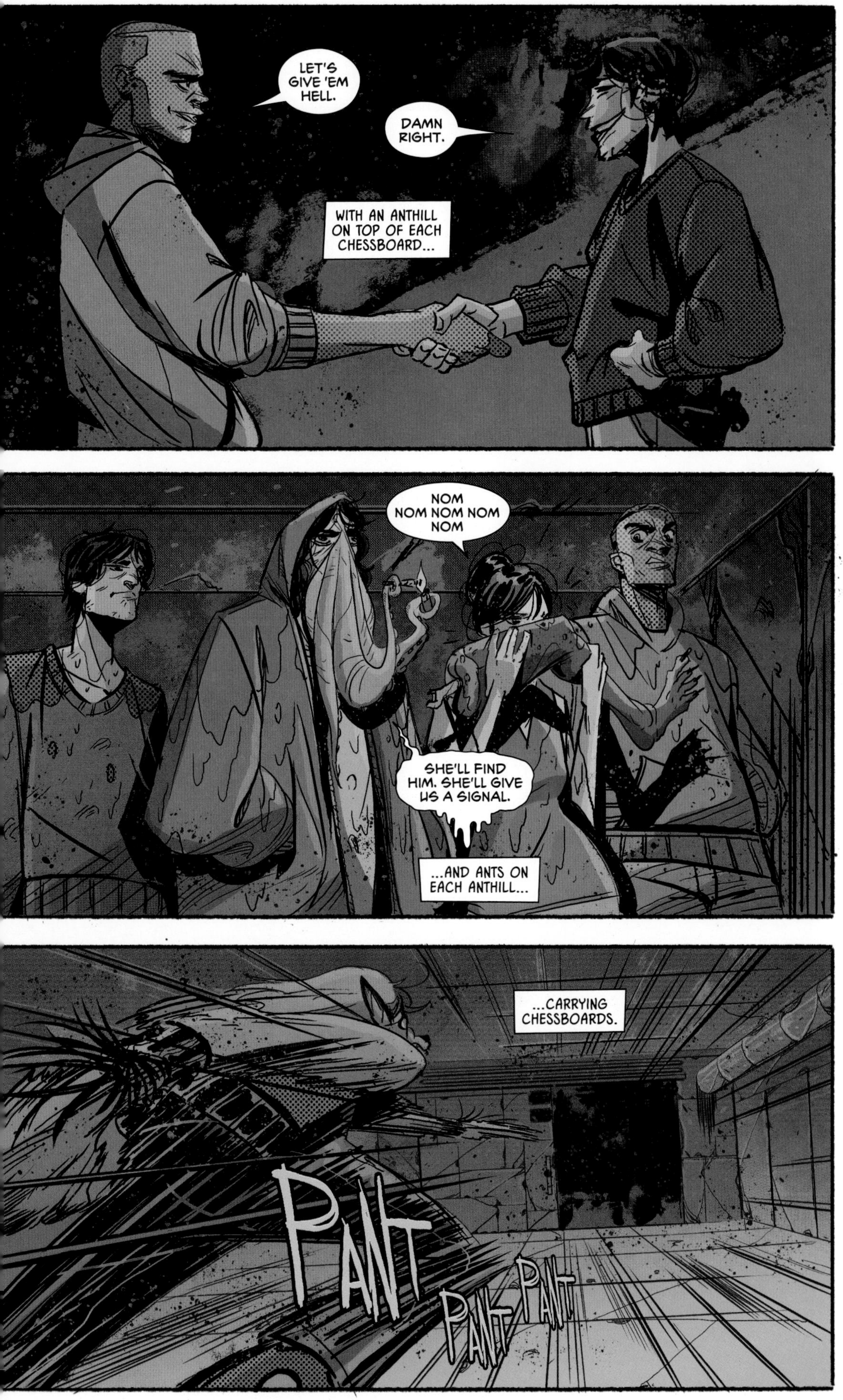
LET'S GIVE 'EM HELL.
DAMN RIGHT.
WITH AN ANTHILL ON TOP OF EACH CHESSBOARD...
NOM NOM NOM NOM NOM
SHE'LL FIND HIM. SHE'LL GIVE US A SIGNAL.
...AND ANTS ON EACH ANTHILL...
...CARRYING CHESSBOARDS.
PANT
PANT PANT

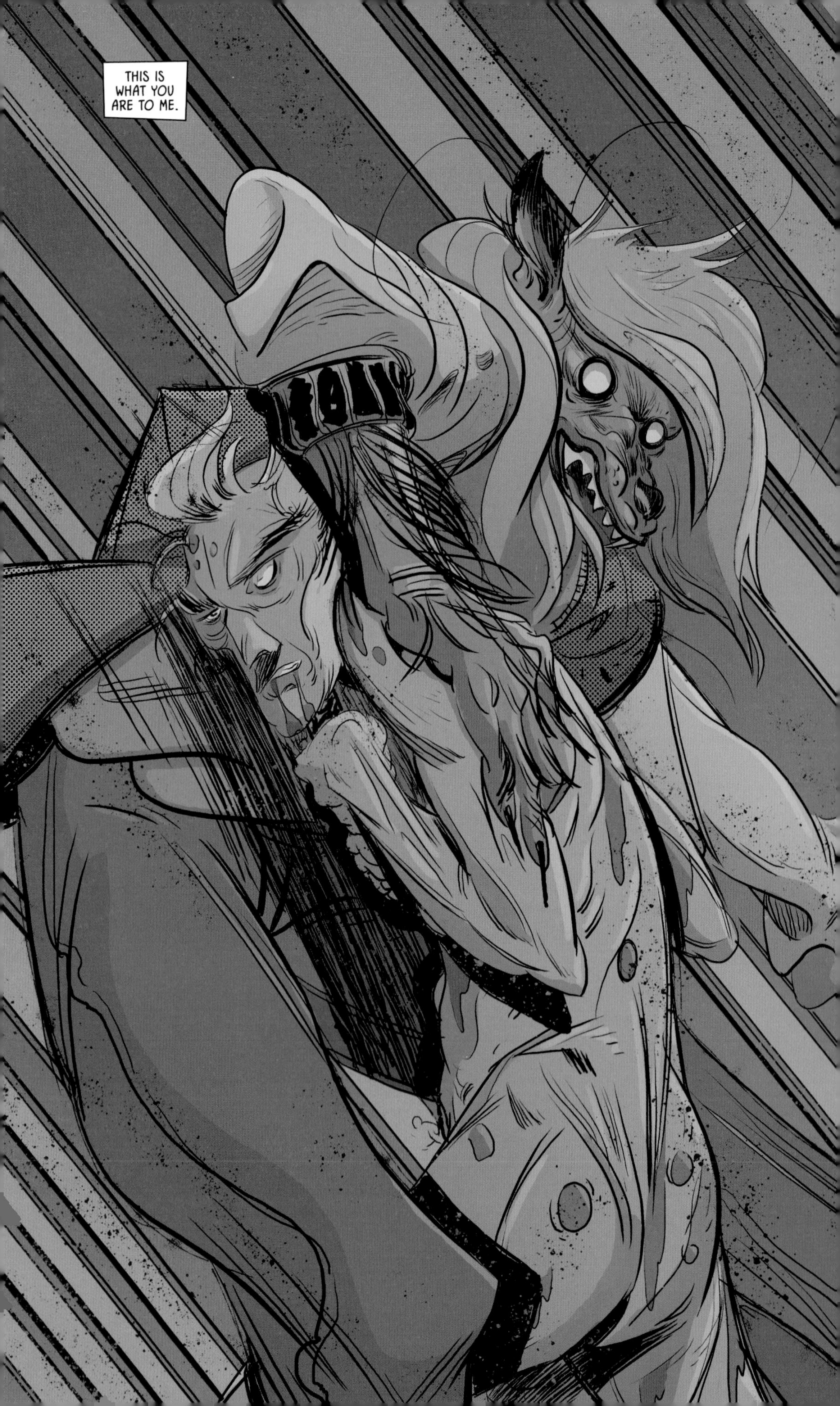
THIS IS WHAT YOU ARE TO ME.

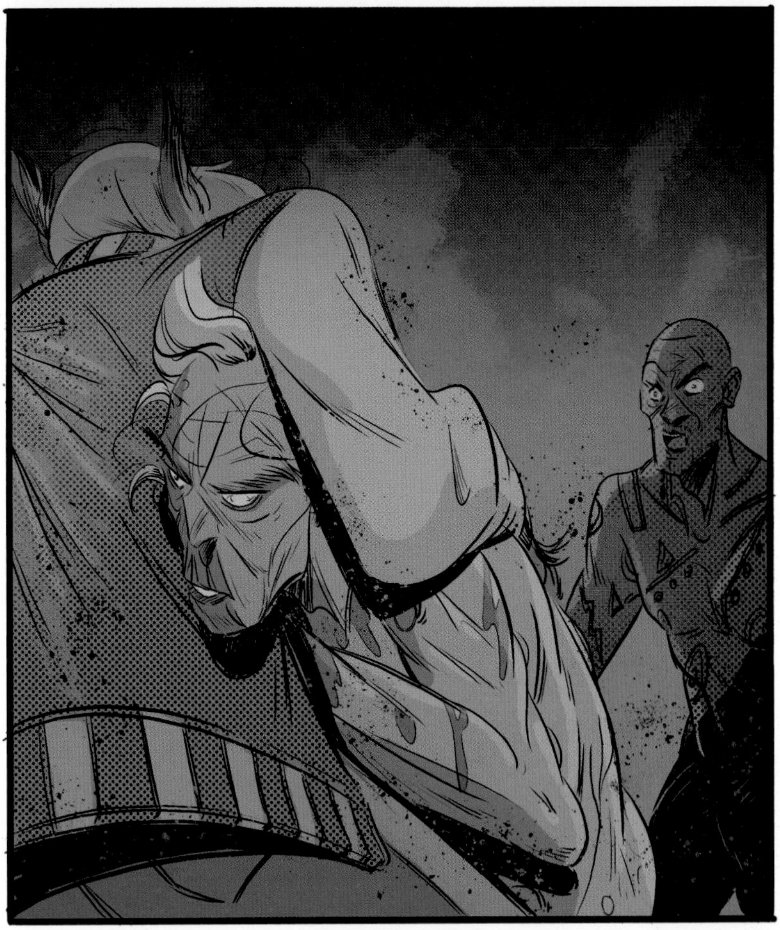

DO YOU
UNDERSTAND?

I AM
THE LACK.

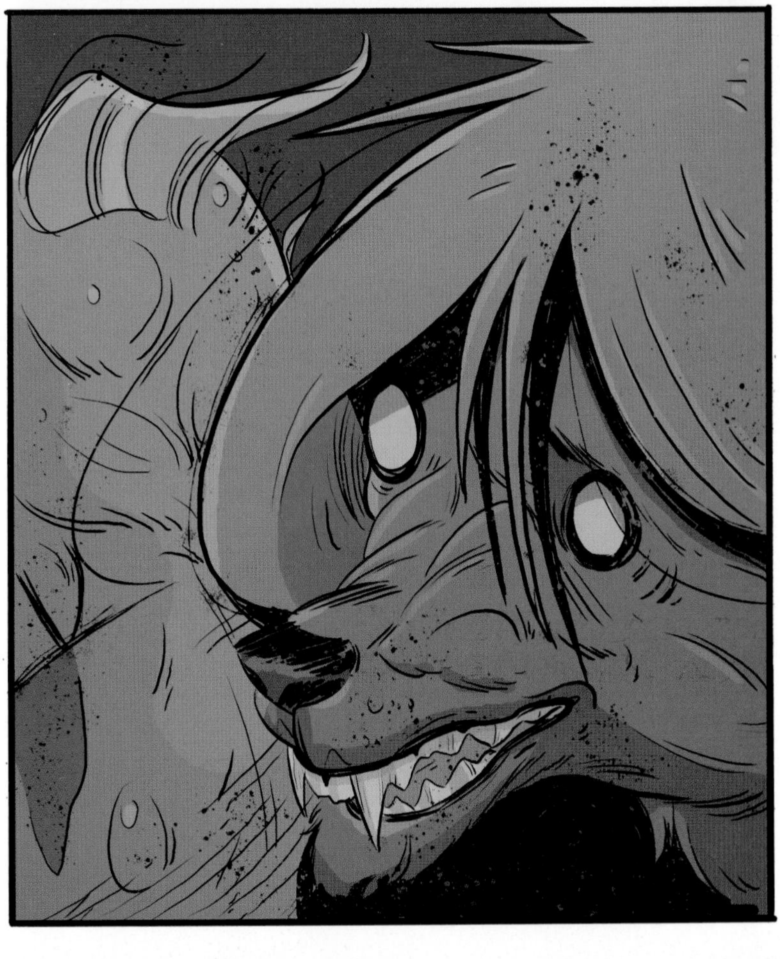

I AM
THE HAND.

I AM THE
ETERNAL VOYEUR.

I AM THE ***GREAT***
MANIPULATOR.

YOU WERE
BAD.

YOU ARE
GOOD.

DO THE
THING.

DON'T DO
THAT THING.

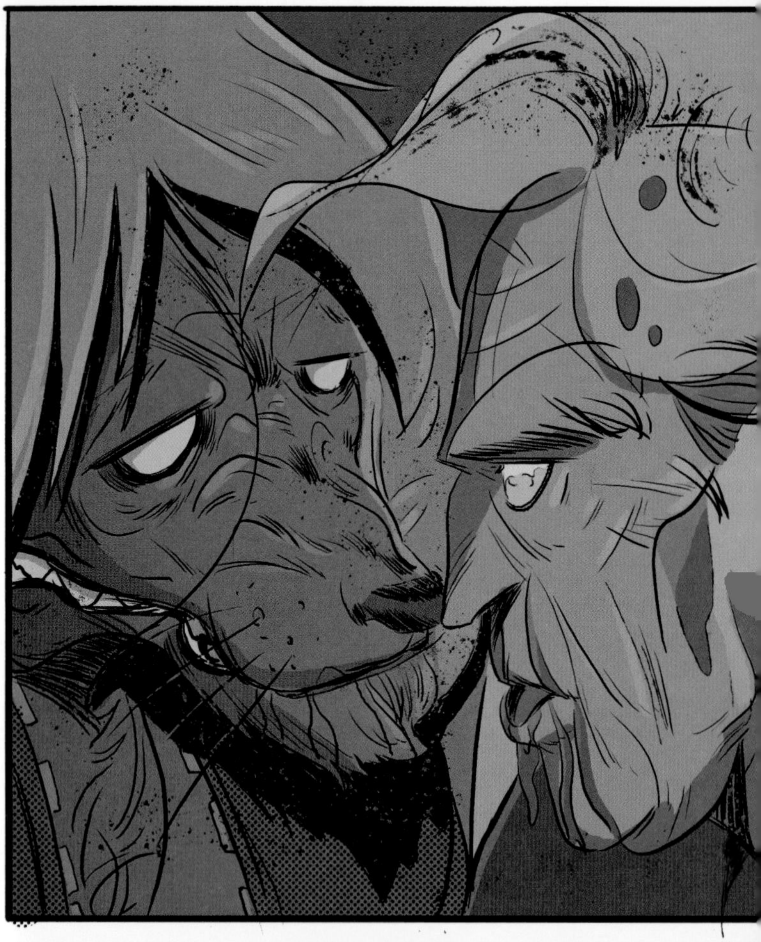

YOU SHOULD
AND YOU SHOULDN'T
AND AND AND--

I AM THE VOICE
INSIDE YOUR HEAD
TELLING YOU WHAT
YOU ARE, AND WILL
BE, FOR ETERNITY.

I AM
THE ANT.

I AM THE
ANTHILL.

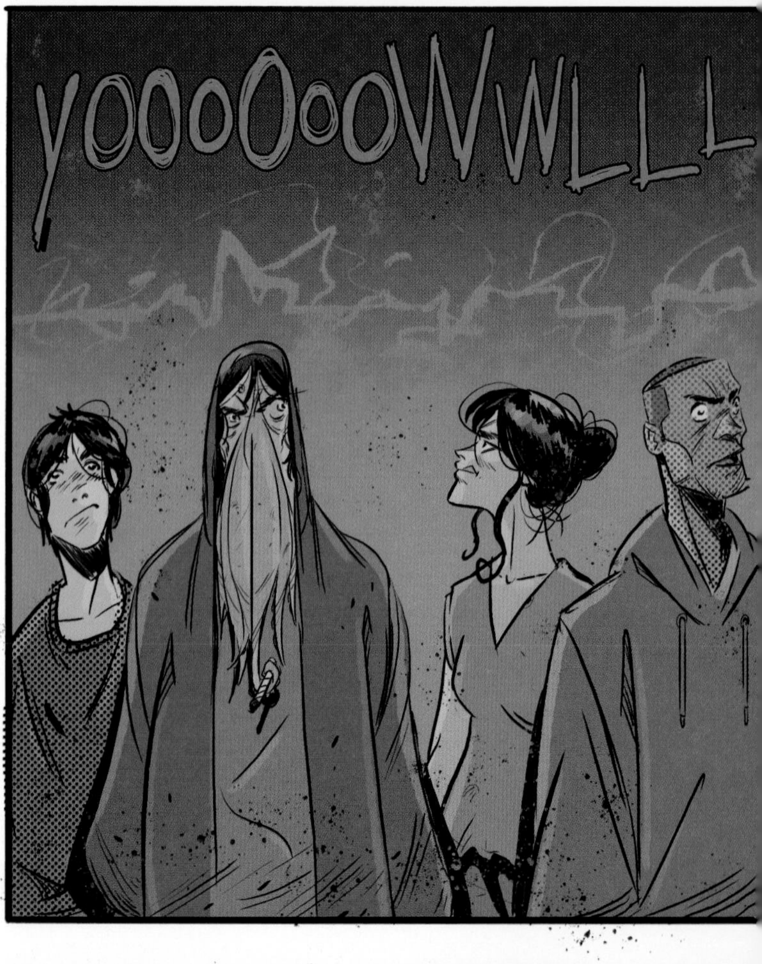
YOOOOOOWWLLL

I AM THE CHESSBOARD
YOU HAVE MOVED ON SINCE
BEFORE YOUR FIRST MOVE.
I AM THE IMAGE OF THE
CHESSBOARD THEY HAVE
CARVED FROM THE
FIRST TREE.

I AM YOUR LOGIC AND
I AM YOUR EMOTION.

I AM THE WORDS
AND I AM THE
GAPS BETWEEN.

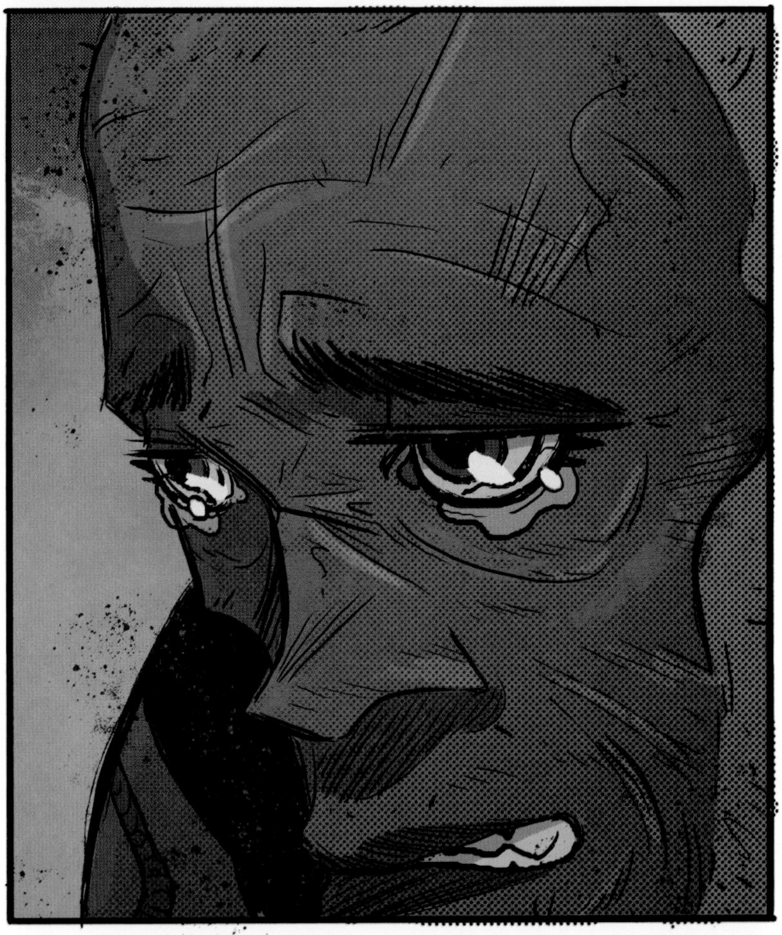

A GIRL NEEDED TO
DIE BY THE HAND OF
HER FATHER, IN THE
BLOOD OF HER FRIEND.

WHO CARES IF
SHE WAS THE
ANTICHRIST
OR NOT?

WHO CARES
ABOUT HER
HOWLING?

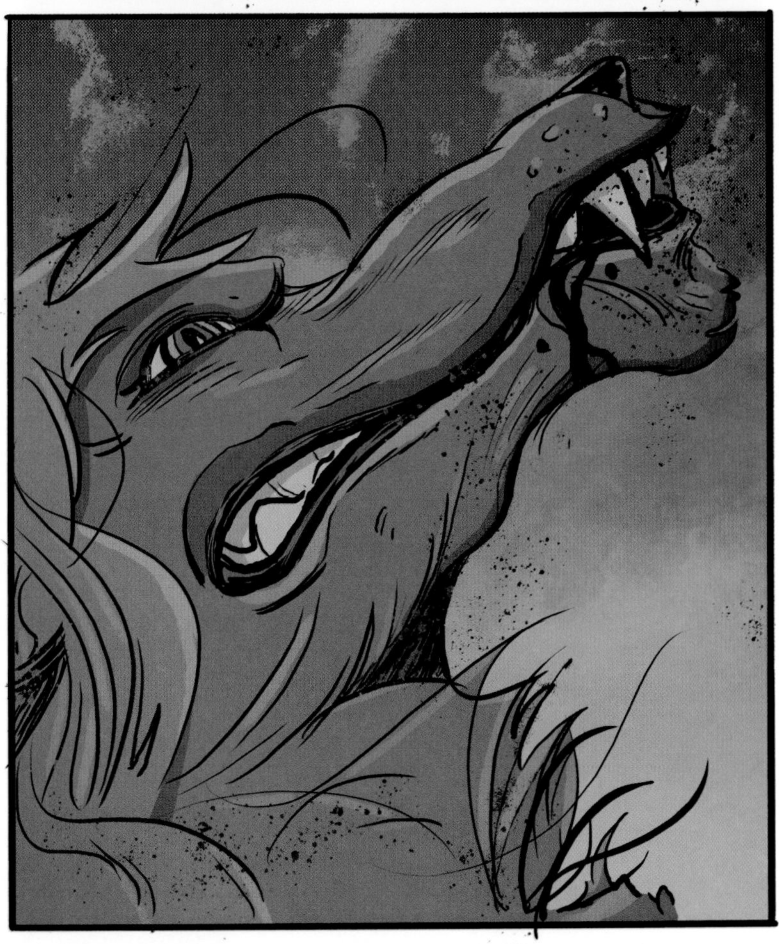

I AM YOUR SYSTEM.

NO-ONE CARES.

ETERNALLY YOURS,

THE ONE WITH MANY NAMES

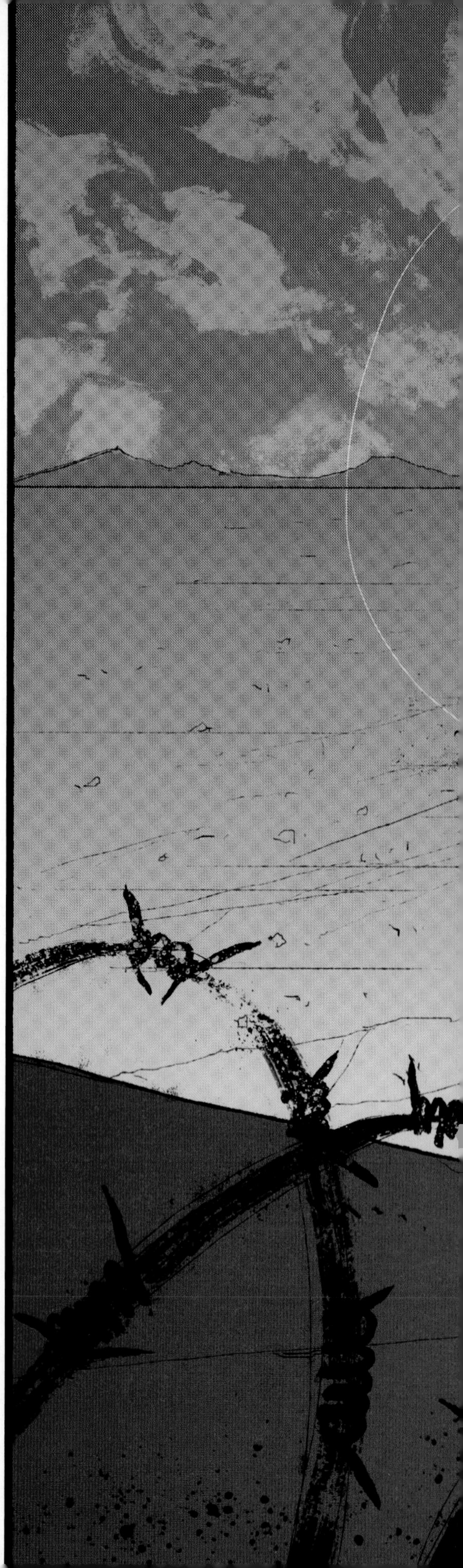

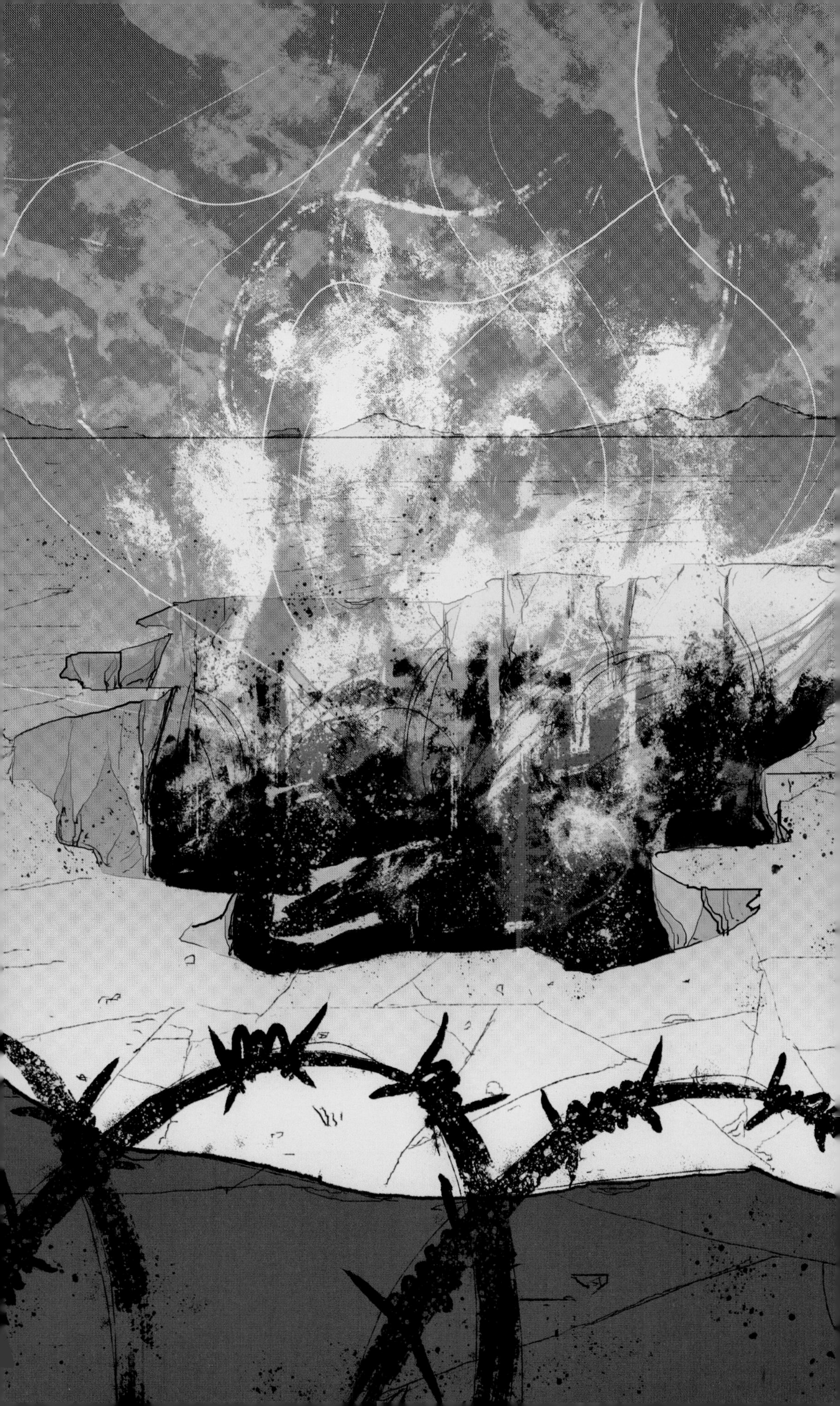

ORIGINAL **Wolf** #5–9 COVERS. ILLUSTRATED BY RICARDO LÓPEZ ORTIZ AND DESIGNED BY TOM MULLER

Apocalypse Soon

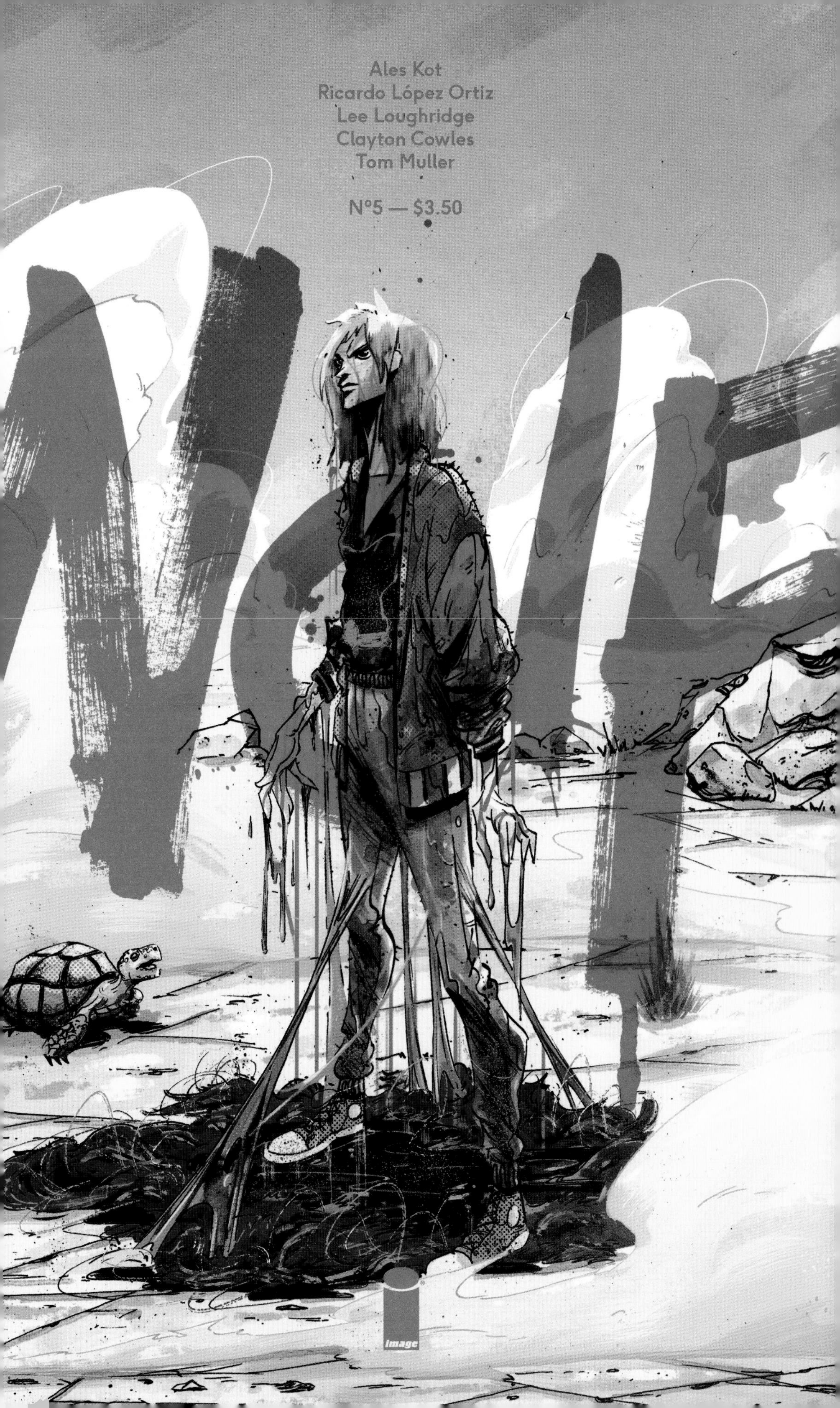
Ales Kot
Ricardo López Ortiz
Lee Loughridge
Clayton Cowles
Tom Muller
Nº5 — $3.50

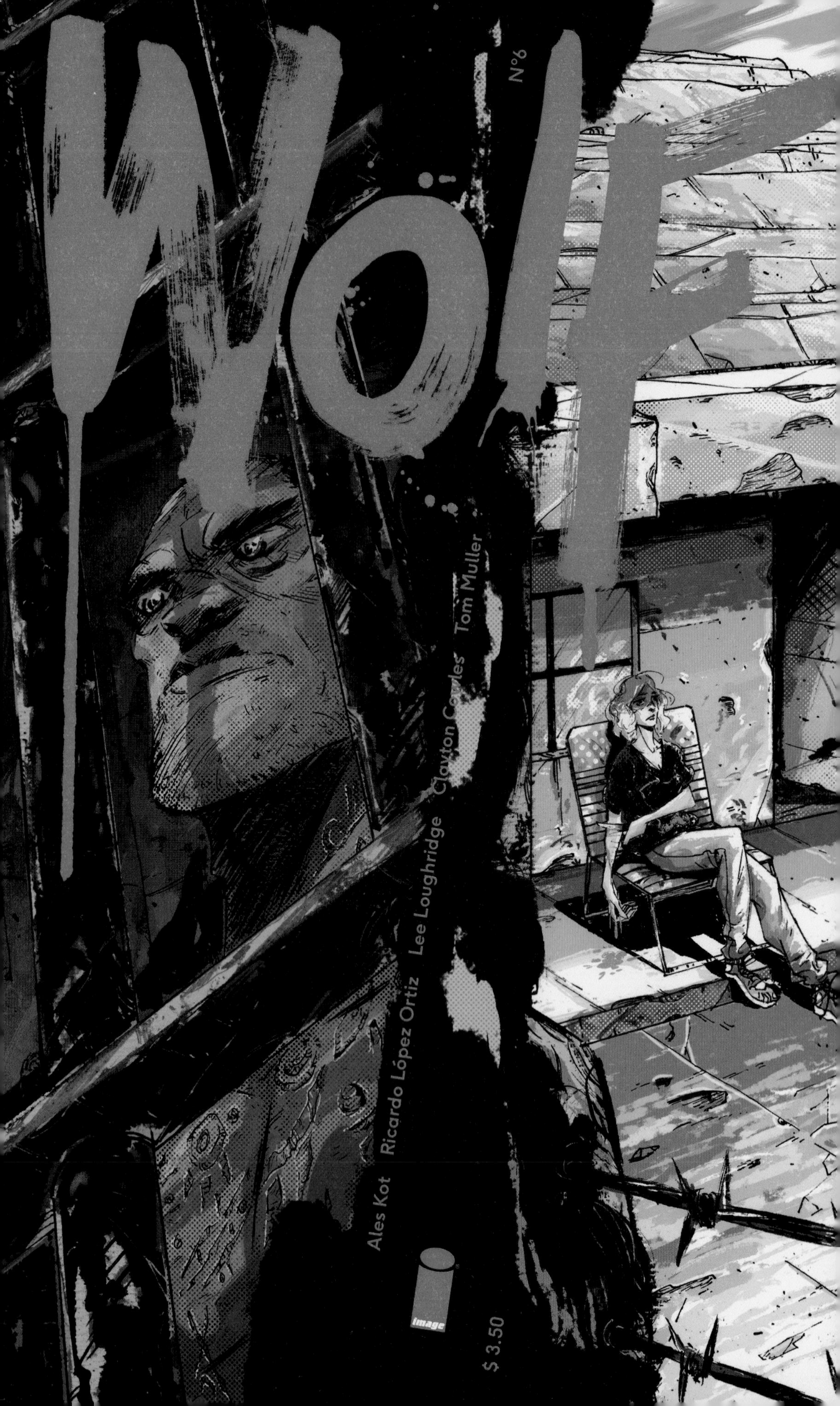

WOLF
N°6
Ales Kot
Ricardo López Ortiz
Lee Loughridge
Clayton Cowles
Tom Muller
image
$ 3.50

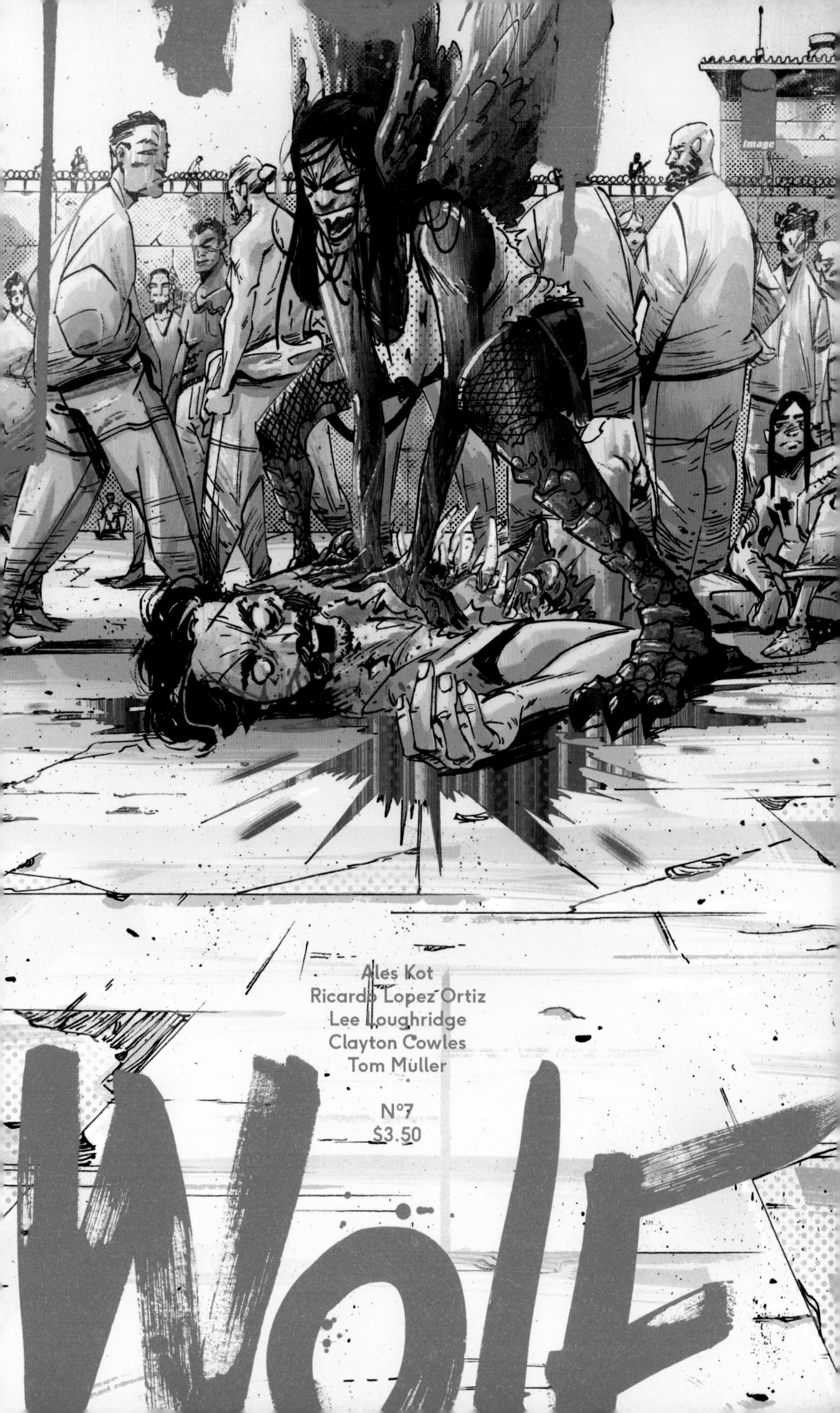

image
Ales Kot
Ricardo Lopez Ortiz
Lee Loughridge
Clayton Cowles
Tom Müller
N°7
$3.50
Wolf

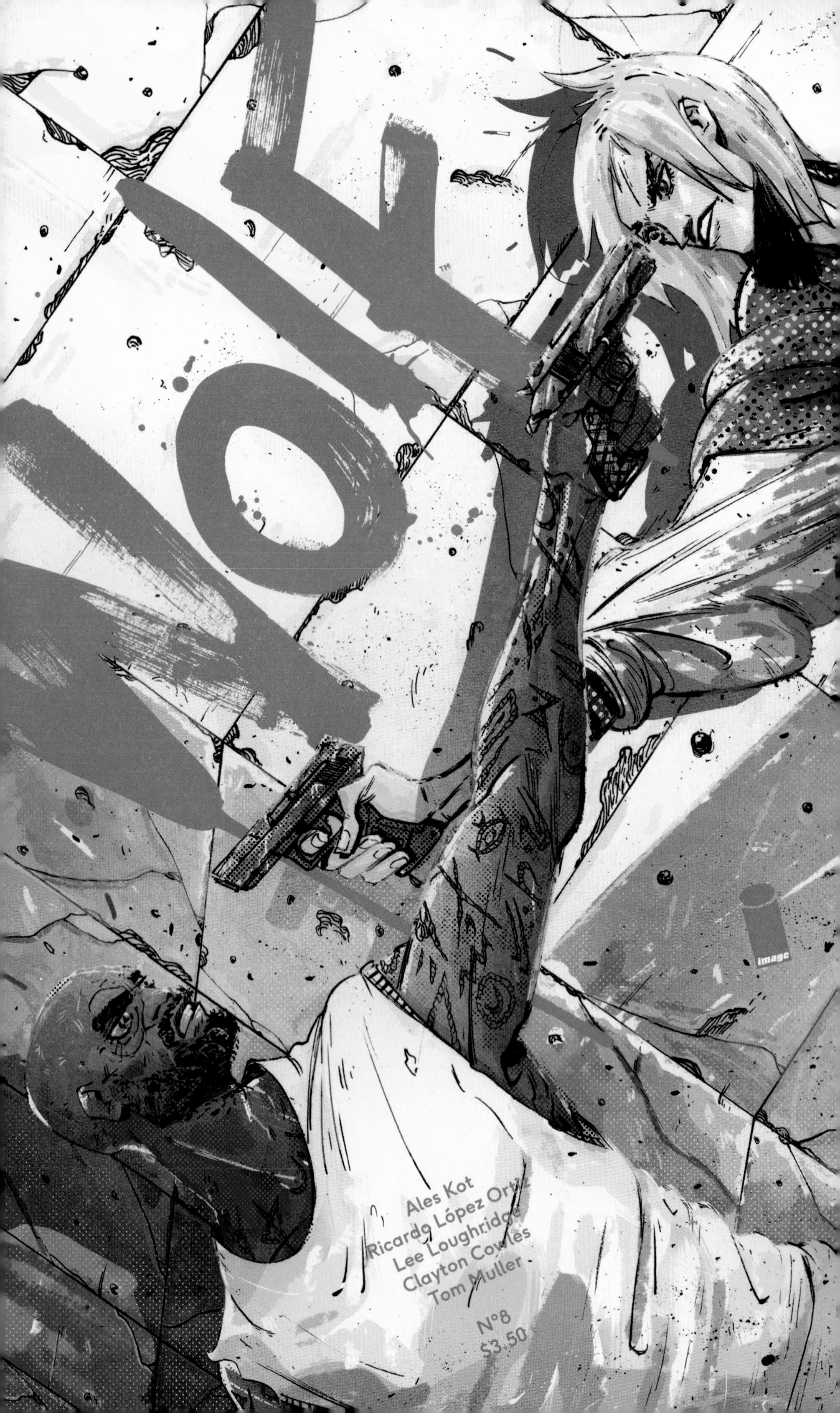
Ales Kot
Ricardo López Ortiz
Lee Loughridge
Clayton Cowles
Tom Muller
N°8
$3.50

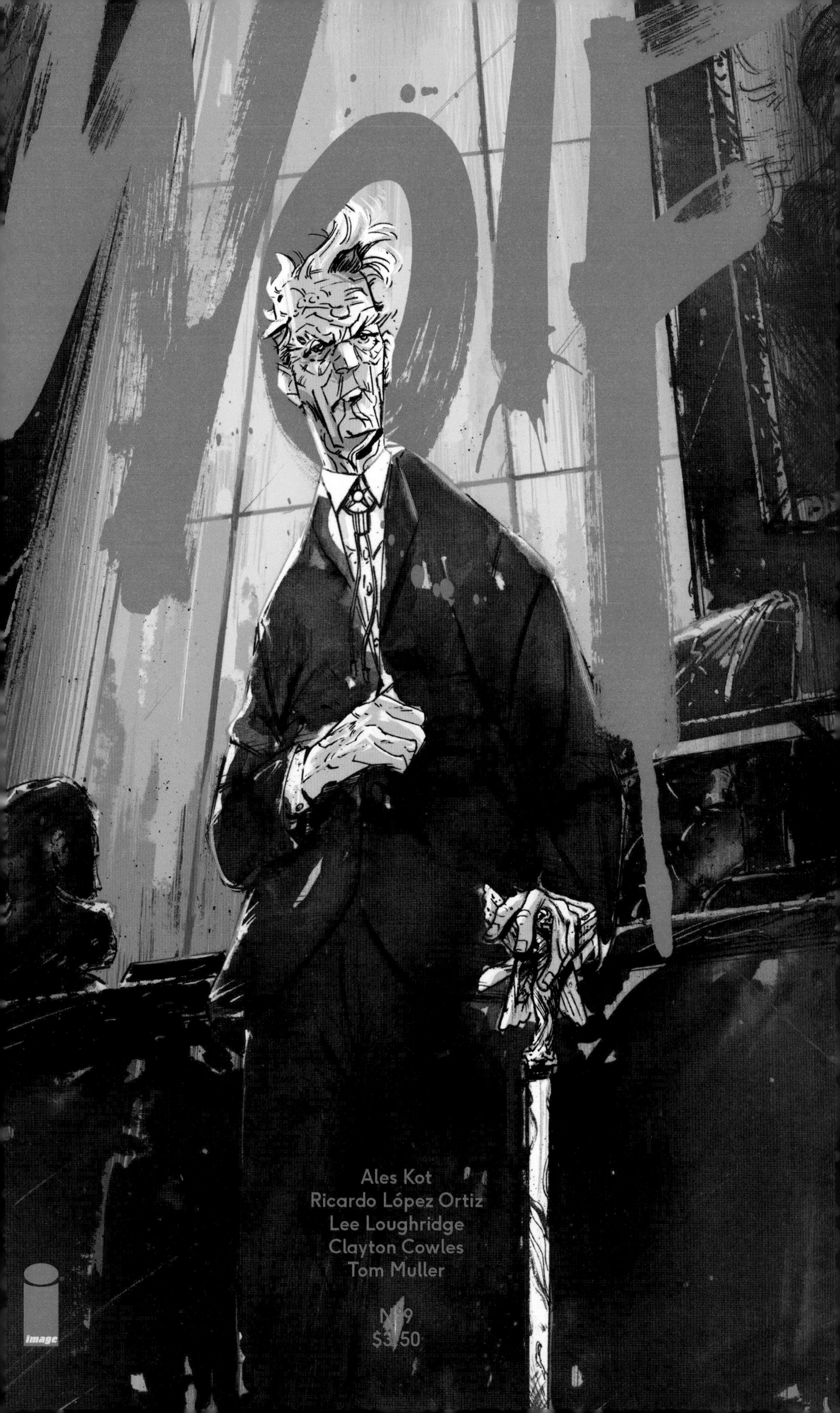
Ales Kot
Ricardo López Ortiz
Lee Loughridge
Clayton Cowles
Tom Muller
Nº9
$3.50

CREATORS:
ALES
KOT, WOLF
RICARDO
LÓPEZ ORTIZ,
LEE
LOUGHRIDGE
CLAYTON
COWLES,
TOM
MULLER.

Photo by Clayton Cubitt

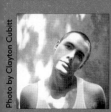

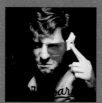

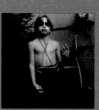

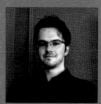

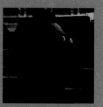

Ales Kot invents, writes & runs projects & stories for film, comics, television & more. He also wrote/still writes: *Change*, *Zero*, *Wolf*, *The Surface*, *Wild Children*. Current body born September 27, 1986 in Opava, Czech Republic. Resides in Los Angeles. Believes in poetry.

@ales_kot

Ricardo López Ortiz was born and raised in Bayamón, Puerto Rico, and studied Illustration at New York's School of Visual Arts. Currently living and working from his Brooklyn studio.

@RLopezOrtiz

Lee Loughridge resides in Southern California. He doesn't think a dog is just like a child and never takes photos of food.

@leeloughridge

Clayton Cowles graduated from the *Joe Kubert School of Cartoon and Graphic Art* in 2009, and has been lettering for Image and Marvel Comics ever since. For Image, his credits include *Bitch Planet*, *Pretty Deadly*, *The Wicked + The Divine*, and less than ten others. His Marvel credits include *Fantastic Four*, *Young Avengers*, *Secret Avengers*, *Bucky Barnes: Winter Soldier* and way more than ten others. He spends his real life in upstate New York with his cat.

@claytoncowles

Tom Muller is an Eisner and Harvey Award-nominated designer and cover artist who works with movie studios, publishers, media producers, ad agencies, and filmmakers. In comics he is best known for his design work on *Zero*, *Material*, *Drifter*, *The Violent*, and *Snowfall* at Image Comics; his logo designs for DC and Vertigo Comics (*Suicide Squad*, *Unfollow*, *Survivors' Club*,...) and his cover work for Valiant Entertainment (*Divinity*, *Generation Zero*, *Book of Death*,...). He lives in London with his wife, and two cats.

@helloMuller

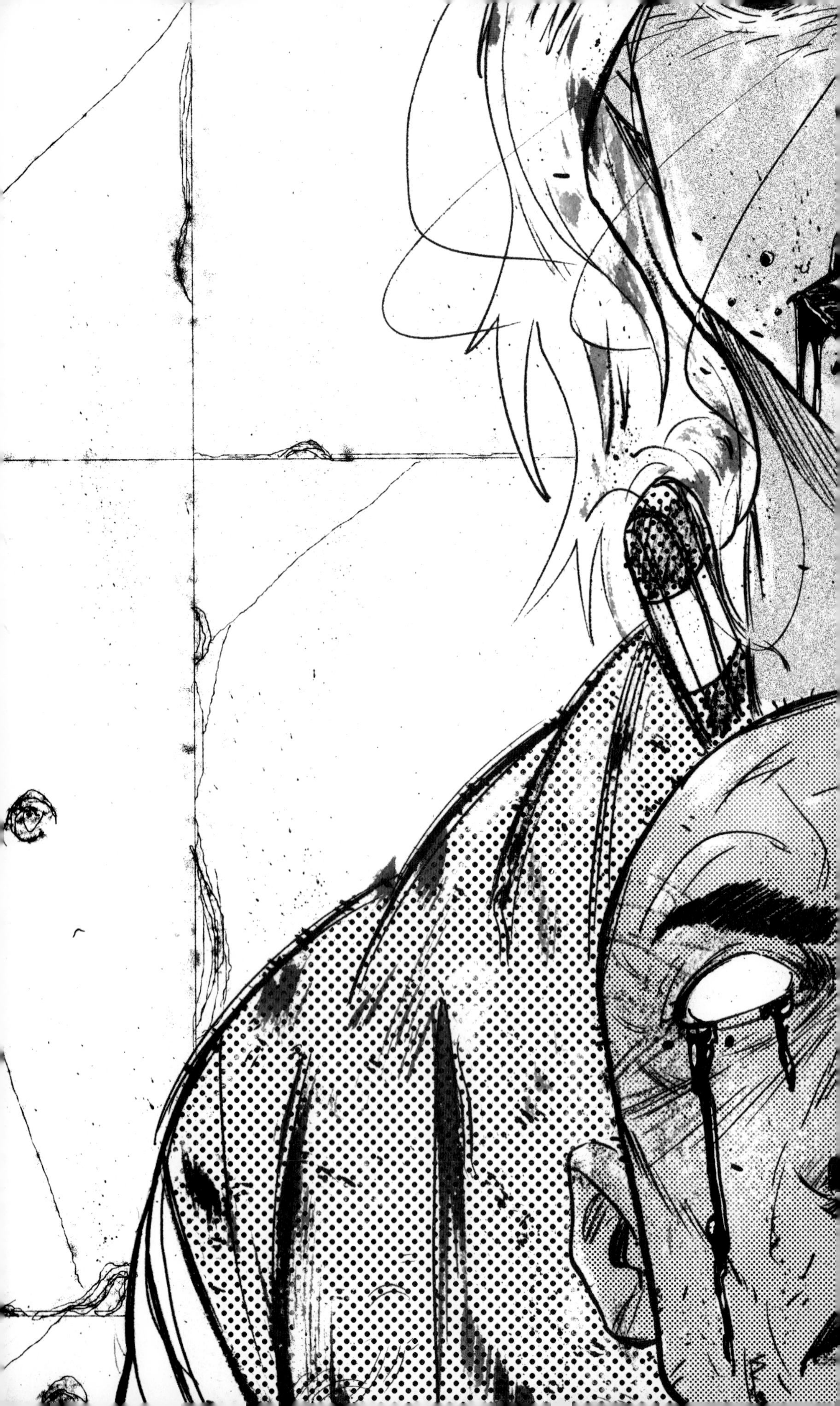

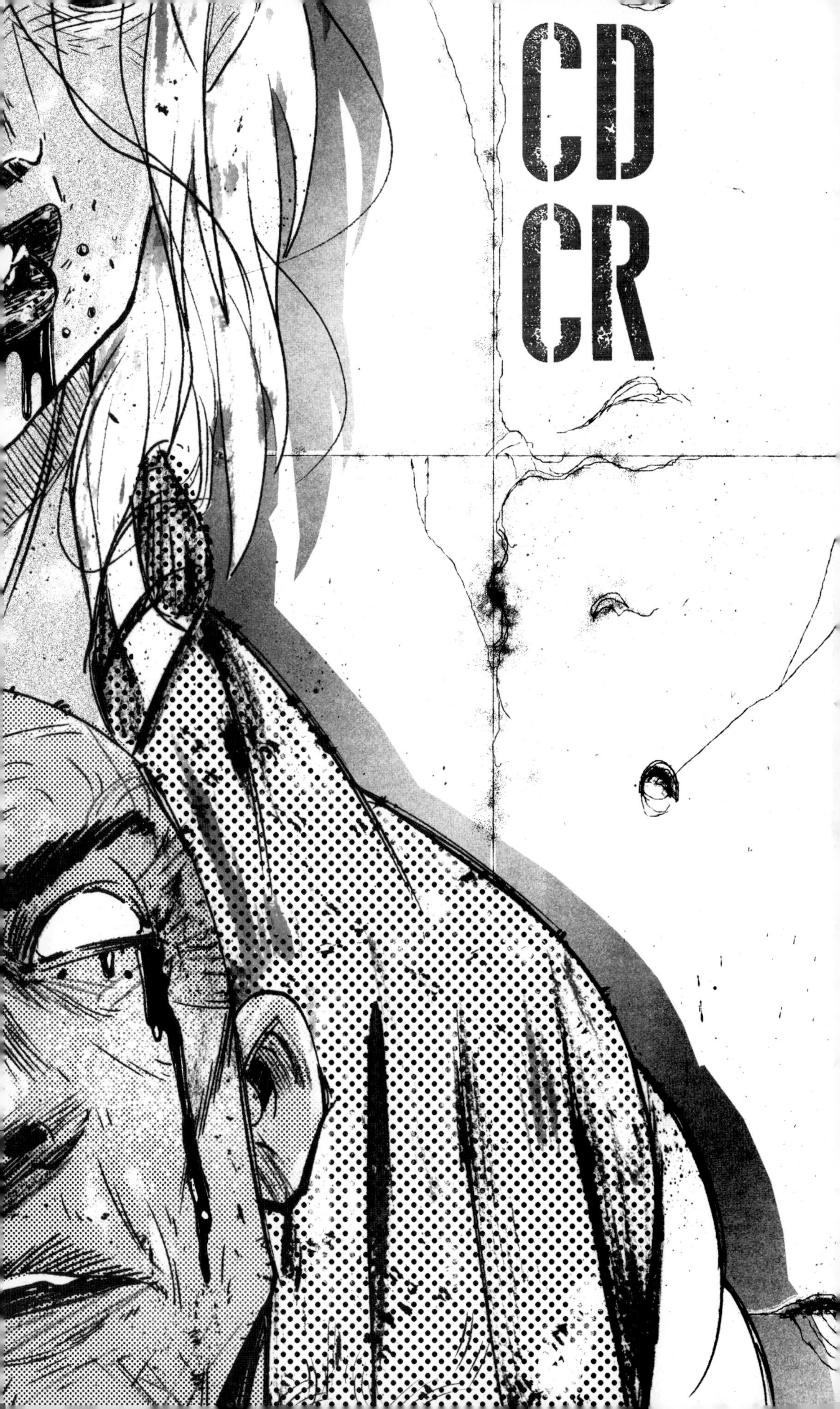
CD
CR

Media inquiries should be directed to Ari Lubet at 3 Arts Entertainment
and Angela Dallas at CAA.

ISBN: 978-1-63215-715-7

Published by
Image Comics, Inc.

IMAGE COMICS, INC — **Robert Kirkman:** Chief Operating Officer, **Erik Larsen:** Chief Financial Officer, **Todd McFarlane:** President,
Marc Silvestri: Chief Executive Officer, **Jim Valentino:** Vice-President, **Eric Stephenson:** Publisher, **Corey Murphy:** Director of Sales,
Jeff Boison: Director of Publishing Planning & Book Trade Sales, **Jeremy Sullivan:** Director of Digital Sales,
Kat Salazar: Director of PR & Marketing, **Branwyn Bigglestone:** Controller, **Drew Gill:** Art Director,
Jonathan Chan: Production Manager, **Meredith Wallace:** Print Manager, **Briah Skelly:** Publicist,
Sasha Head: Sales & Marketing Production Designer, **Randy Okamura:** Digital Production Designer, **David Brothers:** Branding Manager,
Olivia Ngai: Content Manager, **Addison Duke:** Production Artist, **Vincent Kukua:** Production Artist, **Tricia Ramos:** Production Artist,
Jeff Stang: Direct Market Sales Representative, **Emilio Bautista:** Digital Sales Associate, **Leanna Caunter:** Accounting Assistant,
Chloe Ramos-Peterson: Library Marked Sales Representative

imagecomics.com

Volume 2 Apocalypse Soon